IDENTITY AT WORK

This insightful book draws on a range of contemporary and classic studies to explore the connection between the personal experience of work and the wider social structures in which it takes place.

Identity at Work examines key social identities relevant to the workplace, such as those based on gender, sexual orientation, ethnicity and race, disability, age, occupation, class and organizational membership. Using research from a wide variety of countries and academic approaches, the book provides a readable and engaging introduction to the issues, exploring how people experience work, understand and present themselves at work, and relate to others.

Providing an accessible investigation of work and identity, this text will be valuable to students looking at organizational behaviour, HRM, diversity management and the sociology of work.

John Chandler is Professor of Work and Organization in the Royal Docks School of Business and Law, University of East London. His previous publications include *Organizations and Identity* (1994, as co-editor) and *Organization and Management: A Critical Text* (2000, also as co-editor). His research interests include diversity in organizations and public services management.

IDENTITY AT WORK

John Chandler

Routledge
Taylor & Francis Group

LONDON AND NEW YORK

First published 2017
by Routledge
2 Park Square, Milton Park, Abingdon, Oxon OX14 4RN

and by Routledge
711 Third Avenue, New York, NY 10017

Routledge is an imprint of the Taylor & Francis Group, an informa business

© 2017 John Chandler

The right of John Chandler to be identified as author of this work has been
asserted by him in accordance with sections 77 and 78 of the Copyright, Designs
and Patents Act 1988.

All rights reserved. No part of this book may be reprinted or reproduced or
utilised in any form or by any electronic, mechanical, or other means, now
known or hereafter invented, including photocopying and recording, or in any
information storage or retrieval system, without permission in writing from the
publishers.

Trademark notice: Product or corporate names may be trademarks or registered
trademarks, and are used only for identification and explanation without intent to
infringe.

Every effort has been made to contact copyright holders for their permission to
reprint material in this book. The publishers would be grateful to hear from any
copyright holder who is not here acknowledged and will undertake to rectify any
errors or omissions in future editions of this book.

British Library Cataloguing in Publication Data
A catalogue record for this book is available from the British Library

Library of Congress Cataloging in Publication Data
Names: Chandler, John, 1954- author.
Title: Identity at work / John Chandler.
Description: Abingdon, Oxon ; New York, NY : Routledge, 2016.
Identifiers: LCCN 2016001394| ISBN 9781138788305 (hardback) |
ISBN 9781138788312 (pbk.) | ISBN 9781315765624 (ebook)
Subjects: LCSH: Industrial sociology. | Group identity. | Identity (Psychology) |
Occupations--Sociological aspects. | Work--Psychological aspects.
Classification: LCC HD6955 .C43 2016 | DDC 306.3/6--dc23
LC record available at http://lccn.loc.gov/2016001394

ISBN: 978-1-138-78830-5 (hbk)
ISBN: 978-1-138-78831-2 (pbk)
ISBN: 978-1-315-76562-4 (ebk)

Typeset in Bembo
by Taylor & Francis Books

CONTENTS

TABLES AND BOXES

Tables

Boxes

ACKNOWLEDGEMENTS

My work on this book is certainly not the work of someone operating alone. Apart from the contributions of all the writers I explicitly draw on here, I am grateful to many people for sharing thoughts and feelings with me that may, in small or large ways, have informed my writing. Where to draw the line as to who to mention here is difficult, but at the risk of leaving key people out they include (in no particular order) Gil Robinson, Zorlu Senyucel, Andrew Boocock, Andrew Smith, Heather Clark, Jeff Hearn, Jenny Chandler, Robyn Thomas, Jean Helms Mills, Albert Mills, Mike Dent, Matthew Brennan, Liz Harlow, Tony Wailey, Debbie Taylor, Martin Parker, Biebele Alex-Hart, Cathlynn D'Silva, Jeni Gosling, Issa Abdulraheem, Sue Truman and Guy Huber. Above all I have to thank my collaborators on a number of writing projects over the years – Jim Barry and Elisabeth Berg – the work I did with them has entered this book in many ways, not least in providing a model of what work can be: cooperative, interesting, supportive and challenging. I am also grateful to Nicola Cupit at Routledge for providing an efficient guiding hand. It is not their fault if this book is not better than it is.

Finally, I want to acknowledge someone who provided encouragement and relevant critical appraisal during the period in which this book was written, and much else besides: Pam Baldwin.

1

INTRODUCTION

What is this book about?

As I write this book there is a block of flats being built across the street. I find it interesting to observe people doing very different kinds of work to me. I have learnt that even a construction of steel and concrete requires quite a lot of carpentry. A team of carpenters works on the formwork. A man sits on his own way up in the air in a crane which lifts heavy loads, carefully guided by someone on the ground who wears a distinctive high-visibility orange suit, as well as the obligatory hard hat that everyone on the site wears; even the man on the gate who I would imagine is safe from falling projectiles. Sometimes surveyors arrive and squint through theodolites. Almost every worker I see appears to be a man except for one woman, a surveyor seen on one occasion. They are mostly white. I do not hear much of what they say but have heard languages other than English – East European, I would say. They start early by my standards – usually at 7.00am – and finish by 4.00pm, although sometimes a few workers seem to carry on until darkness or beyond (sometimes even late into the night). They seem to work steadily, although occasionally someone seems to be just standing around, or two men sit and chat. Their work is much more physical than mine – 'manual' work. Clearly they have to exercise skill, perform various calculations and stay alert in what is a potentially dangerous place.

As they construct the building I construct this book. Sitting at a desk, typing text using the keyboard. Is the work so different? It too requires planning, relies on the labour of others – those whose work I cite here but also all those who, in various ways, have influenced my thinking, including students, colleagues and teachers. There is also the work of editors, reviewers, printers, accountants. Perhaps there are differences between my work and that of the builders. Is this better work, more intrinsically satisfying? Why? Is it because it is self-directed? No one has told me to do this or is telling me how to do it – at least not directly, although of course there are conventions to follow, publisher's guidelines to consider, as well as the audience whose understanding and interest I seek.

'Identity at Work' – the title is deliberately ambiguous. It can be read as referring to identity in the workplace but also as something that is worked at, upon or with. This 'thing' that can be worked on is the concept itself – but also what it might denote. But what is the meaning of identity? In everyday life, we are often unaware of identity; it is taken for granted. A little like breathing; it isn't something that we think about until, perhaps, it becomes difficult. To the extent that we do become aware of it then we are often quite certain of it as a 'thing' which is relatively stable, fixed, secure, factual. When we describe ourselves as a man or a woman, as white or black, as an academic or a manager we seem to be describing something real and concrete. Part of the purpose of the book is to explore the 'reality' of this. To examine what it means to be a man or woman at work, white or black at work, an academic or a manager. If this is interesting it may be because work is fascinating and people's experience of work is fascinating. It may be because we want to see a representation of our own experience, or, perhaps more likely, we would like to know more about the experience of others. But the book also aims to unsettle such certainties – to examine ways in which what is apparently fixed and concrete is rather unstable and fluid – potentially at least.

What is identity?

Identity is something that has the potential to be individual or collective. I have a sense of identity as an individual but in so far as this involves me being a man, an academic, etc., this also makes me a member of a larger social category. The concept of identity is a bridge between the individual and the social or collective, although we might usefully distinguish *self-identity* (you or me as an individual) from *collective identities* (you or me as a manager or man, etc.). A similar but more commonly used distinction is that between personal and social identity, but I prefer self-identity and collective identity because I would want to emphasize that all identities are social and relational. The term self-identity can be used to denote the individual that we feel ourselves to be and imagine everyone else is, too (see Ricœur 1992 for a sophisticated philosophical discussion of this). Collective identity, on the other hand, is associated with social categories or groups – the identities of manager or professional, for example. Of course, who we are as a unique self is in large part made up of our belonging to particular collectivities, but the self is not reducible to the sum of collective identities that it belongs to.

The concept of collective identity could be seen as similar to that of role, once a central concept in sociology (e.g. see Dahrendorf 1973) but now largely superseded by that of identity. This displacement of role by identity is not an arbitrary one, the mere play of intellectual fashion. One of the differences between collective identities and roles, potentially at least, is that collective identities may be seen as fluid, rather than the apparently stable set of expectations associated with a role. Collective identities may also be very complex, comprising a large number of routinized practices, beliefs and assumptions, not necessarily always easily reconciled. More-over, collective identities may involve rival interpretations, both within a group to which it is attached as well as between observers: there may not be an agreed set of 'expectations' at all. In this way the idea of collective identity may better capture the complexity and fluidity of social being than the relatively static and consensual idea of role.

The idea of identity invokes a concern for both similarity and difference (Jenkins 2004) as well as, in social terms, belonging and exclusion. At the level of the individual my sense of self is partly given by the idea that I am the same person from minute to minute, year to year – even though, as successive photographs of me at different ages would show – I am clearly different. I experience my body as mine and enduring, even as it ages and changes. The sense of self-identity also encompasses the view that I am unique. I am different from anyone else even if I share many characteristics and even if, indeed, my very sense of self depends on being as another self (see Ricœur 1992), sharing an ability to imagine others as having thoughts and feelings that are something like mine (even if, often, they are very different). At the collective level, too, identity implies a similarity (a woman as other women) and difference (a woman not a man). In so far as identity relies on difference it is thus always a relational thing – I am not you and a woman is not a man. We are defined by what we are and what we are not (individually or collectively).

Identity is a noun, something that names me or you, us or them; but it also depends on identification – a process of recognition, of association, of differentiation, of categorization (see also Ashforth et al. 2008). This identification is in part a recognition of what it is that is the same or different, based on categories which are socially available or become available, but it is also, as Ashforth et al. argue (2008), a process in which individuals (and I would add groups) can think, feel and act themselves into identification.

In so far as identification does involve recognition this may be prompted by what might be seen as internal processes (from the perspective of the self or collective that does this identification) or an interactive process involving the other (individual or collective) that identifies. The manager acts the part, and he or she does manage-ment; but others also identify this person as a manager and act on the basis of this understanding or respond accordingly. This is an ongoing process and subject to critical evaluation by both parties. This may well lead to changes in thoughts, feelings and behaviour on both sides (see e.g. Chandler 2010; Marshall 1995). Ashforth et al. (2008) have suggested that identification can take the form of sense breaking or sense giving. By sense breaking they mean a questioning of the identity. A posing of the question 'who am I?' or 'who are we?' in which there is uncer-tainty, opening up the possibility that it can be answered in different ways. Sense giving can be seen as the offering of answers to such questions by others (see Ashforth et al. 2008: 342).

But if processes of recognition are often seen as occurring in the visual realm, identities might be more or less visible, depending on context. I want in this book to deal not just with what is visible and with what is said, but what is invisible and silent or silenced.

Furthermore, if identity rests on identification there is also the possibility of dis-identification and of latent identification. I would like to distinguish between these. Disidentification I see as an active process of refusing a socially available or ascribed identity. Latent identification, on the other hand, might be described as an identity that is currently inactive, possibly due to a person's blindness to the relevance of a particular identity (even though, to others, it might be obvious that they should identify with it). In all this I take the view that identities are always socially constructed. Even those that might seem to be biologically 'given' – my sex, my skin colour – derive meaning and substance from the social context in which they are placed. And not just the immediate context but the historical context (in living memory and beyond). This in turn means that however fixed and certain these identities seem, they are always subject to interpretation, contestation and change as circumstances change. Time is of course a crucial factor here and identification as a process occurs over time. Indeed, we might move between identification, disidentification and latent identification (in any order) as we negotiate our interactions with others.

To study identity at work might be to study identification in all the forms it takes in the workplace. Identity work is something that we do and is done to us. Identity is not just something we have but something we work at or on, although not under conditions of our own choosing. Identity work is negotiated work. In this work we might both do and undo identity, in the sense that Judith Butler (2004, 2011) has suggested we might do or undo gender.

What is the meaning of 'work' in the title 'Identity at Work'?

Having looked at the issue of identity in some detail, what about the other term in the book's title – that of work? I expect most people to think of this as referring to paid employment and this is, mostly, what the book is about. However, I would like to extend the consideration to forms of unpaid work and to the absence of work. This is not least because this sheds light on what we value, and sometimes take for granted, in employment but also because of the importance of such work or non-work in its own right.

Work can be seen as transformative activity and Karl Marx (1974: 327–32, written in 1844) saw human beings as a species that needs to work in order to live. If this, at the beginning of human history, took the form of collecting food or hunting for food and preparing it, as well as preparing shelter, now we would see a need for a wider range of objects and activities to sustain us, perhaps including holidays abroad, nights at the movies, meals in restaurants. All of this requires work in the making of things such as planes, restaurants and cooking implements, as well as in service delivery. Consumption rests upon work. But work is not only of instrumental value, it also has a moral dimension. In many religions work has value not just as a means to an end but as something of worth in its own right. In adopting secular views, too, we often associate work with human fulfilment as well as a contribution to society. Of course work can also be a curse as well as a blessing and the fatigue or wear and tear associated with it calls forward a need for rest and recreation.

Work can be, and often is, considered in opposition to leisure but as many have observed the boundaries between the two can be hard to draw (Ibarra and Petriglieri 2010). An associated distinction is that between work and play: we might associate play with pleasure and work with seriousness, or work with purpose and play with enjoyment, or play might be associated with process – with the means rather than the end (Caillois 1961). And of course 'play' often takes place in different places. As children we become used to leaving the classroom for the 'playground' and at work we often see the workspace as a place for 'work' and the local bar, or perhaps work canteen, as a place for 'play'. I do not hold these distinctions very tightly, however; work can be enjoyable for its own sake and can take place in the bar, while play can take place in the workplace. The word 'play' in English also has another meaning – that of adjustment or movement around a point, and in this sense, too, play might be a useful concept in looking at identity; for seeing how identities can flex and move. Indeed, perhaps a more inventive title for this book would be 'Identity at Play', although that might raise different kinds of expectations. In any case flexing and moving might also be seen as the outcome of the kind of transformative activity that is usually associated with 'work'. I see the processes of identification and disidentification as different forms of *identity work*. Watson and Watson (2012, but see also Sveningsson and Alvesson 2003 on which they draw and Brown 2015) define identity work as: 'the process whereby people strive to shape a relatively coherent and distinctive notion of personal self-identity' (Watson and Watson 2012: 687). This is a truncated version of a longer definition Watson provides in an earlier work:

> Identity work involves the mutually constitutive processes whereby people strive to shape a relatively coherent and distinctive notion of personal self-identity and struggle to come to terms with and, within limits, to influence the various social-identities which pertain to them in the various milieu in which they live their lives.
>
> *(Watson 2008: 129)*

While I am sympathetic to Watson's approach, however, for me this definition is too narrow in that it puts self-identity at the centre and seems to emphasize the moment of stabilization rather than destabilization. I would want also to consider how, collectively as well as individually, people create a distinctive notion of collective identity (as well as self-identity) and to consider how such notions are rendered uncertain or unstable as well as secured.

Theoretical approaches

There is an enormous body of writing on the subject of identity and I cannot hope to do justice to the variety of theoretical approaches that can be adopted; here I will be content with sketching some of the major theoretical approaches and point to those that figure most prominently in the following chapters. If there is a variety of theoretical approaches these might be seen as complementary rather than as at odds, however. Academics have a proclivity for dividing themselves into tribes that rarely talk to one another – and when they do so it is often with a degree of animosity that is sometimes amusing, sometimes rather disturbing (to me, anyway). Poststructuralists can be contemptuous of realists, and vice versa, but most often they simply fail to address one another.

I am a theoretical and methodological pluralist. I see different theoretical approaches and different methodological approaches as different lenses through which to approach the social world we seek to understand and change. The metaphor of the lens is often used and I think it is appropriate (e.g. see Okhuysen and Bonardi 2011, who also discuss the potential and difficulties involved in combining lenses). Any one theoretical or methodological approach is a lens that brings certain features into focus but leaves others blurred. Like most metaphors this is imperfect, of course. It suggests that there is a true and perfect representation of reality to be had, as well as a distorted and unfaithful one. I am not sure this is so and to switch the metaphor perhaps we should consider the knowledge we generate as more of a hall of mirrors – each view is partial but it is our attempt to represent the world.

In seeking to address both self-identity and collective identities we inevitably need to draw upon psychological and sociological theory. A smattering of philosophy and political theory may help, too. For my purpose here I think it is useful to distinguish between three broad approaches, two of them more psychological and one more sociological. These are the psychoanalytic, the social psychological, and the social constructionist. I will consider these various approaches in turn.

The psychoanalytic approach originates in the work of Freud but it has a rich history and has developed in various directions since. I do not wish to enter the minutiae of the theory but I think it is clearly relevant to understanding self-identity as well as the identity work involved in relations with others. Freud famously drew attention to the unconscious, to the operation of complex processes driven by our desires. For students of identity at work I think this has potentially great potential in understanding the psychodynamics of workplace behaviour – of our thoughts, feelings and behaviour in the workplace. The workplace is sometimes portrayed as an arena dominated by rationality but psychoanalytical approaches might alert us to the operation of subterranean forces that are far from rational. Indeed, rationalization might itself be seen as a psychological defence mechanism. A psychoanalytical approach might let us consider repression, narcissism and anxiety as processes that can be used to understand our 'rational' and irrational behaviour alike. It might lead us to consider and comprehend the kind of crises that arise in people's lives which might sometimes take the form of ruptures in the smooth operation of careers or which might be experienced quietly and worked through more or less satisfactorily. To give a flavour of what it might mean to adopt such an approach I will refer to Schwartz (1987: 51–2), who provides an account of one of his student's descriptions of his situation:

He was employed by a large corporation in a unit whose function had almost ceased to exist. Yet his supervisor spent all his time trying to expand his empire by hiring more people. All my student did all day, when he did anything at all, was to play up to the vanity of the supervisor and tell him and others how important the supervisor and the department were. He had to do this because he hated it there and wanted a transfer, which politically required the blessing of the supervisor. The heart of the dilemma turned out to be that the more he was successful in building up the supervisor's image, the more the supervisor refused to permit him to transfer, because the department was, according to the drama, already short on personnel. I asked him why he hated this so much; what he would do if he could do whatever he wanted to at work. He said: 'I am an engineer. All I want to do is build cars.'

This everyday story has pathos, but it also points to some of the processes psycho-analytical approaches might alert us to: in this case the student feeds the supervisor's narcissism but in doing so finds himself hating what he does and also trapped. Schwartz argues that such psychodynamic processes produce 'organizational totali-tarianism' in which there are constant attempts to construct the ideal organization. Anxieties and desires fuel a search for organizational perfection, but this has perverse consequences. Psychoanalytical perspectives can give a rather bleak view although with some hope of redemption, at least contingently and temporarily, if we can work through the difficulties (see Elliott 2009). The psychoanalytic perspective is not very commonly represented in the organizational literature and although I have drawn on it in places, other approaches are much more in evidence.

The second approach I want to emphasize here, the social psychological approach, most prominently takes the form of social identity theory and the related self-categorization theory (see Capozza and Brown 2000; Haslam and Ellemers 2005; Haslam et al. 2014). This is largely based on the psychology of groups and tends to focus on how members of a particular social group define themselves as a group in relation to others. Studies in this tradition tend to focus on the specific characteristics that members use to define membership of a group and often focus on relations between in-group and out-group characteristics which may involve relying on stereotypes. An example of this work is Emerson and Murphy (2014), which looks at identity threats in the US workplace, focusing on ethnicity. They identify, for example, a number of cues used to increase or decrease threat levels, as perceived by people of colour, including the numbers of people perceived to be in the same group in their workplace. They also emphasize cues relating to stereotypes. The operation of the latter may be subtle, for example they refer to findings from other researchers suggesting that: 'black participants perceived White participants more negatively when they praised the athletic ability of African Americans compared to those who never mentioned the positive stereotype in the first place' (Emerson and Murphy 2014: 510). This social psychological approach, like psychology in general, tends to adopt a self-consciously 'scientific' approach, with a careful framing and testing of hypotheses, often, although not always, under experimental conditions and using quantitative methods. Ellemers et al. (2003: 16) have argued that, 'It is only through formal theory development accompanied by rigorous experimental analysis that the approach has proved successful'. There are exceptions to this dominant approach in social psychology, but they are unusual (e.g. Shotter and Gergen 1989). In the following pages I do make the occasional reference to psychological work and I am not dismissive of it in principle, but I do think it tends to narrow the focus rather too much, and in my view in the search for 'rigour' much seems to be lost in the portrayal of the social processes at work.

The third theoretical approach I want to distinguish here is social constructionism. This represents a broad range of mainly sociological work that shares much with social identity theory in assuming that social identities are constructed around difference and through social processes. If it differs it is largely brought about through allegiance to different foundational theorists as well as to methodological differences. While social identity theorists often draw upon experimental situations or quantitative methods, those I am calling social constructionist usually prefer qualitative and interpretive methodologies. The work also often appears in different journals, reflecting the academic divisions between social psychology on the one hand and sociology on the other.

In using the social constructionist label I am deliberately skating over many different varieties of sociological work, and many might see this as a rather dubious catch-all category that masks difference. Certainly one influential theorist, Stuart Hall (1992: 275), has distinguished sociological from postmodern approaches and it is the latter that are sometimes seen as more thoroughly 'social constructionist'. However, it seems to me that while there are many differences between different theorists and approaches in this category, there are certain similarities that I consider to be important. If they differ it is largely in having attachments to different foundational theorists (e.g. Foucault, Bourdieu, Butler, Giddens, Goffman). If the social constructionist approach features most in the following chapters this reflects my own bias but I think they do provide a rich picture of how identities are formed and employed. As Hall (1996) and others suggest, identity is founded on difference. If social identity theory conceptualizes this as the in-group and out-group, social constructionists have a broader view. While social identity theory focuses on the group, social constructionists emphasize discourse and belonging in ways that might be more fluid than suggested by the idea of a group with boundaries.

Social constructionists, as I am employing the term, share the assumption that categories such as man, woman, black or disabled, while they may appear natural and perhaps based on biology or nature, are in fact shaped by social processes, their meaning shifting over time and place. Recent work – particularly that influenced by postmodernism – has often emphasized fragmentation, fluidity of identity categories, but I think the assumption of dynamism is not new and that it has more in common with the symbolic interactionist approaches from the Chicago School onwards than some would like to admit. Moreover, even someone like Hall (1996), who emphasizes fluidity and fragmentation, is also concerned with stabilization – with social processes that tend to 'fix' identities in certain ways (at least contingently and for a while). Above all I see the similarities between varieties of social construction-ism as based on an emphasis on meaning and interpretation. While there may be differences between those of a more realist persuasion, such as Elder-Vass (2012), who has argued for a moderate form of social constructionism, and those adopting what could be seen as more extreme or radical forms of social constructionism associated with postmodernism, all emphasize a need to unravel the meanings of social interaction and it is this that I would want to emphasize here.

The politics of identity

This concern with identity in the academic literature is not isolated from wider political developments; indeed, academic work can be seen as contributing to what is often referred to as a politics of identity – a politics that is based on identity categories connected with race and ethnicity (from the civil rights movement to black power and beyond), gender (varieties of feminism and women's movement activity), disability (the disability rights movement) and sexual orientation (the LGBT movement), as well as what could be seen as the more traditional basis for politics, that of class (workers' movements). The politics of identity is controversial, however. It might be criticized for encouraging a limited political vision associated with single-issue politics or a kind of messy pluralism that might thwart change as well as further it. It seems to me that whatever its limitations or potential we cannot ignore the politics of identity; this politics is central to identity work and to identity in the workplace for reasons that should become clear in the chapters that follow. Identity I take to be a profoundly political issue: the social construction and trans-formation of the aspects of identity to be explored here are steeped in issues of power, oppression, justice, fairness. I doubt that reading this book will change anyone's political stance a great deal, but it might inform it, or extend horizons a little; alert the reader to key questions and debates so that they might engage in discussion and dialogue, as well as in action that is informed by this analysis.

The book's structure and content

The book is structured as it is partly in order to deal with issues that are central to the study of work – focusing on occupations and the organization as sources of identity and sites of identity work as well as the perennial sociological themes of class, gender and ethnicity. If I also focus on age, sexual orientation and disability it is because these seem to me to be important issues in their own right, something reflected in their status as 'protected characteristics' in the UK's Equality Act 2010. I do not consider these to be issues only of minority interest, either: I think the literature on disability and sexual orientation, for example, deserves attention from beyond those self-identifying as gay or disabled.

It might be objected that in dealing with these issues in separate chapters I am failing to deal with the relationships between them, failing to recognize the importance of what has come to be termed intersectionality – of how these characteristics cut across each other and interact. However, I hope it will be apparent from reading these chapters that I do not doubt the importance of such intersections. If I separate these identity categories into separate chapters it is for analytical purposes and also to reflect the emphasis in the literature; it still offers scope to consider the interplay of identity categories within individual chapters. However, I address the issue of intersectionality more directly in the conclusion.

The writer

Finally, the reader might want me to reveal something of myself, at least in so far as this might inform the present work. There is a risk, of course, that this might undermine my credibility rather than enhance it, from certain perspectives. Would the fact that I am a white man make me less credible in the eyes of a black woman, say, particularly when discussing the experience of black women at work? I would imagine it might, but I hope this will be judged by what is said (or not said) rather than by who is saying it. I would be the last to deny that my position as a white, British, male, late-career academic with a primarily sociological orientation did not make a difference to what is said and how it is said. I am what I am and this work is inevitably a product of who I am – and of my experience. The critical reader might be wise to bear this in mind, just as they might consider how their own position affects their reading of the book. However, I hope the reader is at least charitable enough to recognize that I have made an attempt to understand the other, to hear their voice and also be attentive to the possibility of the voice being silenced. In this work I have drawn eclectically on a wide range of scholarship. If this range is still biased towards white men then this reflects the current state of play in the academy. I have attempted to mitigate it by seeking out different voices, although the extent to which I have done so might be insufficient. If so I leave it to others to pursue the work and produce fresh insight and merely hope I have at least done some useful work. Just as those builders over the road leave the building to those who would use it, I must leave this for others to use.

References

Ashforth, B. E., Harrison, S. H. and Corley, K. G. (2008) 'Identification in organizations: An examination of four fundamental questions', *Journal of Management*, 34(3): 325–374.
Brown, A. D. (2015) 'Identities and identity work in organizations', *International Journal of Management Review*, 17: 20–40.
Butler, J. (2004) *Undoing Gender*. London: Routledge.
Butler, J. (2011) *Gender Trouble: Feminism and the Subversion of Identity*. Hoboken: Taylor and Francis.
Caillois, R. (1961) *Man, Play, and Games*. New York: Free Press.
Capozza, D. and Brown, R. (2000) *Social Identity Processes: Trends in Theory and Research*. London: Sage.
Chandler, J. (2010) 'Women and men as managers: The importance of disappointment', *Gender, Work and Organization*, 17(5): 590–611.

Dahrendorf, R. (1973) *Homo sociologicus*. London: Routledge and Kegan Paul.

Elder-Vass, D. (2012) *The Reality of Social Construction*. New York: Cambridge University Press.

Ellemers, N., Haslam, S. A., Platow, M. J. and van Knippnberg, D. (2003) 'Social identity at work: Developments, debates, directions' in Haslam, S. A., van Knippenberg, D., Platow, M. J. and Ellemers, N. (eds), *Social Identity at Work: Developing Theory for Organizational Practice*. New York: Psychology Press.

Elliott, A. (2009) 'The constitution of identity: Primary repression after Kristeva and Laplanche' in Elliott, A. and Du Gay, P. (eds), *Identity in Question*. London: Sage.

Emerson, K. T. U. and Murphy, M. C. (2014) 'Identity threat at work: How social identity threat and situational cues contribute to racial and ethnic disparities in the workplace', *Cultural Diversity and Ethnic Minority Psychology*, 20(4): 508–520.

Hall, S. (1992) 'The question of cultural identity' in Hall, S., Held, D. and McGrew, A. G. (eds), *Modernity and Its Futures*. Cambridge: Polity Press in association with the Open University.

Hall, S. (1996) 'Who needs identity' in Hall, S. and Du Gay, P. (eds), *Questions of Cultural Identity*. London: Sage.

Haslam, S. A. and Ellemers, N. (2005) 'Social identity in industrial and organizational psychology: Concepts, controversies, and contributions', *International Review of Industrial and Organizational Psychology*, 20: 39–118.

Haslam, S. A., van Knippenberg, D., Platow, M. J. and Ellemers, N. (2014) *Social Identity at Work: Developing Theory for Organizational Practice*. New York: Psychology Press.

Ibarra, H. and Petriglieri, J. L. (2010) 'Identity work and play', *Journal of Organizational Change Management*, 23(1): 10–25.

Jenkins, R. (2004) *Social Identity*. London: Routledge.

Marshall, J. (1995) *Women Managers Moving On: Exploring Career and Life Choices*. London: Routledge.

Marx, K. (1974) *Early Writings*. Harmondsworth: Penguin.

Okhuysen, G. and Bonardi, J.-P. (2011) 'Editors' comments: The challenges of building theory by combining lenses', *Academy of Management Review*, 36(1): 6–11.

Ricœur, P. (1992) *Oneself as Another*, translated by Blamey, K. Chicago: University of Chicago Press.

Schwartz, H. S. (1987) 'On the psychodynamics of organizational totalitarianism', *Journal of Management*, 13(1): 41.

Shotter, J. and Gergen, K. J. (eds) (1989) *Texts of Identity*. London: Sage.

Sveningsson, S. and Alvesson, M. (2003) 'Managing managerial identities: Organizational fragmentation, discourse and identity struggle', *Human Relations*, 56(10): 1163–1193.

Watson, T. J. (2008) 'Managing identity: Identity work, personal predicaments and structural circumstances', *Organization*, 15(1): 121–143.

Watson, T. J. and Watson, D. H. (2012) 'Narratives in society, organizations and individual identities: An ethnographic study of pubs, identity work and the pursuit of "the real"', *Human Relations*, 65(6): 683–704.

2

UNPAID WORK AND UNEMPLOYMENT

Introduction

If a person's self-identity is often closely allied with their employment and occupational identity, what happens when someone is unemployed? And to what extent might a person's self-identity be tied to work that is not done in exchange for money?

Those who are not in paid employment are in a number of categories which may overlap or be difficult to distinguish at times:

1. The unemployed who are seeking work.
2. Those choosing not to take paid employment. This may include those who are of normal working age and health and without disability who rely on welfare benefits, but it also includes those who are wealthy enough to have no need to 'work', as well as those who have retired with a pension that provides for their needs. It may also include those who have taken a break from paid employment – most frequently to raise children or care for the elderly, but possibly also simply to have a break.
3. Those unable to work through chronic illness or disability. But in this chapter I would also like to consider another category:
4. Those doing work which is not part of the employment relationship, including work done by those in employment in their 'spare' time, or by those in any of the preceding three categories. This includes voluntary or discretionary work but might also include work that is seen as an obligation, or necessity. This category overlaps with the concept of the informal economy (see Williams and Nadin 2012: 2), although I exclude work that is 'undeclared' work, hidden from the state for tax, social security or labour law purposes, and that is a part of the 'informal' economy since this can be seen as a kind of employment or self-employment.

I will consider the issue of disability in a separate chapter but each of the other categories I will say something about here. I will not consider here work that is done as unpaid overtime and that could be seen as a simple extension of the job. I will start with the category of unemployment that tends, in official statistics at least, to be seen as made up of those in the first category distinguished here.

The unemployed

According to OECD (2015) statistics, in 2014 the unemployment rate was about 6 per cent of the working age population in the UK and US, but around 25 per cent in Greece and 24 per cent in Spain. Of course these figures are not totally accurate as a measure of those who would want paid employment but cannot secure it. They might include some who do not want to work but are presenting themselves as unemployed in order to secure welfare payments. But, conversely, they might also exclude some who are seeking work who do not wish to present themselves to official agencies as unemployed, or are excluded from the official statistics for one reason or another. We should also be cautious in comparing the figures for different countries as they may be compiled under very different circumstances and according to different methodologies. Nevertheless, they may give some rough indication of the numbers of unemployed and, more importantly perhaps, they can give some indication of trends over time at national level.

Unemployment is widely seen as a social problem as well as an individual one. In a society where most household incomes are expected to come from employment one part of this problem is financial: personal and household income is likely to be lower where there is unemployment and poverty may ensue. At its worst this might make it difficult to secure stable housing, pay essential utility bills and buy enough food for a healthy life. At best it is likely to constrain consumption, making things like holidays difficult to afford. But studies of unemployment suggest that it is much more than the loss of income that is a threat to the individual's well-being. An early and influential approach, based originally on a study of unemployment in the Austrian town of Marienthal in the 1930s, identified the problem of unemployment in deficit terms (Jahoda 1982: 60). From this perspective unemployment takes away:

- shared experience;
- a structured experience of time;
- collective purpose;
- status and identity;
- required regular activity.

All of these emphasize the absence of what employment brings – or at least employment as it came to be seen in the dominant, industrialized and bureaucratized form of the 20th century (see Cole 2007). The fourth of these – loss of status and identity – is important and rests on how others see the unemployed, and thus how they may come to see themselves. To be unemployed can carry a social stigma: one risks being deemed to be unsuccessful, perhaps even a scrounger. It is not surprising that many studies since, across the world, point to the psychological and health costs of unemployment (van der Meer 2014).

The deficit model of unemployment runs the risk of seeing people as passive victims of their position, however. Consistent with the approach adopted in this book it might be better to ask how people become unemployed and how people respond when they do. Of course the roots into unemployment and the reactions to it do not occur in circumstances of the individual's choosing. Structural change, such as the decline of an industry in a particular area, can throw people out of work. Even in such circumstances, however, people sometimes exercise agency in deciding the terms and conditions of leaving. But people also exercise agency in how they react to unemployment and how they present themselves. If there is a stigma in being unemployed people may manage this in various ways. In a US context, Pederson (2013) analyses postings on a website where people had shared stories and searched for stories related to job loss and unemployment. On the basis of this he identified various narratives, which he sees as positioned against the meta-narrative of the American dream in which hard work leads to success. He calls these narratives: (a) victim, (b) redeemed, (c) hopeless, (d) bitter, and (e) entitled and dumbfounded.

An example of the victim narrative is the following (with grammatical errors in the original):

> Just got laid off again!!! that is the second hospital that I got laid off from. I am a sterile Tech certify and still can't find a job. I was working at the hospital until on 7/7/2011 security met us at the door with H.R management and handed us our pink slip all ten of us, so I feel like crap. and to make matters worst am getting evicted with my two puppies, and to make matters even worse I have no family a product of the foster care system... YEAH! for me (NOT) This may not mean to [sic] much but it is the little people that is [sic] being affected by this economy mess. Just expressing feelings I don't know what one could do to fix situations like mine and others thanks for listening.
>
> *(Pederson 2013: 309)*

The narrative of the redeemed is very different. An example of this is the following:

> You get out of life what you put into it... and although this didn't work out, something will one day and all the hard work I endured during my 2 years there, will pay off. I take with me new learnings that I now realize since deciding to step back from the situation. I cherish those learnings, because I learned more about myself in that 2 years there, than I had over the course of my entire life. And that, my friends, is invaluable! :0)
>
> *(Pederson 2013: 310)*

The hopeless is, like the victim narrative, another more negative form but rather than looking to the past, it has, like the redeemed narrative, a future orientation, but a more pessimistic view of the future:

> I was laid off five months ago from a job I worked for five years. I loved my job it kept my life balanced. That was my world. I hate this new world that was forced on me. This is not my world this is not what I thought would happen. My life is now a bit of a bipolar mess. I was not ready for the games that my mind was going to play on me. I am still haunted my memories of my last day. The intense grief I feel is overwhelming. I feel like I lost a part of me that I don't think I will ever get back. I miss my friends terribly and find it very hard to adjust to this new painful reality that is my life now. The job search – I am doing everything right. I sent out like a billion resumes in five months and got 2 interviews that they never called me back on. Nothing is happening and I am getting more and more depressed as each day passes. The Long lonely days are the worst it is a living hell just getting through the day and then I have to wake up and do it all over again. When is this going to end? I want my life back again!!
>
> *(Pederson 2013: 311)*

The bitter narrative is full of regret and disappointment:

> Needless to say, after cross-training a young pregnant relative of theirs for two weeks, who HATED doing my job. They gave her everything she ever wanted... MY JOB. I left with a feeling of panic and relief at the same time. 'This was the push I needed' I keep telling myself. Yet, I still wake in the middle of the night with the list of things I never finished and the contractors I never got to say goodbye to. I'm sure my employers had plenty of lies to tell my fellow employees as far as the reason why I was let go but it doesn't matter. I truly believe what goes around comes around and someday they will get a payback.
>
> *(Pederson 2013: 312)*

Finally, the entitled and dumbfounded displayed a mixture of feeling entitled to something better and bewilderment that they are not getting what they deserve:

> I did everything I was suppose to. I was raised in a home where I was taught that education was everything, and as long as I put my mind to it, I could become whatever I wanted to be. I completed high school and went on to further my education in the dental field. I knew things were tough and I assumed it would take me a few months to find a job after completing my education. Sadly, I was very wrong, and it's been almost three years without any job. Out of the dozens of resumes I've put in, both in person and online, I've had a handful of interviews, all unsuccessful. Majority of offices only want

someone who has years of experience, and/or bilingual. I've went as far as trying to volunteer, work for free, just to get the extra experience I needed. I couldn't even work for free. It's been many months since I've last sent in a resume. I know I should be actively trying to find employment, but it's discouraging after so many failed attempts. And since it's been so long, I know an employer is going to question why I was unemployed for so long.

(Pederson 2013: 314–15)

Of course these narratives are representations of experience. They may illustrate a range of socially available subject positions but these are not fixed. Indeed, this categorization may be questioned as incomplete or inadequate. Clearly there is some potential overlap between feelings expressed in the various postings and one can easily imagine the individuals involved shifting from one position to another over time. The point, though, is that these are ways of making sense of a particular event that rendered the individual unemployed and the stories may be used as a basis for action. In the case of the victim, the hopeless and the dumbfounded we might question the extent to which they will be able carry on seeking work. To be redeemed, bitter or entitled might provide a firmer basis for individual or collective action designed to change the individual's situation or the wider social and economic circumstances. Which of these positions is adopted is likely to be affected by interactions with others, including, in this case, reading the postings of others.

The importance of the social context of unemployment is visibly illustrated in a UK context, by a study by Giazitzoglu (2014) of a group of unemployed men in a semi-rural ex-mining town he called Dramen. He dubbed these men the 'drifters' who were 'consensually' unemployed. These men seemed to accept their status as outsiders, seemed to accept that they were despised by others. As one put it (Giazitzoglu 2014: 342):

this (Dramen) is a dust yourself down kind of place where you must work, like you're not a normal person if you don't work. The first question when you meet is do you work, what is your job? If you don't work then they hate you straight away. If you don't work but you say well I try and work but there's fuck all to do at the job centre that is fine, like if you try and work but if you're honest like me and say I don't work, I don't want to work and I'm on benefits they look at you like you're a murderer.

Not working was, for these men, presented as a rational choice. As one put it (Giazitzoglu 2014: 341):

Work? Fuck work. My routine, like me normal day, might be boring, like I keep saying, but it is better than the other choice. I wake up… and then I can do what I want. I have learned to live without money really but that is hard… So I can eat. I have house (due to benefits). I have me lass [girlfriend] and a couple of mates and I know that will be there like forever. And that is fine by me. There is always a new film to watch, a new fucking computer game to play. Another bottle of vodka or bag of pot to smoke come around at the weekend. And I would rather live like this (Walker).

This of course represents exactly the kind of attitude that many would find abhorrent. It would be understandable if others resent such 'freeloaders'. As another respondent in the same study put it (Giazitzoglu 2014: 339):

the way they (the Drifters) take the piss (by living on benefits) is shocking. We live in a place where we help those who need it, but these days I get pissed off with lazy cunts (not working)... 'cause it's not like they're trying to work and can't get a job it's cause they don't fucking want to work and expect us to pay for them.

Giazitzoglu, rather than passing moral judgement on the men, shows how they are making choices under conditions of constraint:

Because of their educations ('I failed every exam'), lack of work experience ('if I went for a job how do I explain ten years of doing fuck all at interview?') and appearances ('I've got a scar on my face from where I got stabbed and a shaved head and a tattoo over my eye – would you give me a job') the prospect of gaining and keeping dependable, steady work is unrealistic for the Drifters. Even if a Drifter did find work in Dramen's problematic local labour market, that work would be defined by insecurity, low-pay and potential emasculation; akin to that association with the working poor's labour experiences. Aware of their realities, six Drifters convincingly suggested that their lives of apparently consensual non-work is 'a better option for us': the Drifters' non-work is not merely a product of laziness, but a pragmatic choice that ensures the men have financial positions which are comparable to the financial positions they would experience if they worked in local 'shitty jobs'.

(Giazitzoglu 2014: 344)

In emphasizing choice, one might feed into a political narrative that simply blames these men for the choices they make, and seeks to coerce them into more 'respectable' ways of living. But their choices are made in circumstances where there are few positive alternatives for those without education and the kind of appearance and manner expected in service work. Indeed, in many ways these men could be seen as embodying the values of neoliberalism. They are behaving as rational economic men and retreating into a privatized existence in which only their family and friends provide support and comfort. Moreover, their very existence may provide a normative yardstick against which others can be measured. We might, of course, still want to ask what other choices they might have made, other than trying harder to get a job. Perhaps if we are to criticize them it is for failing to adopt a more outward-looking approach which seeks to mobilize with others to change the conditions under which they have few opportunities and where those that do exist are in 'shitty jobs' that are lowly paid.

I do not wish to suggest that the experience of these men is typical of the unemployed. Rather I would want to emphasize that these men are located in a particular time and place. Gender, ethnicity and age are also significant features of the situation. These are white English men whose choices are made against a local historical backdrop in which men were expected, and generally did, work in jobs such as mining, often providing enough income for the whole family. These jobs no longer exist in this locality. It is against this historical backdrop that their reactions, as well as those of their neighbours, can best be understood. Moreover, their stage in the life course is significant since if these men were considered to be past normal working age then it seems doubtful that consensual unemployment would be the issue it seems to be; they would not need to justify their choices, or face the opprobrium of their neighbours in the same way. It is useful here to note Cole's (2007: 1135) critical response to Jahodra's work on the 'deficit' model of unemployment arising from the Marienthal study: 'What is not given due consideration in the Marienthal study is the idea that the sufferings consequent on the loss of paid work might be social constructs, that is, outcomes of an historically-contingent construction of (male) identities in relation to a particular form of paid work.' In other words, when one considers what is lost it is what tends to be associated with the work done by working-class men in the 1930s and is our dominant conception of 'work'.

This suggests a need to consider that the experience of unemployment may differ according to class, ethnicity, gender, disability and age (see Artazcoz et al. 2004) – that there is a need to consider it in relation to the meaning of employment, and the history of employment for particular social groups. But there is also a need to consider it in relation to other forms of work, of 'unpaid' work in various forms, and it is to this that I will turn next.

Unpaid work in the private sphere

Much work might be paid or unpaid. I might wash up my dirty dishes for nothing while someone else is paid to do so in a restaurant. Feminists have pointed out that much of the work that women do is unpaid. In the household they clean, cook, care for children and are often expected to do so out of love or duty. In the 1970s in the UK some feminists campaigned for 'wages for housework', hoping that the work of women might be valued and remunerated (Edmond and Fleming 1975). We are still waiting for this.

We might want to distinguish work from play or from leisure but such distinctions are not without their difficulties. Leisure activities or play might be seen as done for their intrinsic pleasure and will cease once this pleasure is gone, while work can be seen as productive activity, done as a means to an end and often having to be endured beyond the point at which the individual might like to give it up (see, for example, Thomas (1999: xiii–xiv)). According to Caillois (1961: 9), play is based on free will, circumscribed within temporal and spatial limitations, and unproductive in that it creates neither objects nor wealth. However, the work/leisure or work/play distinction is by no means absolute and clear cut. We can enjoy work for its own sake and 'leisure' activities such as gardening may also serve instrumental ends – to provide food on the table or means of exercise. Lee and Lin (2011) show how in the world of multiple-player online games such as *Second Life* and *World of Warcraft*, what can start out as a leisure activity can be turned into something for financial gain with some skilful players selling their labour in playing the game to others who might want to take shortcuts, reducing their time spent on what they see as tedious elements. In this study we find examples of identity work where the gamer (itself an identity which might encompass leisure and paid work) works at separating the 'fun' of gaming from the 'work' of gaming. Thus a woman gamer is described as follows:

> Shin has five computers in her bedroom for collecting currency from the game *Lineage*. Between 10 am to 11pm she refers to this space as her 'workstation'. Unlike office, 'workstation' implies a less formal, limited space closed off from other space. At 11pm she terminates all production and transactions through the simple ritual of turning off her mobile phone. She later starts playing another game – *Lineage II* – which allows her to interact with friends without thinking of business or profit. According to her, 'I must make these clear distinctions, otherwise my life will get mixed up and I'll never feel relaxed'.
>
> *(Lee and Lin 2011: 462)*

This study shows how some enterprising gamers – often in developing countries – set themselves up to serve others, thus reproducing something like the supply chains found in manufactured goods. But in so doing sometimes they do work that they might see as mundane, repetitive and intensive. It is easy to see, however, that the distinction between work and leisure can become blurred (think of some professional gamblers, or academics). Lee and Lin (2011) reasonably take the view that such situations contradict every part of Caillois' definition of 'play'. (Their work also suggests a blurring of the lines between the 'private' and 'public' sphere in that gaming, even if taking place in the home, can involve interaction with and trading with those elsewhere in what might be seen as a public sphere.)

I would argue that we often want to blur the distinction between work and leisure as much as possible – to see work as a pleasurable activity and leisure as productive. But nevertheless we do, like Shin in the quotation above, often want to separate these out, to distinguish these as separate times, with different qualities. Such a position is not necessarily contradictory: we might usefully employ the language of leisure to enrich work and work to enrich particular kinds of leisure, while accepting that some work might always be drudgery and some leisure might always be unproductive, at least as measured in terms of 'output' and use-value or exchange value.

Unpaid work can of course be of a wide variety of kinds. In his analysis of time-use data, Gershuny (2003: 171–218) distinguishes between four uses of time: paid work, unpaid work, leisure time and personal care. Within the category of unpaid work he puts the activities of routine housework (cleaning, etc.), cooking, shopping, childcare and odd jobs (Gershuny 2003: 180). Leisure time includes out-of-home leisure, such as going to the cinema, and leisure in the home. The latter he sees as often passive (such as watching TV). The final category, 'personal care', includes sleeping, washing, dressing and medical care.

Clearly some of these distinctions are contentious – are gardening or shopping, say, unpaid work or forms of active leisure? Perhaps they might be both. A distinction might be made on the basis of subjective feelings about them – if the activity is an unwelcome chore it is 'work', if we enjoy it as a hobby it is leisure – but there are a lot of grey areas between these states and our feeling about them might even change from moment to moment. It might, then, be wise to see such concepts as socially available distinctions, used flexibly in the course of everyday life and academic work.

This emphasis on non-paid work can be tied to a broader concern with provisioning. A number of writers, economists and other social scientists, seek to move beyond conventional economic discussion and focus on processes that include activity beyond the marketplace. Provisioning can be defined as the work needed to realize the necessities and conveniences of life (Neysmith et al. 2012: 4). This provides a broad conception which includes the kind of unpaid work referred to by Gershuny (2003), as well as personal care, and could include some of what is included in his leisure category. But the emphasis here is on what might be seen as production for use, as opposed to consumption. Here I would include activities such as gardening as provisioning (watching the TV is not).

Of course there is a relationship between unpaid work and paid work for those in employment. The amount one is paid can affect the unpaid work you do. Glucksmann (2000) pointed to the variable ways in which domestic labour might be related to paid work: women weavers were relatively well paid and could afford to purchase the services of other women – for example to do their washing or childcare, something also common in high-income professional households where the woman works full time. She also reported that these weavers had a more equal division of domestic labour with their husbands than did the casual workers with which she compared them. For these lower-paid casual workers there was no money to allow them to buy labour of others to do work in their own households – they had to do it themselves. Also their husbands often worked in insecure and male gender-segregated occupations and saw housework as women's work. So the nature of paid work influences domestic labour and its distribution between partners within the household. Glucksmann (2000) has also emphasized the articulations of work and non-work activities – the difficulty of separating out work from other activities. Certainly, from an experiential point of view, we might sometimes see childcare as hard work, sometimes as pleasurable 'fun'. The importance of thinking about 'interconnecting temporalities of work' is another consideration Glucksmann (2000) points to. At its simplest we might think about how long 'working' hours, understood as time spent in employment, interact with 'non-work' time, or unpaid work. To some extent this is about how the job impacts on one's life outside of it: whether the job requires long hours, cutting into one's time spent with friends or family. Blyton and Jenkins' (2012) study of garment workers made redundant by Burberry in South Wales, for example, show how, prior to redundancy, they often valued the proximity to home and regularity of the hours: 'No bus fare to pay, on the doorstep. I could leave the house at 25 to eight and be clocking on at a quarter to. We used to finish at 4.40 and I'd be home by 4.45. I could get on with my ironing before tea' (Blyton and Jenkins 2012: 31).

In contrast, the jobs increasingly common in the service sector require 'flexibility' in time spent at work. Thus the authors report how one ex-Burberry factory employee after redundancy became a hotel receptionist, working shifts determined on a weekly basis: 'You can't plan anything. I've just had to cancel a dentist's appointment because they've called me in for a shift and I can't make another appointment because I won't know what I'm working next week' (Blyton and Jenkins 2012: 36).

This is more than a sharing of time between different activities. It is also about rhythms and subjective experiences of time, as well as about when different activities take place in time and the effects of this (e.g. for a night shift worker, when do they see their children?). An illustration of the importance of this latter issue is Dermott's (2005) study of fathers' perceptions of the relationship between employment and childcare. Despite often working long hours that minimized contact with children, they often felt they did have an acceptable 'work-life' balance and were good fathers. Partly this seemed to involve a balancing act. As one father put it:

> I knew that it was unlikely that I would be around all day, but I knew that at the end of the day, I should put work behind me and should throw myself into whatever is left to the day for the children... Given that I have a long journey home from work.
>
> *(Dermott 2005: 98)*

Given the shortage of time with their children these fathers seemed to emphasize quality rather than quantity and Dermott makes the point that they focused on play rather than child-related domestic tasks (such as washing their clothes, perhaps?). In this way they felt they could build good relations with their children while also meeting the demands of the workplace. The author also notes gender differences in this in that women as mothers tended to do more of the childcare in the home, including those aspects that might not be so pleasurable. She also argued that conceptions of the good mother for those in her study diverge from that of the good father, with a greater emphasis on time commitment from the mothers.

It might be argued that a key driver of non-paid work is love and care, but this also raises issues of duty and obligation, based on certain social norms. While the work of women in relation to children might be motivated by love and care, it might also be more complex than this. Consider the case presented by Parker (1997: 18):

Take for example a mother's response to an ill child age 7. Suddenly, from having been the mother of a school-aged child she becomes again the mother of a child who cries if she leaves the room. Some mothers return happily to being a life-support system. They feel confident of their capacity to provide the sort of care needed by a sick child – indeed, some prefer the kind of mothering demanded in this situation. Others feel pulled back to a state they had found fearful and claustrophobic. The present stage of mothering takes for granted the child's mobility and viability, while the sick, regressed child suggests a frailty and demands a quality of attention they had moved beyond, perhaps with a sigh of relief.

Note how Parker points to a variety of responses here, but also to responses that may vary over time as the woman's relationship with the growing child changes and her expectations change. The same author provides an example of more directly ambivalent feelings, too:

Mary's children, aged six and nine, were invited to go to Norway for 10 days with a friend's family. She said to me: I long for them to go. I can't wait to see the back of them. When was the last time I had 10 days all to myself? But I also feel terrible about it. I'm scared of losing them. I have images of planes crashing, drowning and abduction, I want to say that they can't go. It's terrible to want to get rid of them and want so much to hold onto them.

(Parker 1997: 30)

The work of childcare can be hard and unrewarding as well as an expression of love which is gratefully received or taken for granted. As one woman put it, talking about preparing lunch boxes: 'It's just there. It's just got to be done. It would be much easier for me if I didn't have to do it, because it would be one less thing to have to do. But it has to be done, so you just get on with it' (Harman and Cappellini 2015: 769). Why it 'has to be done' is, as this study shows, bound up in culturally specific notions of what it means to be a good mother. Parallel processes are reported in Allison's (1991) study of mothers in Japan and Donner's (2006) study of mothers in Calcutta. Such studies show how this kind of domestic work can have instrumental value in providing nutrition for growing children but it can also be used as a sign of being a good mother – a sign displayed to the child concerned and to those others, such as other children, mothers and teachers, who witness the display. Such work might well figure in the construction of a valued self-identity – that of motherhood.

Much of the literature relating to unpaid work concerns housework and emphasizes the importance of gender. Cleaning, cooking, shopping and looking after children are commonly seen as women's work. Gershuny's (2003) analysis of time-use data, over a number of different countries and over time, does report some convergence between the sexes in the amount of unpaid work done in the home, although women still doing more than men. In particular there seems, in Western countries, to have been a substantial increase in the amount of time fathers spend with their children and that it is now considered masculine to be an involved father (Coltrane 2009).

In a recent qualitative study Lyonette and Crompton (2015: 28) report that: 'Respondents were overwhelmingly supportive of domestic sharing'. However, this was often qualified as being contingent on the circumstances: 'I think it depends on what your paid working arrangements are. We divide them up according to how much time each of us has because of our outside-the-house responsibilities, and I'm very comfortable with what we do (A1, female WEM, earning £90K; female responsibility for housework)' (Lyonette and Crompton 2015: 29). There are also traces of older attitudes as in the statement that:

> It should be a shared thing because if the woman is going out to work I think, you know, you're paying money. I feel it should not be just for a lady to do. I mean if, for example, I'm staying at home, I'm not going to work and my husband is going out to work and he's coming home tired, I'll expect him to come and find a clean house, his dinner is ready and stuff like that for him. So I wouldn't expect him to do that much, really.
>
> Interviewer: But if you're working, it should be shared? Equally shared, yes.
>
> *(Lyonette and Crompton 2015: 29)*

This is also echoed in the sentiments of the men in Natalier's (2003) study of all-male shared households in Australia in which one respondent expresses the view that: 'I wouldn't say that women have some kind of extra housework role. Have you talked to someone who says that? That's pretty rare. Maybe people say it about their wives but that'd be rare anyway now, I'd reckon' (Natalier 2003: 261). Lyonette and Crompton's study shows how the sharing out of domestic work can be subject to negotiation in the household:

> I've made it known to my husband that, listen, I know you don't like ironing but… it would help to just shove a wash load on so that at least I can come home and whatever… but I have hinted it would be nice to come home and not have to think about dinner every night, so we share, but I mean if you ask me who does the ironing, the hoovering, the majority, then I still do it… when my husband cleans he surface cleans, when I clean, I clean (R1 female WEM, earning £45K; female responsibility for housework).
>
> *(Lyonette and Crompton 2015: 33)*

Moreover, among those who shared, some in the higher-paid group shared what was left after paid domestic help had done some of it – a cleaner, nanny or aupair – invariably a woman. Studies have also shown a tendency for men to prefer some kinds of housework – often the most visible, such as cooking – than others (Coltrane 2009).

The gendering of household duties can also occur in all-male households. In Natalier's study the author concludes that:

Opting in, rejecting responsibility and deprioritizing housework define housework as marginal to the daily lives of the male share householders of the study. In this, their enactments reflect those of most husbands. As Omar [one of the respondents] so neatly puts it: 'I'm not his wife'... In this study, even in the physical absence of women, masculinities are played out in over-whelmingly traditional ways. The men consistently disengage from any systematic involvement in housework. They opt in to work, undertaking it when they think it needs to be done and they are prepared to do so. They rarely feel that it is finally up to them to ensure their home is tidy and food is on the table. These men behave as though they are husbands even in the absence of women who might act as wives.

(Natalier 2003: 265)

This idea of 'husbands' clearly rests on a disidentification with domestic labour – or at least a desire to marginalize its importance. There seems to be, among this generation, an awareness of the potential role of housewife which for much of the 20th century was a key source of identity for many women. Many of the women in Oakley's (1982) study of housework in the 1970s describe themselves as housewives. Indeed, faced with the open-ended invitation to complete the sentence 'I am...' out of 40 women asked 25 wrote I am a housewife somewhere in their list of self-descriptions and 20 of these put it in first or second place (Oakley 1982: 176). At the same time many of these women clearly expressed some dissatisfaction with this work they were doing, with problems of boredom and isolation featuring promi-nently in their complaints (Oakley 1982: 173–6) even while the advertising industry valorized their work in keeping the home clean and safe and providing nourishment for children and husbands. The second-wave feminism of the 1960s and 1970s was often targeted at the perceived limitations and constraints of unpaid housework. To a large extent, women's liberation was to be liberation from the home and the identity of housewife: that is, someone dependent on the husband and whose primary role was to work in the home.

The unpaid work that we do may or may not be significant to our self-identity. If we see ourselves as a housewife, mother or gardener it might well do so, but much unpaid work might be seen as of marginal importance to who we see ourselves to be, a chore to be endured but not enjoyed. But even humble routine chores such as cleaning can be tied to key senses of self-identities – the 'good' mother, the 'respect-able' householder. Such tasks can be woven into complex webs of identities, as can the avoidance of such work. Our self-identities are negotiated through our positioning ourselves within a range of possibilities given by income, paid work and social settings, negotiated with those others we encounter in the course of our everyday lives (including partners and children). Significant, too, is public discourse in the media and conversations in the workplace, street or leisure venues, with discussions on issues such as school dinners informing our positions. The public and private realms are often seen as separate, and in the structure of this chapter I am holding them separate for analytical purposes; but they each influence the other.

Unpaid work in the public sphere

Unpaid work outside the home can take many forms and have many motivations. We might start with Taylor's work (2005) in which she examines people working in a voluntary organization which she calls Care Aid. Here we see a contrast between Elizabeth, who is something like the middle-class do-gooder one might associate with voluntary organizations, and Maria, a Philippine woman who was described as having a plethora of unpaid positions working for the Philippine community in London, as well as working for Care Aid in a paid capacity as fundraiser. As Taylor puts it, for Elizabeth her recruitment and subsequent career can be seen as a product of the expectations, obligations and recognition attendant on her social position and relations. She describes her recruitment:

> The president of Care Aid 20 years ago was Lady Somerville and she was at a presidents' conference and my sister, then I think she was deputy president of Cheshire, and she said, 'Surely, you've got three sisters, one of them must live in Berkshire?' And Anne said, 'Yes'. So I got asked to dinner and Lady Alice is a wonderful lady, very frightening, and said I'm about to give up and I want to hand over.
>
> *(Taylor 2005: 128)*

Maria, on the other hand, was described as wanting to serve her own community and her orientation was 'closer to working-class notions of solidarity and mutual aid than to moral notions of helping the less fortunate' (Taylor 2005: 131). These cases illustrate very different routes into voluntary work and very different reasons for doing it.

The motivation to do unpaid work might also be related to the life course (see Chapter 9), even if there is likely to be a large amount of overlap between those at different stages. It may, for example, be more likely that young people volunteer to improve their employment chances than is the case for those in the post-retirement phase.

Unpaid 'voluntary' work might take the form of engagement in charities, in organizing community events or in political work of varying kinds. It can be seen as part of one's contribution to society, as Budd (2011) has explained in discussing work as 'service'. He cites Morone (1998, cited in Budd 2011: 174), who, in discussing the views of those engaged in the American Revolution, stated that:

> The revolutionary ideal lay, not in the pursuit of private matters, but in the shared public life of civic duty, in the subordination of individual interest to the *res publica*… To the first American generation, the political community was a single organic whole, binding each of its members into a single civic body of shared interests that transcended individual concerns. Natural leaders were expected to rise up among the people; others would… contribute their own talents to the common good.

Feminists have also emphasized that unpaid work outside the home is an important part of 'provisioning', defined as: 'formal and informal volunteer activities in community organisations (including places of worship) creating and maintaining networks, visiting and organising social gatherings' (Neysmith et al. 2012: 32). They emphasize what they refer to as invisible provisioning activities: sustaining health, making claims and ensuring the safety of themselves, as women, and their children. Much of this involves networking with others and community activity. In this they emphasize work that goes well beyond the kind of privatized work of the housewife in the home which was the target of women's liberation in the second-wave feminism of the 1960s and 1970s. Consider the words of a volunteer in a food bank (Neysmith et al. 2012: 38):

> It's not so much the food as the emotional support. Since I'm a volunteer there, I've become like part of the family there, been 10 years at this one place, made a lot of friends there. We do Christmases together. My Christmas party of the year is with the volunteers there. We have picnics in the summer. We have social events where we go out pulling together, so they become friends and not just co-workers.

In this it is hard to see a clear distinction between work and leisure or between consumption and production. As the authors point out (Neysmith et al. 2012: 62):

> to provision collectively is not to sell services to customers or clients but to offer public services for the needs and desires of citizens that go beyond technical solutions. At the most activist end of the continuum, this space can offer transformational possibilities for women to explore identities that defy stereotypes.

BOX 2.1 IN THE NEWS: VOLUNTEER LIBRARIANS

In 2011 it was reported that a local resident, Kathy Dunbar, among others, successfully lobbied for the New Cross Library in London to be run by volunteers. This was as an alternative to its closure that had been proposed by the local council in a bid to save money. She was reported as saying, 'There's a gang culture here and this was another thing they would take away from the local children who are already deprived.'

The library was renamed New Cross Learning and reopened in August 2011. Dunbar is joint-volunteer manager of the library and says she spends about 50 hours a week there. Despite this she is not keen on handing all public libraries to volunteers. 'It is not right for all libraries because they will not necessarily have volunteers or support from the community,' she said. 'If you get rid of libraries, they will never come back. I know we have to make cuts, but there are certain things that should not be got rid of.'

Source: Third Sector 2012

The value of work as community service is also a feature of liberal and neoliberal discourse. As Soss et al. (2011: 22–3) observe:

> From Hayek (1960) onward neoliberal discourse has valorized self-discipline as the sine qua non of freedom. Individuals, in this view, have a moral and political obligation to act as disciplined entrepreneurs. They must plan to meet their own needs, accept personal responsibility for their problems, and manage their daily affairs with prudence. The individual who does otherwise fails not just as an economic actor but as a moral and civic being.

This can become the basis for compulsory community service in situations where individuals cannot secure paid work. Of course, what might be seen as a community-service imperative can be satisfied in various ways. In Musick and Wilson's (2007) useful overview of volunteers and volunteering (mainly but not exclusively in a US context), they include both unpaid work providing services to others in need but also political activism as a form of voluntary work, although they go on to say (Musick and Wilson 2007: 26):

> we will not include in the definition [of volunteering] tasks such as child care or informal and casual helping such as dog sitting for one's neighbor. This is because volunteering is 'organized voluntary activity focused on problem solving and helping others'… and the fact it is organized is important.

While I think this is a useful way of distinguishing voluntary work from both domestic labour on the one hand and 'employment' on the other, this does raise the issue of how such work is 'organized'. In a world where social media can be used to facilitate mobilization in ways that may have greater or lesser degrees of formality and permanence, perhaps these boundaries will inevitably be fuzzy. Nevertheless, here I want to explore the world of work that this definition alludes to.

Batson et al. (2002), in a psychological approach to the issue, have suggested that there are four motivations for volunteering: egoism, altruism, collectivism and principlism. Egoism involves a concern with increasing one's own welfare while altruism increases the welfare of one or more other individuals, as individuals. Collectivism is seen as increasing the welfare of a group while principlism is based on upholding some moral principle such as justice. I think these distinctions have some face validity, even if we can expect them to be hard to differentiate in practice or become mixed – the recent graduate who volunteers for charity work may well have ideas about how it will improve their future employability through gaining key skills, while also wanting to serve others and express their 'moral' principles. Indeed, many voluntary organizations appeal exactly to such multiple motivations. To the extent that altruism is a driver of voluntary work, Batson et al. see this as based upon empathy. This might well motivate people to work for those who are seen as suffering in ways that the individual has suffered in the past (as in the case of someone who has had anorexia and chooses to work with people with eating disorders, for example). As Batson et al. define altruism, however, as directed to the welfare of particular individuals, it seems to shade into the kind of informal care that Musick and Wilson (2007) wish to dismiss from their definition of volunteerism. Batson et al.'s third category of collectivism seems to be equivalent to what is more often associated with voluntary work – the desire to work for people with particular needs. Batson et al. make the point that this is often based upon identification with this group: 'Typically, we care about collectives of which we are members' (Batson et al. 2002: 438). But surely many kinds of volunteerism entail a desire for work with groups on the basis of identification with those who are unlike ourselves, sometimes at some emotional cost. An example of the latter is cited by Musick and Wilson (2007) – an ethnographic study of a UK study in which a respondent described the psychological burden imposed by the work of giving emotional and practical support to mothers having difficulty coping with their children: 'You get emotionally involved, you hear things you don't ever want to hear... sleep-losing things. I worry sometimes into the night, for example, once about alleged sexual abuse of a child. I was aghast, and I felt powerless' (Bagilhole 1996: 197). Maria's example above might provide an example of a case of identification with a group she did belong to, but the distinction between this and principlism seems less than clear cut. For Batson et al. it seems to be the distinction between something based on abstract principles as opposed to the concrete needs of a particular defined group but, as Maria's example shows, this might be difficult to distinguish in particular cases.

Musick and Wilson cite Brady et al. (1995: 271) in explaining why more people do not get involved in civic life: 'because they can't, because they don't want to, or because nobody asked'. If people don't want to it may be either because they do not have any of the motivations identified by Baston et al. or that they see the costs outweighing the benefits. An Australian study by Warburton et al. (2001: 588) suggested that for older volunteers, alongside altruistic motivations and a desire to serve others, the benefits included social interaction, filling time, feeling useful and feeling an obligation to society. Interestingly, many of these seem to mirror the deficit model of unemployment, suggesting that voluntary work might fill a gap otherwise filled by paid work. This seems consistent, too, with those who advocate 'active' aging (see Chapter 9). However, others might see the costs as outweighing the benefits, with those not volunteering frequently citing being tied down as a disadvantage and of feeling they were too old to be valued. But if the weighing of costs and benefits make this sound like the rational choice of an individual, the authors also emphasize that this is not a purely individual decision – the support provided by others and the approval and encouragement of others is also important. These others include partners, friends and family but also perceived wider social norms: 'being asked' should not be taken too literally but might extend to a wide variety of social facilitators, including access to information about opportunities and wider social norms. As an illustration of the latter, Baldock (2000) suggests there are differences between the US, Netherlands and Australia in how volunteering is viewed. In the US it is more likely to be seen as resembling paid work and the emphasis is on productive contribution. In Australia it is viewed, at least for the older retired person, as a form of recreation to be enjoyed, while in the Netherlands the emphasis is on integrating the individual in the community – largely through paid work or through engagement in committees. Such differences might well shape individual decisions and expectations. In the US there seems to be more acceptance of voluntary work as unpaid routine service provision, while in Australia the expectation seems to be that it will be intrinsically rewarding and in the Netherlands that it takes the form of community leadership (with any service provision being paid, if it is not done informally).

Musick and Wilson (2007) make it clear that volunteering is very much affected by issues of gender, ethnicity, class and age (or rather position in the life course). For example, with regard to gender, volunteer work often reflects the same kind of division of labour found in paid work (Musick and Wilson 2007: 182). Volunteer fire and rescue work is predominantly a male activity while childcare is female. If it is gendered, this may also be because community activism is fuelled by gendered experience. The drive to provide and campaign for better pre-school provision for children, for example, is, in many countries, a predominantly female activity, but this can be seen as rooted in the experience of women, and identification with other women as mothers, promotes such activity (Neysmith et al. 2012).

All this suggests that identity work involves deciding what we need to commit to where there is at least the possibility of conflicting and multiple commitments. We may answer the call to volunteer or we might resist it. There are, however, important political questions and social policy questions raised by such issues: who should be paid for work and how much; if it is paid, where does the money come from? Voluntary work, by nature of its voluntary nature, might be seen as quintessentially good work, even if it brings its own costs in fatigue or boredom. Yet unpaid voluntary work also raises the spectre of exploitation. In making a contribution freely we are gifting our labour to others. The question of whether such a gift, even one freely made, is unjust is an important one.

Conclusion

This chapter has ranged widely but it suggests that work should not be equated only with employment or with that which we are paid to do. If employment – the job – is a potent source of self-identity, so too is work that is not paid for. Examining unpaid work involves recognizing that work can be done for the benefit of others as well as oneself; it can be done for altruistic or egoistic reasons or a mixture of the two. The discussion has raised issues concerning the extent to which work is pleasurable, freely done and done for the service of others. We have seen also how work and unpaid work are interrelated. In the reflexive project of the self (Giddens 1991), work, in all its forms, is both figure and ground. Through our work we craft ourselves as individuals, but this is not simply the work of the individual. We find ourselves in particular social locations, speaking a certain language, partaking of particular discourses. We make choices, but not under conditions of our own choosing, and if we act, or choose not to act, in particular ways it is through a complex web of relationships, constraints and opportunities. In neo-liberal times the working self seems to be as necessary as the consuming self as to who we are. But there are many kinds of worker, just as there are many kinds of consumer, and we have many opportunities for self-identification in our complex, unfolding lives. Some might retreat into themselves or engage only with a close circle of friends and family, others work collectively to improve the lot of others (others either like themselves or unlike themselves). Work in the public and the private spheres are both significant. Provisioning is not just the satisfaction of individual or household needs but a wider social process. Work is always individual but also always social; but the degree to which it reaches out to others, embodying service, as well as the degree to which it is freely chosen and intrinsically rewarding, is highly variable. Identity work is required to both integrate and differentiate: to play with what is possible and desirable. If we sometimes separate out different kinds of work, splitting up and switching between identity positions, we must weave these fragments together in the fabric of our lives. Perhaps our unpaid work is most satisfying when it is a means of serving others as well as ourselves – giving, learning, growing.

BOX 2.2 AT THE MOVIES: UNPAID WORK AND UNEMPLOYMENT

Movies relevant to the themes in this chapter include:

Grapes of Wrath (1940, director John Ford)
Godfather II (1974, director Francis Ford Coppola)
The Stepford Wives (1975, director Bryan Forbes)
Lost in America (1985, director Albert Brooks)
Tokyo Sonata (2008, director Kiyoshi Kurowsawa)
The Lunchbox (2013, director Ritesh Batra)

References

Allison, A. (1991) 'Japanese mothers and obentōs: The lunch-box as ideological state apparatus', *Anthropological Quarterly*, 64(4): 195–208.

Artazcoz, L., Benach, J., Borrell, C. and Cortes, I. (2004) 'Unemployment and mental health: Understanding the interactions among gender, family roles, and social class', *American Journal of Public Health*, 94(1): 82–88.

Bagilhole, B. (1996) 'Tea and sympathy or teetering on social work? An investigation of the blurring of boundaries between voluntary and professional care', *Social Policy and Administration*, 30: 189–205.

Baldock, C. V. (2000) 'Governing the senior volunteer in Australia, the USA and the Netherlands' in Warburton, J. and Oppenheimer, M. (eds), *Volunteers and Volunteering*. Annandale: Federation Press.

Batson, C. D., Ahmad, N. and Tsang, J. A. (2002) 'Four motives for community involvement', *Journal of Social Issues*, 58(3): 429–445.

Blyton, P. and Jenkins, J. (2012) 'Life after Burberry: Shifting experiences of work and non-work life following redundancy', *Work, Employment and Society*, 26(1): 26–41.

Brady, H., Verba, S. and Scholzman, K. (1995) 'Beyond SES: A resource model of political participation', *American Political Science Review*, 89(2): 271–294.

Budd, J. W. (2011) *The Thought of Work*. Ithaca, NY: Cornell University Press.

Caillois, R. (1961) *Man, Play, and Games*. New York: Free Press.

Cole, M. (2007) 'Re-thinking unemployment: A challenge to the legacy of Jahoda et al.', *Sociology*, 41(6): 1133–1149.

Coltrane, S. (2009) 'Fatherhood, gender and work-family policies' in Gornick, J. C. and Meyers, M. K. (eds), *Gender Equality: Transforming Family Divisions of Labor*. New York: Verso.

Dermott, E. (2005) 'Time and labour: Fathers' perceptions of employment and childcare' in Pettinger, L., Parry, J., Taylor, R. and Glucksmann, M. (eds), *A New Sociology of Work?* Malden: Blackwell Publishing.

Donner, H. (2006) 'Committed mothers and well-adjusted children: Privatisation, early-years education and motherhood in Calcutta', *Modern Asian Studies*, 40(2): 371–395.

Edmond, W. and Fleming, S. (1975) *All Work and No Pay: Women, Housework and the Wages Due*. Bristol: Falling Wall Press.

Gershuny, J. I. (2003) *Changing Times: Work and Leisure in Postindustrial Society*. Oxford: Oxford University Press.

Giazitzoglu, A. G. (2014) 'Learning not to labour: A micro analysis of consensual male unemployment', *International Journal of Sociology and Social Policy*, 34(5/6): 334–348.

Giddens, A. (1991) *Modernity and Self-Identity: Self and Society in the Late Modern Age*. Cambridge: Polity Press.

Glucksmann, M. (2000) *Cottons and Casuals: The Gendered Organisation of Labour in Time and Space*. Durham, NC: Sociology Press.

Harman, V. and Cappellini, B. (2015) 'Mothers on display: Lunchboxes, social class and moral accountability', *Sociology*, 49(4): 764–781.

Jahoda, M. (1982) *Employment and Unemployment: A Social-Psychological Analysis*. Cambridge: Cambridge University Press.

Lee, Y.-H. and Lin, H. (2011) '"Gaming is my work": Identity work in internet-hobbyist game workers', *Work, Employment and Society*, 25(3): 451–467.

Lyonette, C. and Crompton, R. (2015) 'Sharing the load? Partners' relative earnings and the division of domestic labour', *Work, Employment and Society*, 29(1): 23–40.

Musick, M. A. and Wilson, J. (2007) *Volunteers: A Social Profile*. Bloomington, IN: Indiana University Press.

Natalier, K. (2003) '"I'm not his wife": Doing gender and doing housework in the absence of women', *Journal of Sociology*, 39(3): 253–269.

Neysmith, S. M., Reitsma-Street, M., Collins, S. B. and Porter, E. (eds) (2012) *Beyond Caring Labour to Provisioning Work*. Toronto: University of Toronto Press.

Oakley, A. (1982) *Subject Women*. London: Fontana.

OECD (2015) 'Unemployment', at https://data.oecd.org/unemp/harmonised-unemployment-rate-hur.htm (accessed 30 October 2015).

Parker, R. (1997) 'The production and purposes of maternal ambivalence' in Hollway, W. and Featherstone, B. (eds), *Mothering and Ambivalence*. London: Routledge.

Pederson, J. R. (2013) 'Disruptions of individual and cultural identities: How online stories of job loss and unemployment shift the American Dream', *Narrative Inquiry*, 23(2): 302–322.

Soss, J., Fording, R. and Schram, S. F. (2011) *Disciplining the Poor: Neoliberal Paternalism and the Persistent Power of Race*. Chicago: University of Chicago Press.

Taylor, R. (2005) 'Rethinking voluntary work' in Pettinger, L., Parry, J., Taylor, R. and Glucksmann, M. (eds), *A New Sociology of Work?* Oxford: Blackwell.

Third Sector (2012) 'The libraries that have been taken over by volunteers', at http://www.thirdsector.co.uk/analysis-libraries-taken-volunteers/policy-and-politics/article/1146150 (accessed 7 December 2015).

Thomas, K. (ed.) (1999) *The Oxford Book of Work*. Oxford: Oxford University Press.

van der Meer, P. H. (2014) 'Gender, unemployment and subjective well-being: Why being unemployed is worse for men than for women', *Social Indicators Research*, 115(1): 23–44.

Warburton, J., Terry, D. J., Rosenman, L. S. and Shapiro, M. (2001) 'Differences between older volunteers and nonvolunteers: Attitudinal, normative, and control beliefs', *Research on Aging*, 23(5): 586.

Williams, C. C. and Nadin, S. (2012) 'Work beyond employment: Representations of informal economic activities', *Work, Employment and Society*, 26(2): 1–10.

3

OCCUPATION AND CLASS

Introduction

Consider the work of Lynsey Gidman, as described by Biggs (2015: 17). Lynsey decorates commemorative mugs:

> She starts by nicking the rim of the mug three times with pencil and signing each piece with her initials. The first element to go on is a crown... Then hearts, laurels, the date, another crown, more hearts, 68 tiny dots placed by hand all over the mug and a row of 31 hearts inside the rim. Her hands weren't tense: either loosely balled inside the mug, drawing figures of eight with her sponge in the paint and squeezing it out; or slowly turning the potter's wheel as she pocked the mug with dots... Moments of concentration dissipated and returned easily; she hovered the moment before the first crown went on. Sponge decorators are paid by the number of pieces they finish in an hour, which adds up to a rate slightly above the minimum wage. We 'just try to keep our heads down really', as Gidman put it, 'because every second counts'.

This might be seen as skilled work, requiring dexterity and concentration, but it is relatively lowly paid, not much more than the minimum wage we are told. She works in this way for 9 hours a day including breaks totalling 55 minutes for breakfast, lunch and tea. This might be seen as 'manual' or 'blue-collar' work – largely based on working with the hands, although this of course requires judgement and concentration. It does not involve the control of others, or much interaction with others in doing the work itself: the interactions are largely with the physical objects and tools of the trade.

Compare Lynsey's job with that of Caroline Pay, a 'creative director' in an advertising and media company in London, also interviewed by Joanna Biggs and who, Biggs states, 'must earn somewhere in the region of £250,000 a year' (2015: 50). This is something like 18 times the minimum wage for a full-time 40-hours-a-week job. Caroline Pay is a working mum and tries to ensure her working days are 9–7pm. On the underground going into work in the morning:

> she'll write emails that will ping off as soon as she is above ground. 'And from the moment I get in, I talk, until the moment I go home'. She tries to avoid long meetings, even though 'my job is meetings: if it's not a creative review, it's a briefing, and if it's not a briefing something like this interview. I would never ever sit in front of my computer and open a document and write something.' At lunch she might ask one of the teams to take her to eat somewhere she hasn't been before, or meet up with a friend, or just let off steam on a walk. 'Lunch is like a reward!'
>
> *(Biggs 2015: 50)*

These two people certainly do different kinds of jobs, for very different levels of financial reward and in different sectors of the economy (one 'manufacturing', one 'services'). In these and in many other ways we can differentiate occupations: we might do so by pay, by the nature of the skills required, by the level of training required, by the level of education required, by whether or not they require control over others, by whether they are 'dirty' jobs or 'clean' jobs, secure or insecure, routine or non-routine, high or low status, visible or invisible, fulfilling or demeaning. I will start by considering selected occupations, in an attempt to bring out some key points, including those relating to differences between occupations. I will then go on to consider the broader issue of class and its relation to occupational divisions.

Craft and service

The idea of a craft has a very long history. A craft is embodied practice – where practice is (as Sennett 2008 emphasizes) the key. It takes practice to master a craft, practice that in the traditional apprenticeship system in medieval Europe (e.g. Sennett 2008: 55–65) often took years. It involved 'doing' the task and learning from others more experienced than oneself – but the doing was all important. One does not learn a craft from watching others or from books, but by doing it.

Examples such as pottery making may suggest that crafts and the skills associated with them are long-lived and yet, as Thompson (1980: 270) argued, referring to the 19th century, 'we must also bear in mind the general insecurity of many skills in a period of rapid innovation and weak trade union defences'. He showed how the old craft of the millwright was threatened by the rise of the engineer. If such arguments are relevant to the 19th century they are no less so today. Changes in technology and globalization impose challenges to particular craft occupations associated with particular places (such as printworkers in London's Fleet Street in the 1980s and work in the Stoke-on-Trent potteries in the 1980s onwards).

Indeed, some might be surprised to find Lynsey still doing such work in Stoke-on-Trent in the 21st century. While Stoke-on-Trent was a major centre for the production of pottery, much of this work is now done in China, even if the traditional names associated with the industry, such as Wedgewood, are still on the pots. And the firm Lynsey works for is unusual, occupying a niche in the market. It can be useful, therefore, to think about how particular occupations change over time or are affected by contextual socio-economic factors.

Apprenticeships still exist, of course, if often in truncated forms, and certainly craft work still exists, sometimes involving very advanced skill. Holmes (2014), perhaps controversially, provides an example of craft work in a service context – the hairdresser. I say controversially because many might not see hairdressing as a craft, but this might be an example of our undervaluing work that is often associated with women. Certainly in their use of scissors, hairdressers do exercise skill and dexterity which is an outcome of many hours of practice and goes beyond their use in everyday life:

> She combs through the hair, moving the scissors into the crook of her right hand as she does so. Stopping where she wants to cut, she places two fingers where the comb was, while simultaneously moving the comb out of the way to sit between the left thumb and forefinger. Swiftly moving the scissors into prime position, holding with the right thumb and first two fingers, she begins to cut from left to right. This sequence is repeated over and over until the section of hair has all been trimmed. It then begins again as another section of hair is let down. The smooth rapidity of this routine, repeated sometimes hundreds of times on one person's head within a matter of minutes, is incredible. The hairdresser and scissors are one.
>
> *(Holmes 2014: 487–8)*

The last expression may seem a clichéd metaphor but the partnership between worker and the tools used is, in craft work, a close one – to the extent that the hairdresser can tell if someone else has used their scissors. Their practice shapes the tool, wears it in ways that are distinctive, if not to the eye, then to the worker's 'feel'. This sense of 'feel', as well as the coordination of hand and eye, the coordination of different tools and the rhythm of the work, are all elements common to craft work. So, too, is a sense of a quality – of a 'good' outcome. Holmes mentions the moment of 'reveal' when the hairdresser typically shows the customer the back of their head in a mirror and asks 'is that okay for you?'. This is the moment when the work is judged by the customer, but presumably also by the worker (who may, of course, since these are aesthetic judgements, have a different opinion).

Knowledge of results, intrinsic satisfaction and pride in the work seem an integral part of such craft work. Possibly status, too, from having a scarce skill (although status might be highly variable and affected by the efforts of the occupational group to acquire status, as well as the perceptions of others, including perceptions of difficulty and value).

It is easy to see the value of craftsmanship and certainly writers such as Sennett, as well as many craft workers, would testify to this. However, it is also perhaps important not to have too romantic a view of the work. Even Sennett reminds us that it might have its more questionable aspects. For one thing 'Obsessing about quality is a way of subjecting the work itself to relentless generic pressure; workers given over to this passion can dominate or detach themselves from others less driven' (Sennett 2008: 245). Craft workers can also, by restricting entry or creating barriers to entry, enhance their labour market position by limiting the supply of particular kinds of labour. Cockburn's (1983) important study of printers also shows how, in this occupational group, men worked to exclude women from the craft, partly because of masculinist notions of what constitutes the 'proper' work for women and men, and partly, explicitly, because of fear it might lower wages at a time they were seeking to preserve a male breadwinner model (see Cockburn 1983: 174–90). Moreover, the bodily practice of a craft might well impose physical challenges – fatigue, in the hairdresser's case, say, from standing all day. It might even impose occupationally related diseases and ailments from repetition of certain movements and the strain of certain operations. Psychologically, too, craft workers might not be immune from boredom or stress.

The work of hairdressing also allows us to explore two other aspects of work: emotional labour and practices of aesthetic labour. Neither of these figure largely in traditional conceptions of craft work, which is largely concerned with manual work involving inanimate materials, however.

Hochschild's (1983) conception of 'emotional labour' has been very influential in the sociology of work. She developed this idea in the context of a study of service work, and in particular the work of flight attendants and bill collectors. Emotional labour she defined as: 'the management of feeling to create a publicly observable facial and bodily display; emotional labour is sold for a wage and therefore has *exchange value* (1983: 7, emphasis in the original). This management of feeling is something that is accomplished on a day-to-day basis by the competent employee in a service job. If this is managed it is therefore managed by the person involved, but the management of feeling is also brought about by deliberate management strategies such as training in particular ways of behaving. This raises, of course, issues of authenticity: do we want to be greeted by someone whose smile seems false when they wish to us a good day? Hochschild distinguishes between surface acting and deep acting – with the latter being a way of generating the feelings that one considers to be appropriate. Of course both are forms of acting, attempts to display the 'right' feelings. In the day-to-day work of flight attendants and bill collectors surface acting, as well as deep acting, becomes routinized. The idea of aesthetic labour is a related term (Chugh and Hancock 2009; Williams and Connell 2010). This is a matter of looking good and sounding good, something that is often seen as important in service industries.

The studies of hairdressers referred to here do little to set these workers in a wider context but Simpson et al.'s (2014) work on butchers does provide an example of a study with a broader frame of reference. This study focused on a kind of craft work that involves skill of a very different kind: that of butchery, but in the context of relatively small retail butcher shops (not supermarkets, where meat tends to arrive ready prepared). They found that these workers did not express a strong preference for this as a form of work but found themselves doing it anyway:

> Well it's get on and do what you've got to do isn't it? It was a job weren't it? I left school and went straight into work the next day… 15 and that's it. That's all I've done… it's OK yeah, it's all right. I don't mind you know if you don't work you don't get nothing.
>
> *(Simpson et al. 2014: 762)*

The physicality of the job is a feature of the job that the workers emphasize. It requires considerable strength: 'the sheer weight of things, you know, to do the job you are required to lift and even, sort of, if you've got a quarter of a cow put in front of you, even pulling the muscles back to separate things, it's very, very hard' (2014: 762). But it also calls for speed and dexterity: 'I can cut it [a lamb] in seconds, you know, literally seconds. It's only experience but I'm still careful what I do. I don't like, I don't make a mess of it, it's a proper job, you know, because that's the way I've been trained' (2014: 762). In this case there seems to be some pride in being able to do the job quickly but also well.

The authors point out that these butchers' attitude to the work is associated with traditional masculine working-class ideas. In jobs some would regard as 'dirty work', sometimes hidden from the public who might find it revolting, these men gain some sense of respect from the difficulties involved and the skill involved, as well as from the way it leads to a wage with which they can support a family. But while there are thus elements of continuity between these workers' attitudes and those of previous generations, the article also points to change. Even in the course of these workers' lifetimes, significant change had taken place, partly as a result of new hygiene and safety regulations: 'It's always been a physical job… that didn't bother me. And then sort of gradually over the years it's become, you know, you are more like an office worker now than a butcher. Everything has to be recorded… It's become sort of, yeah, it's too clinical' (2014: 764).

It is hard, physical work and they get their hands bloody, but there are also elements of dealing with the customer that requires a different set of skills. The workers emphasized personal service and the relationship with customers, often based on banter and shared humour, rather than a deferential attitude, thus avoiding a feminization of their work. And some referred with pride to an increasingly discerning customer base where quality was appreciated and where advice was sought on the cut of meat as well as methods of preparation. In a context where they were competing with supermarkets, these butchers sought to differentiate themselves, suggesting they had superior knowledge and skill that might be of value to the customer, sometimes drawing on media-endorsed discourses associated with (often male) celebrity chefs to do so.

BOX 3.1 IN THE NEWS: THE END OF DEEP COAL MINING IN BRITAIN

On 18 December 2015 the end of deep coal mining in Britain was reported, with the closure of the last colliery. One miner was reported to have said:

'There's a few lads shedding tears, just getting all emotional. It's a bit sad really. I've been here 30 years, I don't know what to expect now, got to get another job.'

Another who had worked at the pit for 32 years said he would be part of the team capping the shafts his father had sunk in 1959.

He said: 'Everything I've had in my life has come from this mine here. I wish my dad was here today, because he'd have a lot to say about it. What's happened here is absolutely a travesty.'

Source: BBC, 18 December 2015

The call centre, where employees respond to customer queries and/or attempt to sell products or services over the telephone, is of course very different from manual work such as butchery. Typically taking place at a desk with a headset and computer screen there is limited physical movement and fewer physical demands. But it is still embodied work, with the worker using hearing and voice in direct interactions with customers or service users. Call centres have sometimes been seen as a new form of sweatshop (e.g. Fernie and Metcalf 1999, but see also Fleming and Sturdy 2011) – not because of the sweat imposed by physical work but because of the relentless pace often imposed on the employee who is expected to deal with a high number of calls, sometimes in stressful circumstances where service users are rude or abusive. Call centres, like factories in the manufacturing sector, are often characterized by high levels of supervision and managerial control, with the number and quality of calls closely monitored. Since calls are human interactions, 'quality' in dealing with a call is not merely a technical process of getting it right, as in, for example, providing the correct answer to a question; it also involves emotional labour. Qualities of patience and empathy may be called for, with a display of respectful cheerfulness. One of the difficulties here, which also occurs in many cases of manual work, is a possible trade-off between quality and speed. Managers may want employees to deal with a large number of calls, but also insist on high standards. Getting both right might be challenging. In Brannan's (2005) study, for example, performance was assessed through monitoring employees against both numerical targets of the number of calls dealt with and customer satisfaction surveys. According to Brannan (2005: 427), the call centre employees he observed:

> were often confused and anxious about the relative priorities and how these should be managed. Like other call centres, each team has its 'stats' publicly displayed on a moving message sign strategically placed above the workspace occupied by the team. The moving message sign displays the number of calls

taken that day, the number of CSRs [customer service representatives] currently not engaged on active calls, the number of current incoming calls and a figure which was referred to as 'Grade of Service'. Whilst the exact formula used to calculate this figure remained a mystery, it was considered both in the team and the wider call centre to be a reflection of general performance.

Employees, under pressure to make numerical targets and respond to incoming calls quickly, were also anxious to please service users who sometimes wanted to chat. Brannan found that male employees followed their team leader's lead in treating this as a competitive game and found it pleasurable: 'it doesn't really seem like work, it's just having a laugh' (2005: 431).

But some of the tensions in doing so were clear:

> Liz: It's OK, I guess, I know you lot like it [referring to male CSRs] but sometimes they don't know when to stop.
> Researcher: What do you mean?
> Liz: Sometimes the banter, you know, goes too far. They [the clients] get too personal and I just try to change the subject.
>
> *(Brannan 2005: 432)*

In this case it seemed to be expected that male CSRs would maintain informal relationships with clients through aggressive flirting and relationship building. For female CSRs, relationships with male clients were expected to be built on the basis of 'womanly charm' (Brannan 2005: 434). This shows how even in doing the 'same' work, men and women might do it differently. Emotional labour might take different forms. But while it might evoke pleasure (as it did in this case for the men), it might also provoke anxiety and vulnerability (as it did in this case for the women whose views were reported here).

The manager

Many employees have the role of manager, and there might be little in common between the manager, say, in a large insurance company and that in a local bike shop. Even within the insurance company different managers might perform very different kinds of work. Here though, I shall focus on just one example of a manager (Smith and Elliott 2012). This examines the case of Fiona, a food retail store manager of a city centre store that was open seven days a week. She worked long hours – often 60 hours or so a week, sometimes covering for absent staff and requiring working weekends and evenings. She had to manage staff and do various administrative tasks associated with the job and had a budget for the store that she was expected to work to. But she also had to cope with unexpected demands:

> I've just been informed that an extra-curricular activity has been arranged for Sunday night after the store closes and there's no cover been arranged for it at

all, and basically my boss has said to me, 'This is going ahead, you have to cover it.' If no one volunteers to do it, then basically I have to be in from 10 o'clock closing through night shift until the job [which involves contractors modernizing the store lighting system] is finished. And I've had five days' notice. Basically I've been told it has to happen and it doesn't matter what plans I have, I have to cancel them. So basically it doesn't matter what your plans are, you are sort of handcuffed to the front doors at times, it does feel like that. Sometimes you're worried about making plans because they're never guaranteed on a week to week basis; if something changes or crops up, then you may have to cancel your plans.

(Smith and Elliott 2012: 679–80)

Scheduling shifts of a diverse range of staff, many part time, was one thing she did, apparently with due regards to their needs:

Well, basically the staff don't have set hours in here, as such. I generally schedule it on a Friday, for their hours the following week. What I try to do is give them all at least a minimum of one full weekend off each month. If possible, I try and give them one or two weekends off. They all know that they can come and speak to me if they have a function, something coming up. With students, I'm very conscious with them too, I don't like them to work the night before they have an exam. So I get them to give me their exam dates so that I've got a note of them when I do the schedule, I try to schedule round exams. I try when I'm recruiting as well not to take on two students that are on the same course, so that I can get flexibility there.

(Smith and Elliott 2012: 680)

She also has to deal with customers who can become abusive:

I have no security guards here to help me, so you're out there on your own basically. Senior management don't believe that we need a guard here per-manently because incidents don't happen every single day, every day of the week, so they put them in sporadically. That's the guard just arrived just now, so he's here for a few hours tonight. He might be here for a few hours over three or four days this week. Senior management say they don't feel we need a permanent guard here because incidents aren't happening every shift, every day.

(Smith and Elliott 2012: 682)

This example shows how managers are sometimes caught in the middle between dealing with the needs of staff and the demands of their own managers and employer: they have to reconcile these two pressures. Sometimes it is easier to do this than others and the strain it imposes is no doubt variable over time and between managers, but it can be considerable. The effect on home life and partners is also significant. Fiona does not have children but does have a partner who is affected by the uncertainties demanded of the job.

The embodiment here is of multiple levels: there may be the demand to be 'professional' to customers and staff, and to engage in emotional labour towards staff, more senior managers and customers. There is the sheer embodied presence required, imposing the strains of working long hours and negotiating these complex relationships:

> I was actually off work for a year with depression and it was due to a work-related incident. I put a complaint in against my area manager at the time, who I felt was bullying me and that caused my health to suffer. I was on medication for a year... I am now anaemic, which I wasn't before, and I think that's down to the job and the pressures of the job: So now I know physically within myself when I can't do any more, I say, 'No, I'm sorry, that's it'.
>
> *(Smith and Elliott 2012: 682–3)*

The professional

We might look to Kosmala and Herrbach's (2006) study of auditors in the big four auditing firms to provide an example of another kind of work – of 'professional' work, requiring, as does craft work, relatively lengthy training and requiring specialist knowledge and expertise. While this is often acquired through practice, formal training and the acquisition of knowledge is also emphasized, and this is tested in formal examinations. But such professional work also requires a particular set of attitudes and values, reflected here in one of their respondents stating that: 'I am a hyper conscientious person. In fact, as an auditor, I had a real love for well performed work. And I could not stand it when a file is not well done' (2006: 1407). This fits with a common view of professionalism as associated with conscientiousness, with careful work involving rigour, attention to detail and competence. But these authors also found ambivalence and distancing or what I would call dis-identification: distancing themselves from the firm and other people within it as well as distancing themselves from the professional ideal and from the work methodologies involved. These professionals can be critical of the firm they work for, as indicated in the following quotation: 'Auditors get quality training like nowhere else. The major problem is the lack of any individualised career track. As a result, this feeling of being a pawn only disappears on departure day' (2006: 1414). They can be critical of each other or even of their own behaviour to others: 'Sometimes it can get very difficult because of work pressure. Working relations are then no longer professional. There is no... no restraint left. I recall I've been talked to as if I were a dog, I've been yelled at, I've been made fun of' (2006: 1416). This might of course be seen as behaviour that might be confined to the high-pressure end of professional work, but from personal experience I can confirm that it also occurs in what is considered to be the rather less pressured and commercial environment of the university. The professional ideal may be one of cooperative, collegial relations but the reality is often somewhat different.

The distancing from work methodologies can take the form of cutting corners:

> For procedures like analytical review, for instance, you can do it very super-
> ficially. Your manoeuvring room on this type of tasks is very large. You can
> save a little, we can go very far. You must find a compromise. With the
> increase of the paperless audit, there is much more room for a 'plug'.
>
> *(2006: 1417)*

Perhaps, as Kosmala and Herrbach suggest, this is a more ambivalent and cynical
working of professional identity than is normally associated with the term. Indeed,
they see it as a sign of the existence of a postmodern condition and it certainly
seems a long way from the kind of view of the profession presented by authors
such as that leading analyst of modernity, Max Weber (1970: 135), who suggests
that in the case of the scientist, they should be passionate as well as rigorous: 'For
nothing is worthy of man as man unless he can pursue it with passionate devotion.'
(The use of the male pronoun is of course an indication of the time it is written,
originally in 1918, although science, especially natural science, remains an
overwhelmingly male preserve.)

Ibarra (1999) suggests, on the basis of a study of investment bankers and
management consultants, that in the transition to more senior roles professionals
engage in three kinds of tasks: the first is observing role models to identify potential
identities, the second is experimenting with provisional selves and the third is
evaluating experiments against internal standards and external feedback. In other
words, professional identities, like other occupational identities, have to be worked
at and can change over time.

In presenting these accounts of different occupations I have deliberately selected
contrasting cases. I hope that in doing so I have brought out some of the variety
that exists between occupations. These accounts bring out something of the
experience of these workers; something of what it means to work in these jobs and
how they are embodied. In exploring occupations, however, there are many
questions we might ask and which the literature on work and occupations has
explored over the years. In this chapter I cannot hope to cover every aspect of
work that makes occupations what they are and makes them different. However,
I wish to draw attention to several dimensions that seem to me particularly
significant. These are issues of career, class and social relations.

Careers

There is a large literature dealing with careers. The traditional view of the career, as
embodied in Weber's idea of a bureaucracy (see Chapter 4), is of a movement
upward within an organization. We might, however, expect that some individuals
will move between organizations in order to pursue their career. Indeed, perhaps
we expect this to be the case for many in professional occupations such as teachers,
doctors and accountants. If, at one time, an individual might have expected to

work for one employer throughout their 40 years or so of working life we would probably find this unusual now. The early literature on careers, such as that of Super (1957), suggests a progressive and logical sequence of phases in the individual's career. First the individual aligns themselves to an occupation that suits their particular personality and strengths and then moves through phases of establishment, maintenance and decline. However, early studies in the sociology of work also suggest an alternative view of the career as simply a movement through time, not necessarily linear or progressive (Barley 1989). It is this that seems to me to be a better way of looking at the individual's working life. This might involve movement between employers and even between occupations over time. It might involve promotion or sideways moves or even downward movements. The new careers theory (e.g. Arthur et al. 1999) emphasizes the fluidity of careers as people move between jobs, employers and even occupations. We might also emphasize how jobs themselves change over time, carrying the individual with them in a changing and sometimes unpredictable trajectory. Much of the current literature on careers (e.g. Baruch 2004) suggests that we need to move beyond career planning in the sense of a plan or sequence of well-thought-out steps over the course of one's working life and instead adopt an individualized form of career management in which we constantly try to maximize our employability by extending our skills and capabilities. There is some evidence that such a view is taking hold among certain groups, with Martin and Wajcman's (2004) study of Australian middle managers, for example, suggesting they adopted marketable images of themselves in universalistic terms such as being innovative and even aggressive. Such a view, however, risks adopting an overoptimistic position in which individuals successfully ride the waves of change. If we adopt the surfing metaphor the issue is to what extent we expect people to find themselves in various degrees of difficulty or facing 'wipe out'. In Sennett's (1998) book *The Corrosion of Character*, for example, he talks to ex-IBM employees who find themselves the victims of organizational and technological change. Careers are affected in turn by other identities such as those discussed in other chapters in this book: gender, age, disability and so on. The traditional view of the career is based on a white male model of progression, aided by a wife who looks after the home and children; but when we factor in a range of identity positions things become much less certain. Careers require identity work.

Social class and social relations

How we define different classes has been the subject of much sociological debate throughout the 20th and into the 21st century. In everyday life the concept of class is persistent, even if its meaning is slippery. Here I do not wish to settle the issue of how class is to be defined, but point to some key features that are relevant.

Much of the literature on class addresses the issue of categorization, the separating out or identification of the various classes. This involves difficult decisions concerning the criteria we use for distinguishing classes and where we draw the boundaries between them. One issue here is the extent to which occupation is

TABLE 3.1 Eight-class version of the socio-economic classification

1.	Higher managerial, administrative and professional occupations.
2.	Lower managerial, administrative and professional occupations.
3.	Intermediate occupations.
4.	Small employers and own account workers
5.	Lower supervisory and technical occupations.
6.	Semi-routine occupations.
7.	Routine occupations.
8.	Never worked and long-term unemployed.

Source: Adapted from Office of National Statistics 2015a

taken as the criterion for determining class position. One commonly used classification in the British context is that of the Office of National Statistics' 'Socio-Economic Classification' (2015a), which is occupationally based and comes in three-class, five-class and eight-class versions, depending on how groupings are combined. The eight-class version is shown in table 3.1, with the three-class version collapsing the eight categories essentially into a higher, middle and 'routine and manual' class (and leaving the unemployed out). This classification can easily be seen as a hierarchy, although some categories – particularly those of the small employer and own-account worker, might be problematic, ranging from the wealthy small business owner to a struggling odd-jobs person.

Marxists and neo-Marxists seek to define class in relation to what they see as the essential features of capitalism as a social system based on antagonistic social relations. At its most basic level this is seen as consisting of a large class of people who depend on selling their labour power to capitalists for a wage in order to earn their means of subsistence. This is the proletariat or working class. On the other hand, there are the owners of capital who buy this labour power in order to expand their capital. These are the capitalists, or bourgeoisie. Recently, Wright (2005) has attempted to take into account the structural changes in capitalism to create a rather more complex picture of classes, including some positions that are 'contradictory', with managers, for example, being positioned as both wage earners and agents of capital.

Other authors put more emphasis on consumption and lifestyle, with those influenced by Bourdieu, in particular, emphasizing the interplay of economic, cultural and social capital. To Bourdieu (1984), factors such as one's education, one's musical tastes and social networks, as well as one's occupation, all work to define a particular class position, even if it is difficult to define precise boundaries between classes. This was the basis of recent work by Savage and others (Savage et al. 2013; 2015) in collaboration with the BBC and which, on the basis of survey results, suggested there were seven classes, including some seen as new (see Table 3.2). At the bottom of this class structure, and also the subject of work by Guy Standing (2014), is the precariat.

It is important to note that this class categorization is not solely on the basis of occupation and, as these examples show, it is possible for different members of a

TABLE 3.2 Savage et al.'s social classes

Class	Name	Examples of typical occupation
1	Elite	CEOs, judges and barristers
2	Established middle class	Midwives, police officers
3	Technical middle class	Pilots, higher education teachers
4	New affluent workers	Electricians, check-out operatives
5	Traditional working class	Care workers, van drivers
6	Emergent service workers	Chefs, care workers
7	Precariat	Cleaners, van drivers

particular occupation to be members of different classes (for example, care workers may be part of the traditional working class or new emergent service working class on the basis of their possession of different characteristics in terms of their social, cultural and economic capital).

Standing (2014) argues that the changes brought about around the world since the 1980s from the impact of globalization and neoliberalism have diminished the position of the traditional working class but also what he refers to as the salariat (those in salaried positions in bureaucracies and professions) – although these classes still exist. The drive to ever more flexible labour markets has produced a relatively large number of people in precarious employment situations. These are people on temporary contracts, or zero-hours contracts, and with little security. The precariat is thus defined in terms of what its members lack: labour-related security. Standing argues that this class is a dangerous class in the sense that it represents, potentially at least, a fulsome challenge to neoliberalism's dominance, even if its ways of doing so are at odds with the way in which the traditional working class fought for improvements in their situation, largely through formal organization in trade unions and political parties fighting elections. I am sceptical about Standing's claims partly because, as he himself suggests, many people move in and out of this condition and aspire to something different. Moreover, within the precariat there are those who in Standing's own terms might be seen as welcoming the new flexibilities that precarious employment conditions provide. Even zero-hours contracts may be welcome by some – such as students – who do not wish to commit themselves to stable and regular hours of work (Ashton and Noonan 2013). Moreover, Standing may exaggerate the extent to which the precariat is anything new. There has always been temporary work and flexibility in labour markets and in some respects the contemporary situation represents a return to conditions a century or more ago (see Stedman Jones 1971).

Whatever the precise number and definition of classes one issue is that of the inequalities of income. In 2013 Sir Martin Sorrell, WPP's CEO, was reported to have been awarded £29,846,000 (Motley Fool 2014). This is about 23 times as much as someone on the minimum wage at the time (which at £6.31 per hour would earn a full-time employee just over £13,000 for a 40-hour week). As Piketty (2014) has shown, income inequality has been rising throughout the world since 1980 but in the US, Great Britain, Canada and Australia he notes the rise of the supermanager – very highly paid individuals in the top positions of companies. In the case of Britain he reports the top 1 per cent of earners as receiving 15 per cent of all the country's income from employment. In the US it was even higher at nearly 18 per cent. The causes of this he sees as primarily institutional and political rather than economic. Looking at more 'ordinary' jobs in the UK the Office of National Statistics (ONS) (2015b) survey data suggests that in 2015 managers, directors and senior officials earned on average £850 per week (£44,200 per year), while those in 'elementary occupations' earned £333 (£17,316), although these figures are based on Labour Force Survey data and the ONS recognizes that these underestimate actual earnings (partly because respondents earning over £100 per hour are excluded altogether).

Large differences in income, of course, fuel differences in consumption and lifestyle, but the latter is also affected by one's education and social networks. You are less likely to find those in elementary occupations sporting new luxury cars or going on expensive holidays, but they are more likely to visit a football match than the opera.

BOX 3.2 IN THE NEWS: THE POSHNESS TEST?

In June 2015 the Chair of the Social Mobility and Child Poverty Commission was widely reported as criticizing top firms for applying a 'poshness test'. This was seen as systematically favouring those, often from private schools, who had the 'right' accents, behavioural style and mannerisms, as well as experience (such as being well travelled) that made them attractive to employers. One recruiter was quoted as having doubts about a candidate who lacked 'polish'. The chair of the Commission saw this as shutting out working-class people with potential.

Source: *Independent*, 15 June 2015

So far we have considered class positions largely as rather abstract social positions, but there is perhaps a stronger sense in which class figures in the workplace as a set of social relations. At a basic level this might entail consideration of who one socializes with both in the workplace and beyond. We often make friends with those who are similar to ourselves, those with whom we are in close physical proximity and share common experiences with. In this way the differentiation that sociologists point to can be realized in practice through decisions as trivial as who one chooses to sit with at lunchtime. But relations between and across classes also need to be considered. It is in work in the Marxist tradition where this becomes clearest. In labour process analysis (Knights and Willmott 1990) the labour process itself is inscribed with the social relations of capital. Managers become the means by which labour is exploited and in the dynamics of capitalism there is a constant striving for greater efficiency in the use of labour. Braverman (1974), in his seminal work on the issue, associated such drives with Taylor's 'scientific management' as formulated in the early 20th century. The key principles of scientific management were fourfold and were summarized in Taylor's incitement to management to perform the following duties (Taylor 1947: 36–7):

> *First.* They develop a science for each element of a man's work, which replaces the old rule-of-thumb method.
> *Second.* They scientifically select and then train, teach, and develop the work-man, whereas in the past he chose his own work and trained himself as best he could.
> *Third.* They heartily cooperate with the men so as to insure all of the work being done in accordance with the principles of the science which has been developed.
> *Fourth.* There is an almost equal division of the work and the responsibility between the management and the worker. The management take over all the work for which they are better fitted than the workman, while in the past almost all of the work and the greater part of the responsibility were thrown upon the men.

Of course there has been much debate within and around the study of the 'labour process', even among those sympathetic to the idea. It seems to me that one of the strengths of this work is the way in which it situates working practices in the context of wider social processes. In particular, it emphasizes the importance of capitalist social relations in seeking to organize work in ways that extract the most value out of available labour power. In Braverman's (1974) analysis this entailed mechanization and a detailed manufacturing division of labour which separates conception and execution. His analysis also explicitly locates such developments within a particular era, a phase of capitalist development described as one of monopoly capital. Since he wrote this work many would see important changes having taken place in capitalism, variously described as post-Fordism, neoliberalism and financialization (Amin 2008; Epstein 2005; Harvey 2007). Certainly I would side with those who argue that management practice can come in various shapes and sizes, some more obviously hostile to labour and others (Coates 2005; Macartney 2010). Moreover, in the lived relations between managers and workers, capitalist imperatives do not always prevail, not least because managers were sometimes one-time workers or are people who can empathize with the views of others. At the very least this might give rise to the kind of distinction made by one of the men in Nichols and Beynon's study (1977: 34) between managers as bastards or bad bastards. There is, too, something to be said for a Foucauldian attention to ways in which certain discourses, sometimes based on particular occupations which have their own regime of truth, serve to discipline the worker through generalizing certain patterns of subjectivity that hold the subject in its thrall, even if resistance is by no means rendered impossible (Knights and Vurdubakis 1994). In varying ways neo-Marxists, Foucauldians and those of other sociological persuasions might all want to focus on how employees negotiate their working lives. This will include forms of what might be seen as misbehaviour – joking, irreverence, sabotage, conflict (Ackroyd and Thompson 1999), as well as the responses of organized labour in trade unions – something that may be less significant than in the heyday of union power but is still significant in some sectors and occupations (e.g. see Moore 2011). But there are important differences in how different studies conceptualize the context of such negotiation: the extent to which they relate this to what are seen as dominant structures or discourses. In my view the discursive turn associated with the influence of Foucault, has been a useful one drawing attention to subjectivity and cultural forms, but it would be a shame if this was to obliterate a concern with social structures embedded in economic relations. It seems to me that we can use a multiplicity of theoretical approaches, serving to draw attention to different aspects of experience and relations.

However, if forms of conflict and resistance are important a key issue here is solidarity – but with whom and over what? There has long been a search, among certain employers and managers, for solidarity based upon the firm. In the 19th century the chocolate philanthropists Cadbury and others were attempting to forge organizations where the interests of capital and labour coincided. The human relations school of thought could be seen as doing something similar (Rose 1975). But Thompson (1980), in his monumental work on the making of the English working class, shows how solidarity could be based upon a broader conception of class which has distinctive interests. In this view class does not enter the drama fully formed as a character but rather develops through complex processes of interaction, in which memory, conflict and hope combine in unpredictable ways, drawing together people from diverse occupations into something they perceive to be a class, with its own class interests and the possibility of mobilizing as a class in pursuit of those common interests.

Conclusion

The early hopes of Marxists that the self-confident working class would come together as one to challenge the hegemony of capital would seem to have been dashed (see Fletcher and Gapasin 2009 for a US view and Jaques and Mulhern 1981 for an earlier British view). Yet that does not mean that opposition to capital is not in evidence. Rather, solidarity may be contingent and fluid. For example, particular occupational groups may work to reclaim professional integrity that they see as under threat – as has happened in the case of British social work (Goodman and Trowler 2012). But solidarity can also exist across occupational boundaries and across organizational boundaries. The living wage campaign in various parts of the world, including the UK, provides an example made up of a complex alliance of workers on minimum wage or below as well as sympathetic supporters from a variety of faith groups and political parties (Figart 2004). This suggests we need to attend to different levels of analysis – at the micro level of the individual workplace and the micro politics of resistance (Thomas et al. 2004), but also at a macro level to the kind of analysis in the tradition of Braverman (1974) but also of, say, Mills (1956), that looks at the situation of labour under conditions of contemporary capitalism and seeks to identify broad patterns, trends and challenges. In this I think there is a place for neo-Marxist analysis that focuses on the social relations of production within capitalism as well as neo-Weberian approaches that focus on organization. For that matter there is also room for neo-Durkheimian analysis that attends to forms of organic solidarity within the division of labour which is occupationally based.

I am sceptical of the arguments of writers such as Casey (1995: 109, 197), who suggests (on the basis of one case study of a large multinational American company discussed further in Chapter 4) that information technology and a drive towards teamwork and project-based working renders occupational divisions less relevant as we enter a 'post-occupational' age, just as I am sceptical about the claims of new careers theorists that careers are becoming boundaryless (not bounded, that is, by occupation or organizations) – again I think this is to exaggerate the differences from the past and to periodize things too neatly. Certainly there is flexibility and fluidity in occupational boundaries, to greater or lesser degrees. However, this is not new and we need to attend to continuities as well as changes: capitalism rules, but not in quite the same configurations. We may need more sophisticated and varied means of attending to the differences over time. Added to this we might also need a form of political imagination based on conversations between those who are suffering or who are attentive to suffering, leading to mobilization and action – mobilization around a range of demands and a range of issues, but which can be fused into a progressive force for change.

BOX 3.3 AT THE MOVIES: OCCUPATION AND CLASS

Some movies relevant to the themes of the chapter are:

Car Wash (1976, director Michael Schultz)
Gung Ho (1986, director Ron Howard)
Wall Street (1987, director Oliver Stone)
Bread and Roses (2000, director Ken Loach)
Up in the Air (2009, director Jason Reitman)

References

Ackroyd, S. and Thompson, P. J. (1999) *Organizational Misbehaviour*. London: Sage.
Amin, A. (2008) *Post-Fordism: A Reader*. Oxford: Wiley.
Arthur, M. B., Inkson, K. and Pringle, J. K. (eds) (1999) *The New Careers: Individual Action and Economic Change*. London: Sage.

Ashton, D. and Noonan, C. (eds) (2013) *Cultural Work and Higher Education*. Basingstoke: Palgrave Macmillan.

Barley, S. (1989) 'Careers, identities and institutions: The legacy of the Chicago School of Sociology' in Arthur, M. B., Hall, D. T. and Lawrence, B. S. (eds) (1989) *Handbook of Career Theory*. Cambridge: Cambridge University Press.

Baruch, Y. (2004) *Managing Careers: Theory and Practice*. Harlow: FT Prentice Hall.

BBC (2015) 'Closure of Kellingley pit brings deep coal mining to an end', at http://www.bbc.co.uk/news/uk-england-york-north-yorkshire-35124077 (accessed 23 December 2015).

Biggs, J. (2015) *All Day Long: A Portrait of Britain at Work*. London: Serpent's Tale.

Bourdieu, P. (1984) *Distinction: A Social Critique of the Judgement of Taste*. London: Routledge and Kegan Paul.

Brannan, M. J. (2005) 'Once more with feeling: Ethnographic reflections on the mediation of tension in a small team of call centre workers', *Gender, Work and Organization*, 12(5): 420–439.

Braverman, H. (1974) *Labor and Monopoly Capital: The Degradation of Work in the Twentieth Century*. New York: Monthly Review Press.

Casey, C. (1995) *Work, Self and Society: After Industrialism*. London: Routledge.

Chugh, S. and Hancock, P. (2009) 'Networks of aestheticization: The architecture, artefacts and embodiment of hairdressing salons', *Work Employment and Society*, 23(3): 460–476.

Coates, D. (ed.) (2005) *Varieties of Capitalism, Varieties of Approaches*. Basingstoke: Palgrave Macmillan.

Cockburn, C. (1983) *Brothers: Male Dominance and Technological Change*. London: Pluto.

Epstein, G. A. (ed.) (2005) *Financialization and the World Economy*. Cheltenham: Edward Elgar.

Fernie, S. and Metcalf, D. (1999) '(Not) hanging on the telephone: Payment systems in the new sweatshops' in Lewin, D. and Kaufman, B. (eds), *Advances in Industrial and Labour Relations*. Stamford, CT: JAI Press.

Figart, D. M. (ed.) (2004) *Living Wage Movements: Global Perspectives*. London: Routledge.

Fleming, P. and Sturdy, A. (2011) '"Being yourself" in the electronic sweatshop: New forms of normative control', *Human Relations*, 64(2): 177–200.

Fletcher, B. and Gapasin, F. (2009) *Solidarity Divided: The Crisis in Organized Labor and a New Path toward Social Justice*. Berkeley and Los Angeles: University of California Press.

Goodman, S. and Trowler, I. (eds) (2012) *Social Work Reclaimed: Innovative Frameworks for Child and Family Social Work Practice*. London: Jessica Kingsley.

Harvey, D. (2007) *A Brief History of Neoliberalism*. Oxford: Oxford University Press.

Hochschild, A. R. (1983) *The Managed Heart: Commercialization of Human Feeling*. Berkeley, CA: California University Press.

Holmes, H. (2014) 'Transient craft: Reclaiming the contemporary craft worker', *Work, Employment and Society*, 29(3): 479–495.

Ibarra, H. (1999) 'Provisional selves: Experimenting with image and identity in professional adaptation', *Administrative Science Quarterly*, 44(4): 764–791.

Independent (2015) 'Poshness test is the new glass ceiling' at http://www.independent.co.uk/news/uk/home-news/poshness-test-is-the-new-glass-ceiling-lack-of-wealthy-background-denies-working-class-people-top-10319541.html (accessed 23 December 2015).

Jaques, M. and Mulhern, F. (eds) (1981) *The Forward March of Labour Halted?* London: NLB in association with Marxism Today.

Knights, D. and Vurdubakis, T. (1994) 'Foucault, power, resistance and all that' in Jermier, J. M., Knights, D. and Nord, W. R. (eds), *Resistance and Power in Organizations*. London: Routledge.

Knights, D. and Willmott, H. (eds) (1990) *Labour Process Theory*. Basingstoke: Macmillan.

Kosmala, K. and Herrbach, O. (2006) 'The ambivalence of professional identity: On cynicism and jouissance in audit firms', *Human Relations*, 59(10): 1393–1428.

Macartney, H. (2010) *Variegated Neoliberalism: EU Varieties of Capitalism and International Political Economy*. London: Routledge.

Martin, B. and Wajcman, J. (2004) 'Markets, contingency and preferences: Contemporary managers' narrative identities', *Sociological Review*, 52(2): 240–264.

Mills, C. W. (1956) *The Power Elite*. New York: Oxford University Press.

Moore, S. (2011) *New Trade Union Activism: Class Consciousness or Social identity*. Basingstoke: Palgrave Macmillan.

Motley Fool (2014) 'The five highest paid CEOs in the UK', at http://www.fool.co.uk/investing/2014/10/24/the-5-highest-paid-ceos-in-the-uk/ (accessed 11 December 2015).

Nichols, T. and Beynon, H. (1977) *Living with Capitalism: Class Relations and the Modern Factory*. London: Routledge and Kegan Paul.

Office of National Statistics (2015a) 'SOC2010, volume 3: The national statistics socio-economic classification', at http://www.ons.gov.uk/ons/guide-method/classifications/current-standard-classifications/soc2010/soc2010-volume-3-ns-sec–rebased-on-soc2010–user-manual/index.html#7 (accessed 11 December 2015).

Office of National Statistics (2015b) 'Annual survey of hours and earnings, 2014–2015', at http://www.ons.gov.uk/ons/search/index.html?newquery=pay (accessed 11 December 2015).

Piketty, T. (2014) *Capital in the Twenty-First Century*. Cambridge, MA: Belknap Press of Harvard University Press.

Rose, M. L. (1975) *Industrial Behaviour*. Harmondsworth: Penguin Books.

Savage, M., Devine, F., Cunningham, N., Taylor, M., Li, Y., Hjellbrekke, J. and Miles, A. (2013) 'A new model of social class? Findings from the BBC's great British class survey experiment', *Sociology*, 47(2): 219–250.

Savage, M., Devine, F., Cunningham, N., Friedman, S., Laurison, D., Miles, A. and Taylor, M. (2015) 'On social class, anno 2014', *Sociology*, 49(6): 1011–1030.

Sennett, R. (1998) *The Corrosion of Character: The Personal Consequences of Work in the New Capitalism*. London: Norton.

Sennett, R. (2008) *The Craftsman*. London: Allen Lane.

Simpson, R., Hughes, J., Slutskaya, N. and Balta, M. (2014) 'Sacrifice and distinction in dirty work: Men's construction of meaning in the butcher trade', *Work, Employment and Society*, 28(5): 754–770.

Smith, A. and Elliott, F. (2012) 'The demands and challenges of being a retail store manager: "Handcuffed to the front doors"', *Work, Employment and Society*, 26(4): 676–684.

Standing, G. (2014) *The Precariat: The New Dangerous Class*. London: Bloomsbury.

Stedman Jones, G. (1971) *Outcast London: A Study in the Relationship between Classes in Victorian Society*. Oxford: Clarendon Press.

Super, D. E. (1957) *The Psychology of Careers. An Introduction to Vocational Development*. New York: Harper and Bros.

Taylor, F. W. (1947) *Scientific Management: Comprising 'Shop Management', 'The Principles of Scientific Management' and 'Testimony before the Special House Committee'*. New York: Harper.

Thomas, R., Mills, A. J. and Mills, J. H. (eds) (2004) *Identity Politics at Work: Resisting Gender, Gendering Resistance*. London: Routledge.

Thompson, E. P. (1980) *The Making of the English Working Class*. Harmondsworth: Penguin Books.

Weber, M. (1970) *From Max Weber: Essays in Sociology*, trans. and ed. H. H. Gerth and C. W. Mills. London: Routledge and Kegan Paul.

Williams, C. L. and Connell, C. (2010) '"Looking good and sounding right": Aesthetic labor and social inequality in the retail industry', *Work and Occupations*, 37(3): 349–377.

Wright, E. O. (ed.) (2005) *Approaches to Class Analysis*. Cambridge: Cambridge University Press.

4

THE ORGANIZATION AND IDENTITY

Introduction

If you worked for Apple would you be proud of it? If you worked for the prison service would you be less proud? To what extent do employees identify with the organization they work for? To what extent are organizations a source of identification, a shaper of self-identity and of collective identities? These are some of the questions I want to grapple with in this chapter.

When we enter an organization as an employee we are usually recruited to a particular job, but we enter an organization which might be seen as involving a 'patterning of relationships which is less taken-for-granted by the participants who seek to co-ordinate and control' (Silverman 1970: 14). Silverman does not specify who *might* take the patterning for granted, but I imagine he might have in mind people like the new employee for whom the organization just 'is' – it has a structure and a solidity, while those who have to manage it may be more likely to see this as contingent and even problematic.

This organization may be said to make certain demands on us as an organization, even though we know 'the organization' cannot speak; instead it is usually managers or HR staff who speak for 'it' (see again, Silverman 1970: 9 on the 'reification' of the organization – that is with 'the attribution of concrete reality, particularly the power of thought and action, to social constructs'). At the very least we have to interact with a number of others – others in job roles like our own or unlike our own. We are likely to have a boss and to be aware of a hierarchy, we encounter certain rules, certain ways of behaving. Organizations can be seen as needing to integrate the individual, by definition, since it is a set of relationships.

If I look at this from the standpoint of the organization, and assume its reification, the problem is one of ensuring that the individual does the job that is expected, conforms to organizational norms and works cooperatively with others in the organization. We can also look at this from the standpoint of the individual employee and consider the ways in which that individual comes to terms with the organization. Schwartz (1987) suggests that organizations serve an ontological function for the individual – they can create a sense of being. They do this, he suggests, through presenting us with an *organization ideal* – a sense of the 'good' organizational member. This is not to maintain that everyone will live up to the ideal; indeed, we might prefer to see ourselves as individuals who are not entirely cut out of the cloth the organization provides. Even if we wear the uniform (a powerful sign of belonging and a means of identification as a member of the organization) we might wear colourful socks (if we can get away with it). Who wants to be, entirely, an organizational conformist? And yet to fail to conform and reject the organization ideal entirely is likely to be an uncomfortable stand and, indeed, might threaten one's place in the organization. Schwartz suggests, from a psychoanalytic perspective, which is one that can present a richer perspective on the processes at work than any superficial instrumentalism, that working towards the organizational ideal and submitting to it might be a way of serving one's own psychological needs. These needs might include deep-seated insecurities, even if we do not recognize them as such (see Schwartz 1987). Even if one rejects such a psychoanalytic approach, one can still argue that conformism makes sense from a purely instrumental viewpoint: one is likely to be rewarded for conformity to norms (perhaps financially, or in other ways), while infringements seen as damaging to organizational interests (or those taken to be damaging by those who are in a position to make such judgements) are likely to be punished in some way (ultimately by dismissal).

Most of the time such processes seem benign. From the consumer's or producer's perspective they can be a way of ensuring shelves of supermarkets are stacked with food, insurance claims are processed and diseases are treated. From the employee's point of view, they may be a way of ensuring that the salary keeps getting paid and there is no criticism from the boss. However, the price of conformity to organizational norms might sometimes be high. There are examples of terrible things occurring: the processes by which organizations serve an ontological function can also, it would seem, make concentration camp guards participate in genocide or make nurses stand by while patients starve to death (as in the case of Mid-Staffordshire Hospital even in the 21st century – see Francis 2010). We might, of course, explain this with reference to the power of social conformity, but the pressure on us to conform can stem from deep-seated ontological insecurity and an unwillingness to take the risk of standing against the demands placed upon us by others representing the organization. Organizations can unleash the best and the worst in people, and everything in between: they can be a collective effort for good but there is always a risk that they convince us of the need to do harm or to let harm be done. Perhaps most often, however, they lead to a middle-of-the-road blandness, something that excites neither admiration nor contempt; and perhaps that is no bad thing.

Some classic studies

Before considering contemporary organizational life, I think it is worth exploring some classic writings. In particular, the work of Max Weber on bureaucracy seems particularly pertinent. Of course, bureaucracy can be seen in negative terms, associated with red tape and excessive regulation. Yet I would argue that most organizations still have some bureaucratic characteristics, however flexible, lean, creative or even 'post-bureaucratic' (Heckscher 1994) they might be. Max Weber (1864–1920), of course, was writing about bureaucracy in the early 20th century when conditions were very different from today, but he was seeking to understand the characteristics of the organizations he saw around him both in his native Germany as well as other European countries and the United States (see Weber 1970: 14–18). In analysing bureaucracy (1970: 196–204) he was explicitly referring to what was happening in industrial private enterprise as well as in state organizations. The characteristics of bureaucracy, as he identified them, included the division of labour with officials having particular jurisdictional areas ordered by rules; it included a hierarchy, written documents or files; it required expert training to run the office; it demanded the full working capacity of the official. Weber was seeking to emphasize how modern bureaucracy differs from arrangements associated with feudalism and traditional forms of organization which often rely upon nepotism, tradition and relationships based on birth and hereditary. It is worth also remembering what Weber said about the position of the official in bureaucracies. The first point he makes about this is that office holding is a *vocation* and requires a course of training. The position of the official is in the nature of the duty, and loyalty is devoted to impersonal and functional purposes. The office holder usually enjoys a distinct social esteem and the official is appointed by senior authority, based on purely functional points of consideration. Also, the position of the official is held for life: the official receives regular pecuniary compensation of a salary and pension that is enough to ensure their welfare.

While bureaucracy today tends to have negative connotations, Weber emphasized its technical superiority (Weber 1970: 214):

> The decisive reason for the advance of bureaucratic organisation has always been its purely technical superiority over any other form of organisation. The fully developed bureaucratic mechanism compares with other organisations exactly as does the machine with the non-mechanical modes of production.
>
> Precision, speed, unambiguity, knowledge of the files, continuity, discretion, unity, strict subordination, reduction of friction and of material and personal costs – these are raised to the optimum point in the strictly bureaucratic administration, and especially in its monocratic form. As compared with all collegiate, honorific, and avocational forms of administration, trained bureaucracy is superior in all these points. And as far as complicated tasks are concerned, paid bureaucratic work is not only more precise but, in the last analysis, is often cheaper than even formally unremunerated honorific service.

This does not mean that Weber was unreservedly in favour of bureaucratization, but he did see it as superior to many other forms of organization, at least as it provides a means of administering states and organizations. 'The great question thus is… what we can set against this mechanisation to preserve a certain section of humanity from this fragmentation of the soul, this complete ascendancy of the bureaucratic ideal of life?' (Weber 1924, cited in Giddens 1971: 236). Giddens also cites Weber's observation that the individual worker today is a 'small wheel' in the bureaucratic machine, and 'asks himself only whether or not he can progress from this small wheel to being a bigger one' (Weber 1958, cited in Giddens 1971: 236). Moreover, Weber is often associated with the idea that bureaucratization presents something of an iron cage for the individual – seemingly a diminution of freedom. This seems to be something of a misconception but might be based upon the following passage from one of Weber's most important works (Weber 2001: 123, but originally written in 1904–5):

> The Puritan wanted to work in a calling; we are forced to do so. For when asceticism was carried out of monastic cells into everyday life, and began to dominate worldly morality, it did its part in building the tremendous cosmos of the modern economic order. This order is now bound to the technical and economic conditions of machine production which today determine the lives of all the individuals who are born into this mechanism, not only those directly concerned with economic acquisition, with irresistible force. Perhaps it will so determine them until the last ton of fossilized coal is burnt. In Baxter's view the care for external goods should only lie on the shoulders of the 'saint like a light cloak, which can be thrown aside at any moment'. But fate decreed that the cloak should become an iron cage.

However, this passage is in fact a translation from the original German and scholars have pointed out that the metaphor of the iron cage is more the translators' invention than Weber's, whose original German expression would be more accurately rendered in English as 'a shell as hard as steel' (Baehr 2001). This might be seen as quibbling but Baehr argues that this mistranslation changes the meaning and that Weber probably did not mean to convey a state of imprisonment and punishment. Instead (Baehr 2001: 164):

> The habitation of a steel shell implies not only a new dwelling for modern human beings, but a transformed nature; homo sapiens has become a different being, a degraded being. A cage deprives one of liberty, but leaves one otherwise unaltered, one's power is still intact even if incapable of full realisation. A shell, on the other hand, hints at an organic reconstitution of the being concerned; a shell is part of the organism and cannot be dispensed with. The steel shell is… the symbol of passivity, the transformation of the Puritan hero into a figure of mass mediocrity.

I find this argument convincing, but whether it is right or wrong perhaps the most important point is that this discussion suggests two different negative views that might be applied to bureaucracy to go alongside our everyday association of bureaucracy with inefficiency, red tape and overconformity to rules (even though Weber's iron cage/steel shell metaphor in the above quotation seems to be directed at 'care for external goods' rather than bureaucracy). These are, firstly, that bureaucracy might be constraining and cage-like, might be something the individual experiences as confining and wishes to be released from. On the other hand it suggests an alternative in which people may be reconciled to their position and even welcome it, becoming mediocre figures content with petty lives (Marcuse 1964). Moreover, we might note another point about shifting the metaphor from that of the cage to that of a shell. The shell is not only something that cannot be cast off as easily as a cloak, it is something that offers protection from the outside world. Again we might see some of the attraction of conformity to organizational demands as stemming from the need for security, not just in a material sense but in a psychological sense, too.

Before moving on from Weber it is worth saying that, at least as far as private enterprise is concerned, it is clear that Weber associated bureaucracy with the office and management, rather than with the organization as a whole. This already suggests that the organization might be split into different parts and raises the question as to what extent employees in the different parts identify with their part rather than the whole, something I will return to later.

If Weber emphasized rules, Foucault emphasized discipline and surveillance. The school, the factory and the prison all embody disciplinary technologies – timetables, regulations, ways of detecting deviance and testing for compliance, that may produce 'docile bodies'. Foucault (1977: 195–228) spent some time discussing panopticanism, prompted by Jeremy Bentham's ideas for a prison. These proposals for prison design emphasize not the confinement of the individual in a cage but visibility. Foucault describes it as follows (1977: 200):

> at the periphery, an annular building; at the centre, a tower; this tower is pierced with wide windows that open onto the inner side of the ring; the periphery building is divided into cells, each of which extends the whole width of the building; they have two windows, one on the inside, corresponding to the windows of the tower; the other, on the outside, allows the light to cross the cell from one end to the other. All that is needed, then, is to place a supervisor in a central tower and shut up in each cell a madman, a patient, a condemned man, a worker or a schoolboy. By the effect of backlighting, one can observe the tower, standing out precisely against the light, the small captive shadows in the cells of the periphery. They are like so many cages, so many small theatres, in which each actor is alone, perfectly individualised and constantly visible. The panoptic mechanism arranges spatial unities that make it possible to see constantly and recognise immediately. In short, it reverses the principle of the dungeon; or rather of its three functions – to enclose, to deprive of light and to hide – it preserves only the first and eliminates the other two. Full lighting and the eye of the supervisor capture better than darkness, which ultimately protected. Visibility is a trap.

Such a panoptican may seem a long way from most organizational life, although the way some call centres operate might resemble it (Brannan 2005; Clarke 2014 and see Chapter 3). However, through mechanisms as routine as appraisal and supervision by managers, the employee's work behaviour is often subject to observation and this serves a disciplinary function. The employee, conscious of being observed, may modify their behaviour. If organizations seek to use rewards as well as punishments for the right kind of behaviour this renders it a more favourable set of circumstances, but the threat of punishment, of the sack, is also there. Foucault is also associated with the recognition of what might be seen as a more insidious form of control and discipline. Through particular forms of knowledge people become regulated. With the idea of governmentality Foucault (Bratich et al. 2003; Burchell et al. 1991) suggests that we come to think in ways that govern our conduct as well as those of others. There are dangers here of posing an over-socialized conception of people (Wrong 1961) here: people entirely shaped by disciplinary technologies and forms of knowledge. People who, in internalizing the norms of the organization surrender any individuality, any sense of self-identity, that is out of keeping with the ideal organizational self. This would be an unfair reading of Foucault, however, who does also emphasize resistance and a plurality of discourses and contexts (see Foucault 1980 and Knights and Vurdubakis 1994). Such resistance and the complex interplay of potentially rival discourses may result in organizational conflict and disrupt the orderly life of the organization. But the question remains of how far the individual aligns themselves to the organization ideal. In the following pages I want to deal with some relevant studies that deal with the issue of the extent to which the individual becomes a corporate person.

For the moment I think it is useful to stay with classic studies and introduce Gouldner's (1957 and 1958) distinction between cosmopolitans and locals.

(1) *Cosmopolitans*: those low on loyalty to the employing organization, high on commitment to specialized role skills, and likely to use an outer reference group orientation.

(2) *Locals*: those high on loyalty to the employing organization, low on commitment to specialized role skills, and likely to use an inner reference group orientation.

(Gouldner 1957: 290)

In making this distinction Gouldner is seeking to emphasize those identities that are active in more subtle ways than the manifest identities such as specific 'jobs'. Both cosmopolitan and local identities are latent in the sense of being implicit rather than explicit. Moreover, both forms of latent identity can take various forms. For example, he distinguishes between those locals who are, among other orientations, the 'dedicated' from the 'homeguard'. The former are: 'the "true believers" who are identified with and affirm the distinctive ideology of their organization' (Gouldner 1958: 446), while the latter 'are not characterized by a commitment to the distinctive values of the local organization; nor, for that matter, are they especially oriented to the local community... They seem to be bound and loyal to the organization for peculiarly particularistic reasons' (Gouldner 1958: 448).

One reason for a 'cosmopolitan' orientation is that commitment to one's occupation or profession may be more important to the individual than the organization (see Chapter 3). However, managers have sought ways of reconciling cosmopolitan orientations with local ones, particularly in employing professionals who are recruited for their expertise and are expected to be oriented to the norms of the profession while still loyally serving the organization for as long as they are employed by it. Organizations, in so far as they adopt a functional form which puts members of a particular professional or occupational group together, could be said to be seeking to secure organizational commitment while accepting the possibility of a cosmopolitan identity. Even in multidisciplinary project groups the same thing might apply – the individual might be a member of the group precisely on the basis of their cosmopolitanism identity, but still be expected to contribute to the team and show loyalty to the organization as a result.

Organizational culture and identity

While Weber emphasized formal rules, much of the organizational literature points to the importance of informal norms of behaviour. Indeed, the literature on corporate and organizational culture emphasizes that organizations are more than the formal rules and relationships that exist and more than the tangible artefacts of the organization, which might include logos, uniforms, walls and gates.

If the idea of organizations having a culture might encourage ethnographic approaches that provide sophisticated and complex accounts of the patterns of behaviour values and relationships within the organization, it has to be said that much of the literature on corporate culture is superficial and managerialist. Peters and Waterman's (1982) attempt to delineate the characteristics of excellent corporations is very much a management consultant's view rather than an anthropologist's view of the companies in question, for example. Their prescriptions such as 'stick to the knitting' often seem banal to me. Deal and Kennedy's (1988) work is of the same ilk. In it they define culture in standard dictionary terms as 'the integrated pattern of human behaviour that includes thought, speech, actions, and artifacts and depends on man's capacity for learning and transmitting knowledge to succeeding generations' (1988: 4). What they were keen to promote was the idea of strong cultures as being associated with success. Organizations such as IBM, Procter and Gamble and Johnson and Johnson were seen to have strong cultures.

> Whether weak or strong, culture has a powerful influence throughout an organisation; it affects practically everything from who gets promoted and what decisions are made, to how employees dress and what sports they play. Because of this impact, we think the culture also has a major effect on the success of the business.
>
> *(Deal and Kennedy 1988: 4)*

In describing a strong culture they used Tandem as an example – a Silicon Valley tech company. Its culture was described as involving a widely shared philosophy stressing the importance of people, rather than rules or structures, as well as invoking heroes, rituals and ceremonies (1988: 9–13). This, they suggest, leads to people behaving in ways that would probably horrify that critic of 'organization man', Whyte (1960):

> A strong culture is a system of informal rules that spells out how people are to behave most of the time. By knowing what exactly is expected of them, employees will waste little time in deciding how to act in a given situation. In a weak culture, on the other hand, employees waste a good deal of time just trying to figure out what they should do and how they should do it. The impact of a strong cultural productivity is amazing. In the extreme, we estimate that the company can gain as much as one or two hours of productive work per employee per day... A strong culture enables people to feel better about what they do, so they are more likely to work harder.
>
> *(Deal and Kennedy 1988: 15–16)*

One can easily see how managers might be seduced by such rhetoric, and why managers and company leaders might seek to promote such a 'culture' which all can share. However, in this book I am not concerned with promoting productivity or business success, I am more concerned with understanding people's identification with companies or organizations. (Those concerned with business success might find Saffold (1988) a more sophisticated and useful aide than either Peters and Waterman or Deal and Kennedy). But whether one takes a simplistic or more complex view of organizational culture, there are those who, I think rightly, argue that the corporate culture bandwagon was a significant attempt to valorize the corporation (Willmott 1993; Silver 1987).

The idea of a strong organizational culture has much in common with the idea of a clear organizational identity. Those who share a culture have a common collective identity. Albert and Whetten's (1985) classic study of organizational identity suggests three criteria as tests of organizational identity: claimed central character, claimed distinctiveness and claimed temporal continuity. However, they also suggest that identity is often complex – that there can be single, dual or multiple identities. In addition, for dual identities there might be 'holographic' or 'ideographic' forms. The holographic form they see as a blending of two organizational identities together so that each unit within the organization exhibits the two identities (e.g. a university blending teaching and research, so that all academics engage in both activities) while the latter divides itself into two parts, effectively, each different to the other (e.g. a university that separated its research units from teaching departments). Such work suggests that the extent to which any organization can be said to have a unitary culture is, at best, variable and studies such as those by Parker (1999) show how organizations have pronounced sub-cultures. These may not be what management or company leaders would wish to promote; they may even work against company objectives or at least have a questionable relationship to them. If organizations might be seen to have a more or less well integrated and homogeneous identity, those working within it may find different forms of identification possible, depending on how far it might take dualistic or multiple forms.

Organizational commitment?

While Gouldner's (1957, 1958) work suggests that employees might have varying degrees of identification with the organization, later work has explored the relationship between organizational identification and organizational commitment, with the former assumed as likely to be productive of the latter. If you identify with your employing organization you are likely to be committed to its goals and actions in pursuit of the goals (see Meyer et al. 2006). Employers might be interested in this because committed employees are likely to exhibit positive traits such as good attendance, organizational citizenship behaviours and good job performance (Meyer et al. 2006: 666). Meyer et al. (2006: 669) suggest that identifying with a collective can lead to the development of a commitment to that collective. Moreover, it may be useful to distinguish different types of commitment: as Meyer and Allen (1991) argued, employees may maintain an attachment to a given target because they want to (affective commitment), because they feel they should (normative commitment) or because they have too much to lose by severing the connection (continuance commitment). Each of these could be seen as variables and one can have a greater or lesser degree of such commitment. This raises the issue as to what extent management policy and practice in an organization shapes such commitment as well as the related question of how the employee's experience in the organization affects it. In so far as individuals may identify with an organization such as Apple, one possibility is that the organization draws upon prior commitments and values; involvement in the organization may do little to change them. In such a scenario there is no need for the organization to reshape the individual because the individual already fits. But we could alternatively imagine situations where the organization does influence the individual's wants, values and calculations of benefits. The training in religious orders as well as the military has, for centuries if not millennia, been oriented in this direction, seeking to mould often raw recruits into military or religious figures of the 'right' kind, even if it does to a large extent depend on some prior commitments. Is this not still happening in contemporary organizations, albeit perhaps in more curtailed ways? Certainly back in the 1950s, Whyte suggested it was.

Whyte's (2002 but originally published in 1957) study of *Organization Man* is a powerful warning against excessive conformity to organizational demands. In looking at middle and senior managers in large companies in the USA in the 1950s, at a time when such roles were exclusively occupied by men, he expresses concern at the direction of travel of corporate life. He was concerned in particular about the way individualism was threatened by what he called the social ethic. He defines the social ethic as:

a contemporary body of thought which makes morally legitimate the pressures of society against the individual. Its major propositions are three: a belief in the group as the source of creativity; a belief in 'belongingness' as the ultimate need of individual; and a belief in the application of science to achieve the belongingness.

(Whyte 2002: 7)

In examining how the organization man was educated, trained and lived both in the organization and in the residential suburbs, he describes the kind of moulding process going on whereby the individual comes to conform to what he refers to as The Organization. The managers he was discussing do not just work for The Organization, as he says in the introduction, they 'belong to it as well' (Whyte 2002: 3). He goes on to say: 'they are the ones of our middle class who have left home, spiritually as well as physically, to take the vows of organisation life, and it is they who are the mind and soul of our great self-perpetuating institutions'. This does not mean that he portrays individuals as entirely at one with the organization. Indeed, he often conveys the sense of ambivalence that exists. For example, one man 'poised at the threshold' of the top management of a large corporation was quoted as saying (Whyte 2002: 167):

> One of the hazards of the kind of life we lead is the loss of well-defined objectives. What is the purpose, what is the end? I was deeply a part of my job in the chemical division. My wife and I were deeply a part of the community; I was contributing and was effective. Then they asked me to come to New York – the V.P. in charge told me that by coming here I'd have a box seat in the 'Big Time'. If his guess had been bad, it's a terrible waste. I hope the company isn't playing checkers with me. I feel a lack. I don't know what I'm being groomed for. I don't know what contacts to keep alive. A sales manager knows he should keep his current customer contacts, but in the broad management philosophy you can't do this. You have to guess. I felt I trained for 20 years for a tremendous job that had plenty of challenge, and I was in it for only nine months. Somehow I feel this move is out of my pattern whatever that is. I'd hate to lose all that's behind me because somebody is playing checkers with me.

As Whyte puts it: 'one wrong turn can destroy all that is gone before'. He also points out that loyalty to the corporation is far from total, indicated by what he sees as an increasing tendency to switch employers, often prompted by blocked promotion. As he portrays it, there is often a tension between the individual and the organization – rarely a complete 'surrender'. For example, he says this about conformity (Whyte 2002: 155):

> In an inverse way, how much a man thinks himself conformist tells a lot about how much spiritual fealty he feels for The Organisation, and as subjective as this attitude may be, there is a discernible difference between older and younger men. The younger men are sanguine. They are well aware that

organisation work demands a measure of conformity – as a matter of fact, half their energies are devoted to finding out the right pattern to conform to. But the younger executive likes to explain the conforming is a kind of phase, a purgatory that he must suffer before he merges into the area where you can do as he damn well pleases. 'You take this business of entertaining', an ambitious assistant plant manager told me. 'You have to go through all that stuff for ten years or so, but then you can chuck it. It's like running for the President of the United States; during the campaign you have to do a lot of things you might not like, when you get to be president that's all over with.'

Older executives learned better long ago. At a reunion dinner for business school graduates a vice president of a large steel company brought up the matter of conformity and, eying his table companions, asked if they felt as he did: he was, he said, becoming more conformist. There was almost an explosion of table thumping and head noddings. In the mass confessional that followed, everyone present tried to top the others in describing the extent of his conformity.

Whyte presents a rather bleak picture but not one altogether without hope. He ends the main part of the book with an exhortation as follows (2002: 404):

The organisation man is not in the grip of vast social forces about which it is impossible for him to do anything; the options are there, and with wisdom and foresight he can turn the future away from the dehumanised collective that so haunts our thoughts. He may not. But he can.

He must *fight* The Organisation. Not stupidly, or selfishly, for the defects of individual self-regard are no more to be venerated than the defects of cooperation. But fight he must, for the demands for his surrender are constant and powerful, and the more he has come to like the life of organisation the more difficult does he find it to resist these demands, or even to recognise them. It is wretched, dispiriting advice to hold before him the dream that ideally there need be no conflict between him and society. There always is; there always must be. Ideology can wish it away; the peace of mind offered by organisation remains a surrender, and no less so for being offered in benevolence. That is the problem.

(Emphasis in original)

I am pretty sure Weber would agree with the sentiment. Incidentally, these are not quite his last words in the book. There follows an appendix: 'How to cheat on personality tests' – an example of how an individual might fight the organization, even when they aspire to become a part of it. As Alvesson and Willmott (2002: 621) have put it: 'The organizational regulation of identity... is a precarious and often contested process involving active identity work.'

Whyte's distinction between working for the organization and belonging to it is an important one. For many people the organization might not be something they would wish to draw their identity from, or identify *with*; perhaps it just provides the job. If we consider another classic study of organizational life, Beynon's (1975)

Working for Ford (based in Ford's Liverpool plant in the 1960s) we see a very different attitude to that of the 'Organization Man' of Whyte's study. Men like
Eddie, for example, who worked in the paint shop and was a shop steward
(a union representative at 'shop-floor' level):

> I don't know what it is. Some sections like this one are good sections with all
> good jobs. It's because you have had blokes like myself and Kenny and
> George who've come to stay I suppose. We've decided not to be beaten down
> by Fords or to leave. On other sections the jobs are really bad. I can't under-
> stand it. I've been down to talk to the lads on one of those sections, to try to
> persuade them to do something. They say they'll be leaving soon. At the other
> extreme you get the daft buggers in the boiler house who've been here since
> the start up and still haven't done anything. For all we say though, there is no
> easy job in this plant. We're going to have to give way on manning on this
> section soon. We've just been fortunate with the change off in the fascia
> panels. Most jobs in this plant, even the easy ones, are pretty bad really.
> There's no joy in putting things on hooks.
>
> *(Beynon 1975: 132)*

Kenny was even more forthright in expressing what I would see as disidentification
with the organization he worked for:

> I don't know what I am, or what I want to do. I hate Fords. I'd give up a
> wage increase to have Henry Ford on this section and give him a good kick
> up the arse. I'd thought of going to Australia. Of opening a shop. Can you be
> a socialist and own a shop?
>
> *(Beynon 1975: 131)*

Of course Beynon was describing a situation in a Ford plant when the union was
stronger than it is today and men like Eddie had a lot more control over their
working conditions than they do now, even though, as Eddie's words show, it was
far from total.

One issue is how far those who seek to coordinate and control organizations still
demand conformity. In the foreword to the 2002 edition of Whyte's book, Joseph
Nocera argues that things have indeed changed in corporations: that individuality
is now seen as a virtue not a vice (Whyte 2002: ix) and that the common
assumption today is that 'conflict can be healthy, and that most great ideas... are
more likely to come from a single person with an original thought than from any
number of well-meaning task forces'. I am not quite so sure – I think the pressures
to conform are there, although they may exist side by side with an emphasis on
individuality. Perhaps what has changed is the expectation of a job for life within
one organization – but as Whyte himself pointed out, people switching between
organizations has always been common, and it is doubtful whether this is as profound
a change as might be assumed.

Another study that provides interesting insights into organizational conformity and the shaping of individual identities within them is that of Casey (1995). This is an ethnographic study of the relationship between the self and the organization conducted in 1991 to 1992 in a American company she calls Hephaestus Corporation. The company was described as engaged in 'the manufacture and use of advanced technological products and in organisational restructuring and cultural change' (Casey 1995: 198). In this book she describes a process of 'corporate colonisation of the self' (Casey 1995: 138) where:

> The person's values, attitudes and general orientation must correspond with those promoted by the organisational culture. Consequently, specific traits and attitudes that are useful to the work of the team are stimulated and rewarded. Traits and attitudes that are unnecessary or that impede the processes of work place culture, and therefore of production, are thwarted and suppressed. Individuals who display more of these corporately undesired features tend to experience higher degrees of intra-psychic conflict, discomfort and alienation and those more disposed to, or more willing to comply with, a congruent fit with the corporations desired character type.
>
> *(Casey 1995: 139)*

The individual seems to be rewarded for being the kind of person the company wants, and the individual is made to feel discomfort if they do not live up to the organizational norm. Thus one employee is reported as saying:

> I wasn't as competitive as most people. I was more laid back. I figured that I am not one of those people, but I don't like to play their games just to get ahead... But it is a harsh reality, because I found out that since I'm not playing the games I'm not getting promoted as fast as everybody else. I had a manager who had a problem with me, because I tried to do everything good, so that if there is a problem that might take somebody else 10 minutes to solve I may spend an hour or two on it because I want to learn more, and basically it is that other people just blow-off half of it and do one or two things and they look like they did everything, because they make themselves look good that way... A lot of people will cut corners to do things and get the job done, but they didn't do it right, but they say the right things, and they look good. That goes into competitiveness too, because there are ways of cheating as a way of getting ahead. It's deceiving, and looks are deceiving... After a while you kind of lay back because you get tired of being shot down for whatever reason.
>
> *(Casey 1995: 139–40)*

However, if the expression 'corporate colonization of the self' suggests that the self is merely passive and becomes the employee that the organization demands this would be misleading. The process of colonization Casey describes, is a complex one involving identity work, including resistance and defensive reactions. In fact, drawing on psychoanalytic concepts, Casey points to three broad clusters of reaction to the situation, three ways in which individuals seek to deal with the demands placed upon them and adjust to them; these are defence, collusion and capitulation.

The defensive adaptation is often associated with a critical view of much of what is going on in the organization, while still working to or above the required performance standards. Those adopting a defensive approach often keep a kind of psychological distance from what is going on – as one respondent is quoted to have said 'I have always stood back and looked, "Look at this silly game". I've been part of it, but I've always been able to stand back and know that you are a player' (1995: 169). Employees adopting this approach seem to preserve some sense of self as being separate from, if not opposed to, that self that the company offers; and yet they are not immune from the demands of that company to behave in certain ways.

The second adaptation, the colluded self, is a closer approximation to the fully committed employee – to the company man or woman – but it also requires identity work:

> A lot of people are passionate about the product so I think what I have discovered in my own experience, is that if you seize or assume responsibility, it seeks its own equilibrium. People are always looking for leadership at some level, at all levels.
>
> I looked around me and I saw people in management positions and I said to myself, I could do this. I could do that. My ideas were as good as theirs. I was about 20 years old then. And I guess I began to set myself goals in this company. And I have achieved them.
>
> *(Casey 1995: 172)*

BOX 4.1 IN THE NEWS: EXPEDIA – A GREAT PLACE TO WORK?

In December 2015 the *Independent* reported how Expedia, the travel company, had come top in a survey that tries to find the UK's best employers. After visiting the company the reporter quoted a manager saying the London office 'gives a feel of fun the moment you walk through the door' while another says, 'Everyone is passionate about the company' and 'everyone is passionate about travel'. When he visited the office he saw about 50 staff attending a training event, dressed in Christmas jumpers, many in trainers, and 'all of them, by the looks of it, under 40'. He reported that they 'applauded and giggled their way through a diversity session delivered by Britta Wilson, vice-president of inclusion strategies'. Apart from whiskey clubs and cocktail nights, ping-pong tables and an ultra-modern office, the company also seems to offer flexible hours: one employee describes how she could take early calls from home and pick her daughter up from school at 3pm.

Source: *Independent*, 11 December 2015

Aligning the self to the corporation is, in this view, not always easy or straight-forward, however. It requires developmental work and can involve overcoming difficulties, as another employee demonstrates (Casey 1995: 172–3):

> I would say that what I'm criticised most for is the fact that I think I am right all the time. I think that in the last five years I've really tried to conquer this, because it has been that I am not right all the time… I've kind of dampened what I call my arrogance, in the last five years I have really consciously addressed it.
>
> I don't like conflict. I really don't like it, so I try to beat it. I don't like it when Ken gets angry in meetings, I don't like those performances, and they will have to stop. I can see everybody getting uncomfortable with it. And I don't believe in getting angry like that… There are other ways to deal with things.

The final category in Casey's analysis, that of the capitulated, are those that seem either pragmatically or reluctantly to give in to corporate demands. The pragmatic response is one from someone who 'knows how to play the game, and when to retreat. They are pragmatic, strategic selves' (1995: 175). They do not rock the boat and may be ambitious individuals and successful in the organization, who find ways of reconciling their interests to those of the company demands. The 'reluc-tantly' capitulated also accommodate to corporate colonization, but suggest that there is a price to pay.

For Casey organizations like Hephaestus Corporation offer an organizationally based identity that is, in many ways, attractive: the promise is that the employee 'finds gratification in a sense of giving, a devotion to an entity greater than herself and her ordinary, narcissistic, anxiety ridden life'. And yet it is a promise, as Casey makes clear, that carries many risks: the existence of 'regressive sibling rivalry, nepotistic patronage and advancement, and elimination of job security and benefits' (1995: 190) may undermine any ontological security provided by the organization. Loyal employees may encounter situations where they feel shock and betrayal, as was the case with Andrew when his proposals for resolving a crisis were blocked by senior managers, leaving him contemplating resignation from the company (1995: 162).

Casey does recognize the existence of processes of resistance, certainly at a psychological and individual level, but she reports few instances of what might be seen as outright organizational misbehaviour – the kind of anti-management humour, sabotage, strikes or organized union activity that might confront the corporation's definition of the self (see Ackroyd and Thompson 1999). Nor does she deal with the differences between different divisions or departments – the different cultures that might provoke different loyalties and varying definitions of the self (Parker 1999). Moreover, perhaps hers is a somewhat bleaker view of the colonization of the self than is warranted: she seems to focus on individuals' conflicts and troubles, rather than their pleasures and successes (compare Pahl 1995). However, she does point to processes and tendencies that certainly are important to recognize and, like Whyte, points to ways in which success might be viewed ambivalently. Colonization of the self by the organization is certainly something that can be a possibility, even if it is successful to varying degrees and with varying degrees of negative psychological and social consequences. As Goffman (1968) demonstrated in his book, *Asylums*, even in what he called total institutions that impose severe constraints on the individual there is always a capacity for some individual resistance and, usually, if not always, we could find instances of this in organizations if we knew where to look and how to look for it. Attempts by those controlling organizations to create the person they want the employee to be are always likely to be precarious.

Crafting the self

Kondo's study (1990) provides another fascinating ethnographic study of organizational life in Japan, set in its community context in which the issue of the association between the individual and the organization is explored. Hers is not the study of life in one of the giant Japanese conglomerates such as Toyota but a study of life both within a small confectionery company and in the community in which it is situated.

Kondo recounts how in many ways the owners and managers of the company seek to present the company as a family and draw employees into it. The company had around 30 full-time employees and part-time workers and Kondo points out that this is too large for familial face-to-face interactions on a constant basis, but in many respects the company's owners seek to preserve elements of a family. This includes concern for the well-being of its employees. For example, Kondo relates how after a company end-of-year party the 'sensei' called a taxi for a group of employees as well as Kondo, to take them home. The next day he was furious with them for not calling him when they got home: 'I stayed up waiting until all of you got home! If you just thought to call… I worried myself sick!' (1990: 180). This is a striking case of a manager behaving something like a father towards his children. But if this seems culturally specific, surely something like such paternalism is frequently encountered in contemporary organizations in the West, even if it might take a different, less personal form (such as supporting gym membership as a way of promoting healthy lifestyle). Kondo goes on to show a variety of ways in which the company sought to bind employees into the organization. Through company trips, for example, and through parties and social events, they provided what might be seen as favourable treatment to their employees; but while in many respects the company thus presented itself as a good employer at times it worked its employees very hard. At a time of peak production it required its artisan confectioners to work from 2.00 in the morning to midnight for a week in order to meet orders (1990: 215). Kondo recounts how one artisan revealed to her 'the complexities of the Artisan's relationship to the company' (1990: 215–6):

> After a dinner lecture by an ethics teacher who had come to visit the company, [Yutaka-kun] invited me for a cup of coffee at the Artisan's favourite coffee

house, 'Pony'. We played videogames and read comic books for a while, and then Yutaka-kun started to tell me about himself and about work. He... had already been working for the Satōs [the owners] for seven years. It didn't take long before he launched into a litany of complaints. The physical labour was too demanding, the hours were ridiculously long, and you always had to watch how you acted in front of the bosses. He laughed scornfully at his co-workers, 'You see how everybody complained about the ethics retreat, then when they came back, they always go and say "thank you, I learned a lot" to the *shachō*.' Yutaka-kun's tirade went on for some time, and I murmured sympathetically, pleased that it would be so frank. Suddenly, he changed his tune. 'But I am glad I work there. People say if you can work there you can work any-where'... He continued to elaborate this point of view: that they were so busy was really due to the prosperity of the company. No other confectionery in the entire ward, said he, produced such a range of confections in such massive volumes as did the Satōs. Working at the Satō confectionery, then, was a real education in the craft... The long working hours and taxing conditions, though a source of complaint, were proofs of the Artisan's strength, fortitude and endurance virtues – the virtues the ethics retreat extolled so memorably. And not incidentally, this same fortitude acted as testament to their masculine toughness.

(Kondo 1990: 216)

Again, if this sentiment might seem alien to a Western reader it reminds me of the sentiments expressed by managers in Whitehead's study (2001), where he portrays managerial discourses as offering the promise of power and hierarchical status and 'the sense of potency which may come from overcoming and controlling extern-alities: self and others'. Paradoxically, it is suggested (Whitehead 2001: 95), the greater the chaos and risk of failure, the greater 'the potential to achieve a sense of control, self-esteem and self-worth through confronting and "over-coming" these challenges'.

Such sentiments might of course be seen as a form of cognitive dissonance reduction; ways of the individuals convincing themselves that putting up with a difficult situation is a sensible strategy. We might expect that employers will want to offer positive rewards for working for the organization as an inducement to commitment. This is the logic behind attempts to provide a positive employer brand which is often associated with the provision of flexible working and favourable working conditions and opportunities for development (e.g. see Cascio 2014).

Conclusion

We can take from Kondo's observations, as well as those of Casey and Whyte, the presence of ambivalence in employees who see the negative side of working for the organization as well as a positive side. One view of employee engagement is that it depends on the balance of such positives and negatives. And yet we need to be aware of the capacity for individuals to tolerate what might be seen as intolerable conditions. Instances like the case of the Mid-Staffordshire hospital in which care was found to be unsatisfactory to the point of causing deaths, are a salutary reminder of this (Francis 2010). Even while care standards were deteriorating to dangerous levels, this organization survived: employees continued to turn up for work and get paid (although no doubt in many cases patients were treated well, and employees might take comfort in that).

In examining identification with the organization, one can of course consider this as a matter of degree. Gouldner's work suggests there might be other sources of identification that acquire primacy, possibly leading the employee to behave in ways that are different from those suggested by the norms of the organization. In considering the relationship between the individual and the organization one needs to bear in mind these alternative sources of identification both within and without the organization. If the issue is couched in terms of conformity then this raises the potential for non-conformity. An alternative way of construing this is in terms of power and resistance, but for now it may suffice to note that individuals and groups within an organization may well want to exit the organization or else to act in ways which are neither expected nor desired by those who set the rules. While organizations may well be based on certain rules and norms, the extent to which they are internalized or adhered to will be variable. The reasons for lack of conformity though, I would suggest, are often based on alternative collective and individual identifications, whether these be occupational or, in the example of Kenny, referred to earlier, class-based.

Those of us who work in organizations are inevitably organization men and women to some extent. The question is to what extent and with what consequences. In entering particular organizations we may be working with the grain of our existing values and ways of behaving or be cutting across the grain. The extent to which the organization is an iron cage, a steel shell or a light cloak is an open question and highly variable. Marx (1974: 327–32 but originally written in 1844) bemoaned a state of alienation in which the human being is alienated from his or her species being, that of a creative, social and productive animal. Perhaps some individuals do fulfil themselves and develop themselves in organizations, but the danger is that we settle for too little. Like the men in the boiler house that Eddie referred to above, maybe in keeping our heads down and failing to fight, we cede too much; worse still we may embrace our own subjugation, feel safe within the limited horizons of our shells, becoming 'one-dimensional' men and women (Marcuse 1964). For Casey, the organization seems more important than occupational identities as shapers of self-identity. I am not convinced by this, not least because our occupational identities are at least a latent 'cosmopolitan' identity, as we saw in Chapter 3, but organizational life certainly requires identity work and the organization can, at least sometimes, be an object of identification.

BOX 4.2 AT THE MOVIES: THE ORGANIZATION AND IDENTITY

Some movies relevant to the themes of the chapter are:

Company Limited (1971, director Satyajit Ray)
Glengarry Glen Ross (1992, director David Mamet)
Office Space (1999, director Mike Judge)
Up in the Air (2009, director Mike Nichols)

References

Ackroyd, S. and Thompson, P. J. (1999) *Organizational Misbehaviour*. London: Sage.

Albert, S. and Whetten, D. A. (1985) 'Organizational identity', *Research in Organizational Behavior*, 7: 263–297.

Alvesson, M. and Willmott, H. (2002) 'Identity regulation as organizational control: Producing the appropriate individual', *Journal of Management Studies*, 39(5): 619–644.

Baehr, P. (2001) 'The "iron cage" and the "shell as hard as steel": Parsons, Weber, and the stahlhartes gehäuse metaphor in the Protestant Ethic and the Spirit of Capitalism', *History and Theory*, 40(2): 153–169.

Beynon, H. (1975) *Working for Ford*. Wakefield: E. P. Publishing.

Brannan, M. J. (2005) 'Once more with feeling: Ethnographic reflections on the mediation of tension in a small team of call centre workers', *Gender, Work and Organization*, 12(5): 420–439.

Bratich, J. Z., Packer, J. and McCarthy, C. (2003) *Foucault, Cultural Studies, and Governmentality*. Albany, NY: State University of New York Press.

Burchell, G., Gordon, C. and Miller, P. M. (eds) (1991) *The Foucault Effect: Studies in Governmentality*, with two lectures by and an interview with Michel Foucault. London: Harvester Wheatsheaf.

Cascio, W. F. (2014) 'Leveraging employer branding, performance management and human resource development to enhance employee retention', *Human Resource Development International*, 17(2): 121–128.

Casey, C. (1995) *Work, Self and Society: After Industrialism*. London: Routledge.

Clarke, A. J. (2014) 'What a performance! The influence of call centre workflows on workers' skills and emotional wellbeing', *Journal of Organizational Ethnography*, 3(2): 259–274.

Deal, T. E. and Kennedy, A. A. (1988) *Corporate Cultures: The Rights and Rituals of Corporate Life*. Harmondsworth: Penguin.

Foucault, M. (1977) *Discipline and Punish: The Birth of the Prison*, trans. Alan Sheridan. London: Allen Lane.

Foucault, M. (1980) *Power/Knowledge: Selected Interviews and Other Writings, 1972/1977*, ed. Colin Gordon. Brighton: Harvester Press.

Francis, R. (2010) 'Independent inquiry into care provided by Mid-Staffordshire NHS Foundation Trust Jan 2005–March 2009. Vol. 1', at http://webarchive.nationalarchives.gov.uk/20130107105354/http://www.dh.gov.uk/prod_consum_dh/groups/dh_digitalassets/@dh/@en/@ps/documents/digitalasset/dh_113447.pdf (accessed 7 December 2015).

Giddens, A. (1971) *Capitalism and Modern Social Theory: An Analysis of the Writings of Marx, Durkheim and Max Weber*. Cambridge: Cambridge University Press.

Goffman, E. (1968) *Asylums: Essays on the Social Situation of Mental Patients and Other Inmates.* Harmondsworth: Penguin.

Gouldner, A. W. (1957) 'Cosmopolitans and locals: Toward an analysis of latent social roles: I', *Administrative Science Quarterly*, 2(3): 281–306.

Gouldner, A. W. (1958) 'Cosmopolitans and locals: Toward an analysis of latent social roles: II', *Administrative Science Quarterly*, 2(4): 444–480.

Heckscher, C. (1994) 'Defining the post-bureaucratic type' in Heckscher, C. and Donnellon, A. (eds), *The Post-Bureaucratic Organization: New Perspectives on Organizational Change*. Thousand Oaks, CA: Sage.

Independent (2015) 'Expedia: A day as an employee at the best place to work in the UK', at http://www.independent.co.uk/news/business/news/expedia-a-day-as-an-employee-a t-the-best-place-to-work-in-the-uk-a6770281.html (accessed 21 December 2015).

Knights, D. and Vurdubakis, T. (1994) 'Foucault, power, resistance and all that' in Jermier, J. M., Knights, D. and Nord, W. R. (eds), *Resistance and Power in Organizations*. London: Routledge.

Kondo, D. K. (1990) *Crafting Selves: Power, Gender, and Discourses of Identity in a Japanese Workplace*. Chicago: University of Chicago Press.

Marcuse, H. (1964) *One Dimensional Man: Studies in the Ideology of Advanced Industrial Society*. London: Routledge and Kegan Paul.

Marx, K. (1974) *Marx: Early Writings*. Harmondsworth: Penguin.

Meyer, J. P. and Allen, N. J. (1991) 'A three-component conceptualization of organizational commitment', *Human Resource Management Review*, 1(1): 61–89.

Meyer, J. P., Becker, T. E. and van Dick, R. (2006) 'Social identities and commitments at work: Toward an integrative model', *Journal of Organizational Behavior*, 27(5): 665–683.

Pahl, R. E. (1995) *After Success: Fin-de-Siècle Anxiety and Identity*. Cambridge: Polity Press.

Parker, M. (1999) *Organizational Culture and Identity: Unity and Division at Work*. London: Sage.

Peters, T. J. and Waterman, R. H. (1982) *In Search of Excellence: Lessons from America's Best-Run Companies*. London: Harper and Row.

Saffold, G. S. (1988) 'Culture traits, strength, and organizational performance: Moving beyond "strong" culture', *Academy of Management Review*, 13(4): 546–558.

Schwartz, H. S. (1987) 'Anti-social actions of committed organizational participants: An existential psychoanalytic perspective', *Organization Studies*, 8(4): 327–340.

Silver, J. (1987) 'The ideology of excellence: Management and neo-conservatism', *Studies in Political Economy*, 24: 5–29.

Silverman, D. (1970) *The Theory of Organisations: A Sociological Framework*. London: Heinemann Educational.

Weber, M. (1970) *From Max Weber: Essays in Sociology*, trans. and ed. H. H. Gerth and C. W. Mills. London: Routledge and Kegan Paul.

Weber, M. (2001) *The Protestant Ethic and the Spirit of Capitalism*. London: Routledge.

Whitehead, S. (2001) 'Woman as manager: A seductive ontology', *Gender, Work and Organization*, 8(1): 84–107.

Whyte, W. H. (1960) *The Organization Man*. Harmondsworth: Penguin Books.

Whyte, W. H. (2002) *The Organization Man*. Philadelphia, PA: University of Pennsylvania Press.

Willmott, H. (1993) 'Strength is ignorance; slavery is freedom: Managing culture in modern organizations', *Journal of Management Studies*, 30(4): 515–552.

Wrong, D. H. (1961) 'The Oversocialized Conception of Man in Modern Sociology', *American Sociological Review*, 26(2): 183–193.

5

ETHNICITY AND RACE

Introduction

To what extent are you conscious of your race or ethnicity? When are you conscious of it? Does it matter and if so, how? You might take your race and ethnicity for granted and it might rarely enter your consciousness. Even if you are conscious of it, however, you may feel it has little relevance to your working life. In this chapter I explore issues of race and ethnicity and argue that it is often highly relevant to work experience – and to inequality – even if we may sometimes, understandably, want to dodge the issue. I start by dealing with the meaning of 'race and ethnicity' as related and overlapping terms, before sketching some dimensions of inequality and considering possible origins, before I focus on how it is negotiated at work.

Race and ethnicity: what do the terms mean?

What do you think of when asked about your race or ethnicity? In the United Kingdom, when applying for jobs it is common to be asked to complete an 'ethnic monitoring' section of an application form (see Box 5.1). This is intended to monitor selection decisions and is prompted by legislation that makes discrimination on the basis of race illegal in the United Kingdom. 'Race' is defined, in the glossary of terms provided on the Equalities and Human Rights Commission (EHRC, 2015) website, as follows: 'Race... refers to a group of people defined by their race, colour, nationality (including citizenship), ethnic or national origins.' In this definition race and ethnicity (as well as nationality) are conflated. We have to recognize, however, that this definition occurs in a particular historical, cultural, geographical, social and political context. Essed and Trienekens (2008) inform us that, in Holland, 'race is a sensitive if not a taboo word' – it is not used in political discourse or official forms – nor is ethnicity. Instead the emphasis is on culture or nationality or religion. Does this mean Dutch society is more tolerant of 'ethnic' or 'racial' difference? Probably not, if the same article is used to understand how differences are understood and represented there.

BOX 5.1 HOW WOULD YOU DESCRIBE YOUR ETHNICITY?

Please select one of the following:

Asian/Asian British

Asian or Asian British ▢ Indian ▢ Pakistani ▢ Bangladeshi ▢ Any other Asian background ▢

Black/Black British

Black or Black British ▢ African ▢ Caribbean ▢ Any other Black background ▢

Chinese or other ethnic group

Chinese or other ethnic group ▢ Chinese ▢ Any other ▢

Mixed heritage

Mixed heritage ▢ White and Black Caribbean ▢ White and Black African ▢ White and Asian ▢ Any other mixed background ▢

White

British ▢ English ▢ Welsh ▢ Scottish ▢ Irish ▢ Other White background ▢

Other ethnic group

Any other ethnic group ▢

Please state which..

Source: adapted from Acas 2015
Note, though, that other forms are also available on this and other websites and there are a number of interesting differences between the alternatives they present.

It is possible to identify three broad positions on the definitional issue around 'race' and 'ethnicity': firstly, conflation of the terms (as in the EHRC definition), so they might be used interchangeably, secondly, a preference for one or other term as the focus of analysis and, finally, a wish to preserve both terms as having somewhat different and varying meanings and with both being significant. The latter position is adopted here. I do not want to go into the complexities of the shifting and contested meaning of these terms in too much detail. The interested reader could look at Law (2010) for an overview. However, it is worth noting a few key points.

Firstly, the two terms *are* slippery and contested – often used interchangeably to refer to the same thing, sometimes used in a differentiated way, but with different authors using the same term in different ways. As a reader, then, one needs to be alert as to what terms are being used and how they are employed. The second point is that race and ethnicity are obviously, like other markers of identity considered in this book, terms used to denote difference between people. Often a key marker of perceived 'racial' difference is taken to be physiological – particularly skin colour and other features of the body such as hair and eye colour, whereas those who emphasize 'ethnicity' tend to focus on cultural difference (see Jenkins 2008, but also Anthias and Yuval-Davis 1992, for rather different positions). In so far as the marker of 'race' is physiological and embodied this is, as Alcoff (2006) puts it, a visible identity: it is hard to hide our race, even if we might want to. Physiological differences, however, such as skin colour, attain a certain meaning and perhaps emotional charge in a given social context. In the UK, for example, with a history of colonialism and involvement in the slave trade, and with large-scale immigration by non-white people being a relatively recent event (from the 1950s), race and racial differences are loaded with a complex of emotions and attitudes. These meanings and emotions are both the cause and effect of social action and behaviour ranging from violence against non-white people amongst 'white' British people at one extreme and welcoming acceptance on the other.

While racial differences may appear natural, biologically given and enduring their meaning is always socially and historically situated and, thus, potentially open to contestation and change. I will not, as some writers do, generally put 'scare quotes' around the term race to indicate its questionable status as a way of categorizing human beings, but I hope the reader will see it as a problematic category, albeit one that has led to much human misery. The final point is this: that both ethnicity and race involve categorization and group identification, to use a distinction Jenkins (2004: 81) makes. I see the former as a process of *identification-'of'* – one distinguishes one group from another, perhaps our own from the other: she is 'black' or 'white', Jamaican or English and thus like others in this category, unlike others in other categories. Such identification *of* is based on differentiation and what Medina (2003) describes as counter-identification – if I am this I am not that, if you are this you are not that. The latter (group identification) might be seen as a process of *'identification-with'* – we feel the same as others, some affinity with others in the same category, and it is thus based on belonging, on sameness. Of course, as Jenkins makes clear, these are analytical categories and particular behaviours or interactions might involve both elements. As I watch the England team play football I feel solidarity with them and other supporters, but I am also categorizing myself as English; there is identification *with* and *of* and the two go hand in hand.

BOX 5.2 IN THE NEWS: MISREPRESENTING RACE?

On 2 November 2015 the *Daily Telegraph* and many other newspapers reported that Rachel Dolezal, a white US academic and civil rights activist, had misrepresented herself as black although she admitted that she was

> 'biologically born white to white parents'. She was reported to have said she had seen herself as black from a very early age and still self-identified as black.
>
> 'I acknowledge that I was biologically born white to white parents, but I identify as black', she said.
>
> Source: *Telegraph*, 2 November 2015

If I use the terms race and ethnicity in this chapter it is partly because they are both used in the literature and in everyday life. A manager racialized as 'black' in England may also be seen (or see herself) as a (minority?) ethnic group member. To ignore race might be to ignore both racism and racialization – and that would seem to me to be questionable. Conversely, to deny the importance of ethnicity might lead to neglecting what might be important differences between and within races – differences based on culture, say, between a 'black' Jamaican and a 'black' Nigerian. This is a difficult balancing act, however, for if we emphasize race we might neglect ethnic differences that are socially significant, but if we emphasize ethnicity we might draw attention to a multitude of cultural differences and neglect what might be seen as fundamental – racism and racial inequality that cuts across particular ethnic divisions on the basis of crude and general 'racial' categories (such as 'white' and 'black'). As always, when we pose the problem of identity we raise the issue of which identities matter. There is no simple answer to this – it all depends on context and on who is making the decision and why. This is a political issue since it can determine what aims and interests are pursued and who allies with whom in these pursuits. In what follows, then, I employ both the terms 'race' and 'ethnicity' and hope that their meaning is clear in the context in which they are used.

Racial or ethnic inequality

If there are racial or ethnic differences in society one issue is the extent to which there is inequality between different groups. If there is such inequality there is then the question of what gives rise to it. These are complex issues, but we must not overlook simple differences and simple explanations. Where there are inequalities this might be due to one racial or ethnic group systematically securing its advantage and oppressing other groups. However, there might also be complex factors at play that we might usefully recognize.

The UK can be seen as a particular case – perhaps even an extreme case – for how ethnicity and race are played out in the workplace. It has a history as a colonial power that for centuries abetted and profited from slavery, but without having slavery as a feature of employment relations within the UK itself. If it has a particular history that makes it different from other countries it can still serve to illustrate several points.

TABLE 5.1 UK employment and unemployment by ethnic origin and gender, 2015

	Employment rate %	Unemployment rate %
Women		
Black	61.5	11.0
White	70.1	4.9
Indian	61.3	7.2
Pakistani/Bangladeshi	32.8	16.4
Mixed	63.5	8.5
Other	52.0	9.0
Men		
Black	65.6	15.3
White	79.1	5.4
Indian	79.5	5.1
Pakistani/Bangladeshi	69.7	10.2
Mixed	66.8	12.9
Other	69.8	6.8

Source: Adapted from Office for National Statistics (2015)

Recent statistics, for example, show that the proportion of people employed full time varies with race and ethnicity, as does unemployment. If unemployment is taken as a good indicator of labour-market disadvantage then the 'white' population has roughly half the rate of unemployment of those from minority ethnic groups (see Table 5.1). Table 5.2 suggests a complex picture of relative advantage or disadvantage according to ethnicity.

Heath and Cheung (2006) demonstrate how, even when educational levels are controlled for, there is an 'ethnic penalty' for minority ethnic groups in Britain. Men from such groups are more likely to be unemployed, find themselves in lower-level jobs and be paid less. The situation for minority ethnic women is slightly different – their unemployment rates are also higher than white women but they earn as much or, in the case of some ethnic groups, more than white women.

Such statistics suggest the presence of racial/ethnic inequality. They suggest a pattern of disadvantage and relative advantage, but they cannot reveal why and how this comes about. The following sections explore some of the possible roots of such inequality and what it means to live with it.

Sources of inequality

One obvious explanation for any observed ethnic or racial inequality is *direct discrimination* on the basis of ethnicity or race – or racism if this is seen as a 'discourse and practice of inferiorizing ethnic groups' (Anthias and Yuval-Davis 1992: 12).

TABLE 5.2 Ethnicity by standard occupational classification: UK, 2014 (Percentage of each ethnic group in particular occupational categories)*

Occupational group	Percentage of the ethnic group (men and women)						
	White	Black	Indian	Pakistani/Bangladeshi	Mixed	Other	All ethnicities (including White)
Managers, directors and senior officials	10.4	5.9	11.2	9.4	7.1	8.7	10.2
Professional occupations	19.5	19.9	31.7	16.9	21.3	22.5	19.9
Associate prof and technical	14.3	11.8	12.4	9.5	19.4	10.9	14.0
Administrative and secretarial	11.0	10.2	10.2	7.6	11.9	7.7	10.8
Skilled trades	11.4	5.6	4.7	7.7	6.8	8.2	10.9
Caring, leisure and other service	9.1	16.7	6.6	6.9	9.7	10.7	9.2
Sales and customer service	7.6	8.9	9.3	14.6	11.0	8.7	7.9
Process, plant and machine operatives	6.3	5.6	5.2	14.0	3.0	6.8	6.3
Elementary occupations	10.6	15.4	8.6	13.4	9.8	15.9	10.8
Total	100.0	100.0	100.0	100.0	100.0	100.0	100.0

*That is the proportion of a particular ethnic group in a particular occupational category – so the figure of 10.4 for white managers, directors and senior officials in the first cell indicates that 10.4 per cent of all white people in employment are managers (not that 10.4 per cent of managers are white). This can then be compared with the equivalent percentage for other ethnic groups. Calculated from data available from the Office for National Statistics, Annual Population Survey via NOMIS (2015).

Consider the following historical case as discussed by May and Cohen (1974). In 1919 there were disturbances with a 'racial' dimension in several British dock towns (Liverpool, Cardiff and others). These involved stabbings, fighting, robbery and looting. As the *Times* report of the time put it, describing one such incident: 'White men appear[ed] determined to clear out the blacks who have been advised to stay indoors. This counsel many of them disregarded... Whenever a negro was seen he was chased and if caught severely beaten' (1974: 114). At least one black man was killed in the disturbances – drowned in the dock as he tried to flee, to cries of 'Let him drown!' from the mob (114). This is an example of direct action by one racial (white) group against another group. How do you react to such an account? Do you consider it to be a remote historical event – perhaps an indicator of how things have moved on? Perhaps, perhaps not. Even if such extreme violence against those of another 'race' is now rare is it not possible that such racialized animosity still exists? That discrimination and racism still exist? McDermott (2006), a white researcher's study of two communities in the US, vividly demonstrates anti-black prejudice, 'a prejudice that often coexists with friendliness, civility and an avowed opposition to explicitly racial discrimination' (2006: ix). It would be hard to claim that applies to the US but not to the UK, even if its origins or prevalence might vary between the two cases. In the UK *direct discrimination* against someone on racial or ethnic grounds is currently illegal in most circumstances (EHRC 2015). But just as people break other laws, so it may be with direct discrimination. The extent to which it occurs is hard to gauge, however. This is partly because there is a desire to conceal it, by anyone practising it, since it is illegal. However, given the complex nature of recruitment decisions, for example, in which multiple criteria are used and where processes such as interviews are usually conducted in private, it may be easy to cover up any direct discrimination that does occur. It might also be the case that direct discrimination occurs even when people are not conscious of it – as stereotyping and attribution processes might create assumptions that are not tested by the person responsible. In such circumstances the rather small number of cases where racial discrimination resulted in a compensation award by an employment tribunal is poor evidence for the scale of the problem (there were only 38 such awards in 2014/15 with a median award of £8,025 (Ministry of Justice 2015)).

Heath and Cheung (2006: 35), using data from a Home Office citizenship survey of 2003, report considerable differences between ethnic groups in terms of how often they had been refused a job on what they attributed to be 'racial' grounds, ranging from 0.3 per cent for the White group to 15.9 per cent for those of African origin, with all minority ethnic groups being above 5 per cent.

BOX 5.3 IN THE NEWS: RACIAL DISCRIMINATION

In 2014 an employment tribunal found evidence of discrimination against a black woman firearms officer, Carol Howard, employed by the London police force. The tribunal found that not only had she been discriminated against because she was a black woman, she was then victimized for complaining about it. The police were accused of attempting to smear the woman in a bid to deflect attention from its own failings, after allegations appeared in the press that Howard had been arrested for assault and possessing child abuse images. The assault claim, involving her estranged husband, was later dropped, and the image of a child was a photo she had shared with him of their sleeping six-year-old daughter. The tribunal concluded that the smear campaign was part of a pattern of behaviour that was 'insulting, malicious and oppressive'. The actions of another officer who subjected Howard to a year-long campaign of discrimination were also deemed to be 'vindictive and spiteful', and the police force's failure to apologize was considered to have added insult to injury. That the police force also removed evidence of racial and sexual discrimination from documents later submitted to the internal panel hearing PC Howard's case was also severely criticized. The tribunal ordered the force to pay her damages of £37,000.

Source: Guardian, 9 September 2014

Of course, such perceptions of discrimination do not necessarily indicate the degree to which it occurs – they might overestimate or underestimate it. However, Heath and Cheung (2006) point out that the differences seem to be in line with differences in the rate of job refusals between the different groups – which are higher among minority ethnic groups than the white group. In other words these perceptions are a plausible explanation for the differences that exist. Even if they do exaggerate the problem they also show the existence of perceptions of inequality – the ethnic minority 'Other' *feels* excluded.

Heath and Cheung (2006) also use the British social attitudes survey to assess the degree to which there is a 'chill factor' for minority ethnic groups within Britain. They consider responses to the question 'How would you describe yourself... as very prejudiced, against people of other races, a little prejudiced, or not prejudiced at all?' The good news for those of an anti-racist disposition is that those of working age willing to identify themselves as prejudiced declined in the period 1983 to 2003. However, the figures for men of 42 per cent and 34 per cent, respectively, and for women of 38 per cent and 25 per cent still represent a sizable minority willing to present themselves in this way. The authors also analysed the results for 2001–3 by industry and educational level and found significant differences between them. As might be expected, public administration, education and health came out with the lowest degree of prejudice (but still 24.1 per cent), while the highest was transport and communication at 38.2 per cent. In each industry those with post-school qualifications scored lower, suggesting a link between level of educational attainment and degree of prejudice.

The way racism occurs might sometimes be blatant and open, sometimes expressed only perhaps to intimates or to those who the person feels will not censure them. For example, Hite (1996: 13), in a US context, refers to a manager reported as saying that he 'didn't think women belonged in sales and didn't think blacks belonged anywhere'.

Racism could also come from fellow workers or from customers or clients. Healy and Oikelome (2011: 151) quote one nurse saying: 'a patient shouted racist abuse at me, and um, the next time I went into work they said that I had to move wards'. Notice that here the racist abuse by a patient is not tackled – the nurse is simply removed from the situation. The same authors also refer to an incident where a patient refused to have a black nurse treat her child and the hospital was silent and complicit (2011: 142).

But racism can take many forms, sometimes covert or through ways of making people from particular groups feel uncomfortable or unwelcome. In the UK there is an acknowledgement that discrimination can take direct or indirect forms – and both are generally illegal. Indirect discrimination is defined by the EHRC (2015) as: 'The use of an apparently neutral practice, provision or criterion which puts people with a particular protected characteristic at a disadvantage compared with others who do not share that characteristic, and applying the practice, provision or criterion cannot be objectively justified.' Examples of this might be using a particular educational qualification that is less commonly held by people from non-white groups. However, such a definition does little to tackle the sort of behaviour Hite (1996) describes where a consultant ignored a black woman professional to give information to her white intern, assuming their roles were reversed. Notice that this seems to be a case of ignoring, of rendering invisible, a 'black' woman. Racialization might take the form of abuse or singling out on the basis of race, or it might take the form of ignoring, silencing, marginalizing, excluding – these are all mechanisms that can be used to reproduce inequality between different racial or ethnic groups or render their work experience less satisfying.

A term that has been used to capture general processes which structure racialized inequality – whether consciously and overtly 'racist' or not – is that of 'institutionalized racism'. This was a term used by the black power activists Stokely Carmichael and Charles Hamilton in the context of the US in the 1960s (Carmichael and Hamilton 1969) to refer to covert and overt forms of embedding white superiority over blacks. In the British context it came to the fore in the Stephen Lawrence inquiry in the 1990s which examined the way in which the police had investigated Stephen's murder by a group of white youths. The inquiry concluded that there was institutional racism in the police service as well as in other police forces and institutions countrywide. In the report it was defined as:

> The collective failure of an organisation to provide an appropriate and professional service to people because of their colour, culture, or ethnic origin. It can be detected in the processes, attitudes and behaviour which amount to discrimination through unwitting prejudice, ignorance,

thoughtlessness and racist stereotyping which disadvantage minority ethnic people.

(Macpherson 1999: 28)

In this case a key criticism made of the police was that they did not take the 'racially motivated' nature of the murder seriously enough. This is an example where being 'blind' to racialization can disadvantage the minority group. There was also much emphasis in the report on a 'culture' in the police that stereotyped black people. One example given in the report was from the evidence of a member of the MPS Black Police Association: 'as a Sergeant I was in the car and a female white officer on seeing a black person driving a very nice car just said "I wonder who he robbed to get that?", and then she realised she was actually voicing an unconscious assumption' (1999: 21).

Unconscious assumptions and 'unwitting' racism are seen as part of institutional racism – it does not have to rest on explicitly and consciously held racist beliefs but it can be part of providing what Heath and Cheung (2006) refer to as the chill factor. Consider again the case of the 1919 disturbances in British docks, introduced earlier (May and Cohen 1974). One explanation for the disturbances lies in competition for jobs: the aggression by white working-class men could be explained as arising from a fear of losing jobs and having wages being undercut by those who would accept lower wages. This has echoes in current debates in Britain and other relatively prosperous EU countries, about concerns of East European migrant workers or migrants from beyond Europe's borders. 'White' workers can, then, react negatively towards people of colour due to stereotypes (as in the case of the white police officer) or *perceived* threats to their status or interests (as in the docks). Such explanations do not justify racism but they might help explain it.

If 'race' and 'ethnicity' is implicated in structuring inequality these structures are not static, stable entities but subject to change and challenge. People are positioned within these structures of racialized and ethnic inequality in ways that are not of their choosing – but they may also react to such positioning and seek to position themselves in a variety of ways. This is explored in the next section.

Experiencing race and ethnicity at work: the push and the pull towards racial or ethnic identities?

Kenny and Briner (2013) refer to processes in the workplace that either 'push' people towards recognition of an ethnic identity or 'pull' people towards it: the first they refer to as ethnic assignation and the second ethnic identification. Their study is based on a study of 30 'Afro-Caribbean' graduates in Britain. I think theirs is a useful analytical distinction although I would quibble with the labels they attach to these processes. Both the pushes and the pulls they describe are processes of identification and what might be seen in this case as a particular form of identification: racialization. The difference between the two kinds of racialization identified by Kenny and Briner seems to lie, according to their analysis, in the evaluation of the source – a 'push' seems negative and unwelcome, instigated by others, the other is more positive, an attractive force. They provide one particularly vivid example of the push to an ethnic identity – the account of the experience of a uniformed prison officer:

> I remember taking a prisoner to the hospital because he had a punctured lung… I went into the consulting room with him and the nurse said to me… 'you need to stay outside'… It was that assumption that you can't be an officer even when you are wearing a uniform. Somehow people can't see that you might be a professional, you must be the prisoner's mother. Another time I had taken a prisoner to immigration tribunal and the adjudicator had said to the prisoner after he had given evidence that 'you need to go back and sit with the prison officer' and he had to be handcuffed because it wasn't a secure room, so he came and sat next to me and the adjudicator said… 'I didn't mean you to sit with your family'… I stood up and said 'you can see I am actually wearing a uniform I am from the prison service'… It was just seeing a black face and then not noticing the uniform or anything (Anthea, Senior Executive Officer, Civil Service, 39).
>
> *(Kenny and Briner 2013: 733)*

Such an example illustrates how the 'assignation' of ethnicity (although one might also say race – as the only marker of ethnicity would appear to be skin colour) is effectively to deny the individual professional status. It illustrates a process of exclusion, of erasure: 'they can't see that you might be a professional'. This example also shows, of course, resistance. The prison officer reacts by drawing attention to the uniform – they seek to make visible what is invisible; to draw attention to what has been ignored. However, this might be seen as involving a different kind of erasure: don't look at my black face, look at my uniform; but it might still serve to challenge what can be seen as racist assumptions.

The racialization in this case could be seen to be work done by the employee who defines the problem as originating in 'race' – but it was also prompted by the nurse 'just seeing a black face and then not noticing the uniform'. In this case racialization is seen in negative terms. It is of course also associated with a negative stereotype.

Another example of the 'push' to an ethnic identity comes from an HR practitioner:

> I just felt the pressure was on to be professional and not showing my blackness, but what does that mean? I suppose it was just about the way I carried myself or the way I spoke to them, the way I dress even maybe, because here the culture is very relaxed, I wouldn't necessarily wear a suit to work but I found myself wearing suits (Laura, HR Business Partner, Oil and Gas Industry, 30).
>
> *(Kenny and Briner 2013: 734)*

Here again the 'professional' seems to want to erase her 'blackness' – to be viewed as professional which seems to involve not 'showing their blackness'. Here the black employee seems to be pointing to the existence of white normativity – to be 'professional' seems to be racialized, implicitly, as non-black. It echoes the title of Franz Fanon's classic book (1970) *Black Skin, White Masks*. The worker feels compelled to mask her 'blackness'.

The 'push' to ethnicity also occurs, according to Kenny and Briner's (2013) study, when the person is numerically in a small minority and thus becomes aware of their distinctiveness. As one person describes this:

> I can be in a room where everything is very white and English and Anglo Saxon... and that highlights my blackness in a different way. But I don't have to act upon that, my being there is enough... just by your sheer existence. You don't have to do anything on top of that – I'm a black person, whey! And I'm sure other people are there going 'oh no, there's a black person!' You know, but then again... it's just one of those things. I've never really felt it welling up inside me or anything. It's just you deal with things when they come. I suppose (Anna, Senior Accounts Executive, Media Company, 32).
>
> *(Kenny and Briner 2013: 735)*

This seems to illustrate a different reaction to the 'push' to ethnic identification – not an erasure, but an acceptance of it: 'you deal with things' – and the others who push you into this ethnic identity also have to deal with it.

The consequences of such a 'push' to ethnic assignation are, in Kenny and Briner's analysis, variable: they can act as a spur to higher performance in order to defy the stereotype. This is reflected, in a nuanced way, in the following quotation:

> I think as a black woman you are not sort of carrying the black community on your shoulders but you are aware of the image you are presenting, so you work hard, you lead by example, people look at that but you do know that people think – 'oh well she's not lazy'. And people make judgements about black people being lazy so I'm not sort of wearing it on my shoulders all the time but I am aware sometimes if I do a good piece of work, or if I'm presenting a negative image it does have an impact on how black people or black women are perceived (Esther, Senior Executive Officer, Civil Service, 29).
>
> *(Kenny and Briner 2013: 736)*

I find this a particularly interesting response – at once individualized and collective – she is not 'carrying the black community' on her shoulders but she is conscious of how her actions might help to challenge stereotypes. This might be seen as an example of quiet identity politics but even quiet approaches might involve doing a lot of cognitive work in trying to make sense of the situation and deciding how to act:

I wonder sometimes – and the only reason I say that is because I am the only black HR person there… when I got the job it was like a double-edged sword because I thought, are they doing this to make me fall flat on my face? But the other side is 'damn I'm going to have to work hard to prove myself'. And those were the thoughts I had because I am the only black HR person here and you think to yourself, now why is that? Is it because… black people haven't come to the positions? Is it something they are conscious about and now that I am here I am the token black person? Those thoughts have run through my mind (Laura, HR Business Partner, Oil and Gas Industry, 30).

(Kenny and Briner 2013: 737)

Such a situation might well spur action and high performance – but it might also be at the cost of increased strain on the individual. There is some evidence in the US that Latinos, for example, suffer high degrees of workplace stress (Len-Rios 2002), and also that they take on extra work to prove they can do it all. But there is also evidence that they exit organizations because they are frustrated (Zerbinos and Clanton 1993, cited in Pompper 2007).

Turning to the *pull* of identification, in Kenny and Briner's (2013) analysis, here there are opportunities for the assertion of ethnic or racialized identities that seem to be experienced as more obviously positive. For example:

I suppose it… comes more to the forefront maybe when I am in situations where there are other black people there… because the work I do is very global, it's very international. Like yesterday I was at this trade show and a few people from the South African delegation came to visit our stand and everything and it was really kind of like whey! You know I felt I could ratchet up the blackness a bit… you didn't have to hold it down, you could let it rip. You know in terms of language and things (Senior Accounts Executive, Media Company, 32).

(Kenny and Briner 2013: 739)

Other examples of this are associated with situations in which the Afro-Caribbean person finds themselves in a situation where there is a relatively high proportion of minority ethnic group representation among the workforce or clients (or students, in the case of education professionals). It can also occur when a person recognizes someone of their own ethnic identity as an exception to the norm that triggers a particular response, sometimes across hierarchical boundaries as in the case of a senior civil servant described as mixed black/white ethnicity and a black female middle manager of lower rank described by Atewologun et al. (2015: 10):

We know each other, not well, but I knew who she was, she knew who I was… The fact that I had particularly noticed her was to do with the fact that she was a black woman… so when she came up to me and said 'Oh could I have a word with you?', I was pleased 'cos I had a positive vibe about her…

> I had an inkling it was something more personal, and that's flattering... (Later)
> I was conscious that the reason (she) wanted to talk to me was really because I
> am a senior black woman in Govt Plc [the organization pseudonym used by
> the researchers] and I was pleased, I mean I was really pleased and flattered...
> that (she) wanted to talk to me.

Another example of the 'pull' of identity, from a different study, is Marra and
Holmes' (2008) study of a media company in New Zealand serving the Maōri
community (the ethnic group indigenous to New Zealand). The organization's
founders deliberately aimed to serve the Maōri community and incorporate Maōri
cultural values and norms in the way the organization operates – including those of
humility, modesty and respect and care for others. The article is based on an analysis
of a story told by one member of the organization to others in the organization. The
story is a humorous account of an award ceremony in which the master of ceremonies
mispronounces Maōri terms and names, even while making the award to a film the
company had produced. In the telling of the story and in the audience's reactions to it,
the authors find evidence of the operation and valorization of Maōri cultural values.
In this way 'the stories told at work contribute not only to the construction of the
ethnic identity of individual speakers, but also provide a means for co-constructing
a distinctive Maōri identity for the group' (Marra and Holmes 2008: 397). Such
processes involve, according to this analysis, creating insider and outsider status –
the master of ceremonies who cannot pronounce the words properly and thus
might be seen as guilty of a lack of respect or care for Maōri culture is an outsider,
while the audience, who respond to the story with laughter and supportive comments, understand the points being made because they are insiders. There is also an
implicit promotion of Maōri culture (through the value placed on the 'correct'
pronunciation of Maōri words and their use in the narratives). The incident is also
seen as the enactment of an ethnically distinct culture of practice in which narrator
and audience demonstrate self-deprecating modesty, and pre-eminence of the
group over the individual. In this way even through incidents as simple as
humorous conversation, a distinct 'ethnic' identity is constructed and valorized. It
demonstrates how an organization can act as a vehicle for expressing ethnic identity.

Of course the 'push' and a 'pull' towards identity might occur simultaneously.
Ram (1992), for example, considers the case of Asian employers in Britain and
shows how, as employers, they often worked within a predominantly 'Asian'
context – dealing with other Asian businesses and, often, customers. However, if
this might be seen as due to the 'pull' of ethnic identification, some entrepreneurs
faced obstacles that they interpreted as racial in origin. As one of his respondents
put it: 'there is still a racial problem about; it's very important to present a white
face to the customer' (1992: 608). Of course, the extent to which an organization
works within and for a particular ethnic group can serve to reproduce ethnic differences. While it might serve as a vehicle for social mobility on an individual or
community basis it might also serve to continue to marginalize an already disadvantaged group. Holvino (2000) notes that Hispanics hired to fill a particular

niche, serving people of similar ethnicity, may not be able to move out of that specific area to advance in their careers. Such strategies of separation might also serve to reproduce cultural stereotypes.

Which 'races', which 'ethnicities'?

If there is both a 'push' and a 'pull' towards ethnic or racial identity, which 'races' or 'ethnicities' are they? Atewologun and Singh's (2010) study of a small number (seven) of young black professionals in Britain deals with how these men and women interpret and negotiate their identities as minority ethnic employees. In the interview data on which the study is based, the complexity and variability of experience is revealed. For these individuals their very 'ethnicity' is a complex and contestable issue. Asked about their ethnic origin five described themselves as 'Black African' – four from families of Nigerian origin and one whose family was from Ghana. One simply described himself as African (his family was also from Nigeria), while one woman from Guyana described herself as Afro-Caribbean. Such designations make sense in a British context where they are identifying themselves as ethnically distinct from other groups. However, in an African context they might well describe themselves differently, since there are many different ethnic groups in Africa – even within one country such as Nigeria. Their self-categorizations occur in a social context in which they are racialized – where they are viewed as black and come to see themselves as black. Interestingly, the one respondent who simply described himself as African (not black African) was raised in Nigeria and he commented that: 'I've never been conscious of my race in a way that I think a black British person would be conscious of their race... It's not questioned – that identity is not really shaken' (Atewologun and Singh 2010: 336).

Which race or ethnicity one recognizes, and is pushed and pulled towards, as this study demonstrates, is partly a function of descent – of which 'racial' or 'ethnic' grouping, however it is categorized and identified, one is born into. But it is partly also about how others see and categorize you in a particular situation. Forced to choose one category people might emphasize whatever seems most important to them or what they interpret as most important for the questioner. One might have a number of different ethnic or racial identities – 'black', 'Nigerian', 'black British', 'Igbo' (a Nigerian ethnic group) – socially available. Of course this does not mean that there is no 'authentic' ethnic identity here – one is or is not black, Nigerian or Igbo – but the meaning attached to this and the salience of it in any context is variable (Atewologun et al. 2015). Historically, too, these categories can have shifting meaning and boundaries – Nigeria itself is a relatively recent creation.

One cannot consider racial terms such as 'black' and 'white' without considering the history of colonialism and slavery in which people of European origin often treated the 'other' in despicable ways or condescending ways. This is the origin of post-colonial studies of race and ethnicity (see for example Childs and Williams 1997; Gandhi 1998). Of course, if 'whites' have often inferiorized the 'other' (e.g. see Said 1978), then this is not necessarily uncontested or without response from the 'other'. As Leonard (2010), citing Holdsworth (2002), has pointed out, throughout the periods of both colonialism and territorial rule the British have been constructed by the Chinese as other: the terms *gweilo* or *fan gweilo*, literally meaning 'foreign devils', is used by the Chinese to construct a subject position for white people that is derogatory and bears connotations of cultural clumsiness on the part of the British (see Leonard 2010: 348). Still, this history of colonialism and slavery, as well as the more recent history of migration (to which the British docks case referred to earlier is an early response), has left a legacy in the complex responses people have towards race – particularly in places like Britain and the US where the meaning of 'black' and 'white', as racialized terms, carry several centuries of baggage. This can lead to relations between people of different ethnicities and races being charged with tension: the one might feel they are being thought of in negative or hostile terms, racialized as inferior or at least subject to a 'chill factor' or institutionalized racism, while the other might, even if not subscribing to racist notions directly, be conscious of the sensitivity of the issue and seek to avoid embarrassment. More importantly, perhaps, particular racialized conceptions become dominant and normative – in particular in a British context it would seem that to be 'professional' is coded as racially/ethnically white – if one is 'other' then there is pressure to conform to white normativity. This pressure can, of course, be complied with or resisted as an example provided by Atewologun et al. (2015: table 3, 12) from a woman in a 'big four' professional services firm illustrates:

> The first thing that the senior Partner said was 'Oh my God, Bernadette, are you stuck in the disco years wearing that suit?' I guess he was joking, but that one statement was such a big deal for me that I actually threw away all my 'does not fit in' type suits. (Years later, a different) senior Partner said… very loudly in our open office… 'Oh my God, Bernadette, you're in your power suit. Red. Scary!' I just looked up at him and I said 'What do you mean red is scary. Red is good. Red is luck! It's optimistic, It's good, what's scary about red?' (Bernadette, Chinese Female, PSF).

The play of ethnic/racial difference: advantage and disadvantage?

Sometimes 'ethnic' cultural identities might be used as a resource at work, sometimes as a liability. Poster (2007), for example, deals with the case of Indian call centre workers, based in India but serving clients in the US who were encouraged to disguise their Indian national identity in favour of an 'American' one – something that includes changing the name they use, their mode of delivery and showing familiarity with American popular culture and current events. However, they were frequently questioned about their nationality by the people they called and experienced hostility and sometimes extreme abuse – it was reported that American consumers said things like, 'How do I spell my name? F-U-C-K-Y-O-U!'. Poster observed such hostility 'at least once an hour' (2007: 283). Such aggression might not, of course, necessarily stem from racism, although it might. It might stem from hostility to the off-shoring of jobs, something that has attracted much adverse attention in both the US and the UK. But the call centre worker is, through the actions of employer and clients alike, being encouraged to manage their identity in the direction of Americanization and this can be seen to be a case of attempting to erase a non-American ethnicity.

Atewologun and Singh's study (2010: 339) of what they refer to as black British professionals also suggests that the recognition of disadvantage might be gradual:

> When I first started working, I wouldn't notice any kind of difference in how I was treated and how white colleagues were treated. As I've moved around, really I can see it so much more. Like you notice that people who are in charge are always white and the people at the lowest level are black or non-white.

The experience of ethnic or racial discrimination and disadvantage in workplace or trade union can spur trade union involvement and activism. As one local government worker put it:

> I have always been active within the union, because it was another way of showing total dismay at some of the inequality that I saw, and so it was a door that had opened, which said that I could use this as a way for knocking at other doors to let somebody know that something's not right.
>
> *(Bradley and Healy 2008: 127)*

While there is consciousness of the disadvantages of racism among the group that Atewologun and Singh (2010) studied, there was also a recognition that race is not always experienced in negative terms – minority ethnic status and being 'black' might have advantages:

> I almost use probably subconsciously Ghana and my blackness in the work-place... I almost feel like in some situations people almost take to me because I'm black... English colleagues and friends... love talking about Ghana, they love talking about black things. It's almost like I give them the chance (NK, Female).
>
> *(Atewologun and Singh 2010: 339)*

This seems to show how colleagues are interested in the cultural context of the respondent's ethnicity. Far from being erased, here Ghana and 'black things' are the subject of interest. Of course ethnic identities might be what are effectively traded on. Cochrane's (2009) study of Senegalese weavers, for example, shows how weavers can represent their distinctiveness in ethnic terms – as weaving like their ancestors wove to produce products that are valued by wealthy Senegalese of the same ethnic group origin as well as tourists. The same study also shows, however, the complexities and fluidities of such work – for even while representing faithful adhesion to ethnic tradition, weavers can sometimes employ new technologies – what is faithful to the past is open to interpretation.

Another respondent in Atewologun and Singh's (2010) research recognized the possibility of minority racial status conferring advantage but expressed some ambivalence about it: 'There is a general push to have more black faces but I'd agree, I think I've benefited from being hired as the token black guy... but a part of me still feels I would rather not have been the token black guy (NA, Male)' (2010: 343). Consider, also, the following two quotations from different respondents illustrating different strategies for dealing with stereotyping:

> I think there is a general stereotype about being a black guy and being funny, outgoing, athletic. In some of my jobs they've expected me to be Will Smith [an extrovert African American comedy/action movie star] of the office... but I'm very chilled at work – I like to keep to myself and it always comes as a shock to people that I don't make jokes (NA, Male).
>
> *(Atewologun and Singh 2010: 341)*

> I find it very difficult. If I'm too loud, I feel like I'm propagating the stereo-type. It's a very delicate balance... the fact that I'm a black male adds that extra dimension... they might be scared of black men... I know I'm a minority so I just make that all-round general effort to be a little more talkative, outgoing... and make an effort to adjust to the system. That's the way it is (LS, Male).
>
> *(Atewologun and Singh 2010: 342)*

For the minority ethnic professional in Britain, then, there would seem to be a variety of responses and experiences, but people have to deal with the situation they are in based on their interpretation of the situation. The identity work going on here is complex – the individual is positioned as a racialized subject, but they respond through actively interpreting the situation and adopting strategies that may either reinforce or confound the stereotype. Such are the ways race relations are enacted in a recent British context. The experience and situation of the black professionals in this study certainly seem a long way from the violence and inti-midation against black workers recounted in May and Cohen's (1974) account of racialized conflict in British docks in 1919. We might, perhaps, from a UK point of view, comfort ourselves that things have 'progressed' since 1919 or the 1960s when black people were frequently sought out and attacked on the street or in their homes on racial grounds. One might think that there is more tolerance, under-standing and commitment to equal opportunities. But still, in a British context, there would still seem to be the existence of racial prejudice and a positioning of the 'minority ethnic' person as the Other. Sometimes a novelty and point of interest, but different.

Ambiguity and hybridity

The extent to which skin colour or other factors mark out one's ethnicity and the ways in which ethnicity becomes visible is variable. Hite (2007: 27), for example, in her research on Hispanic women in the US, refers to one woman whose ethnic identity as different from her work colleagues was not readily apparent as she spoke with 'unaccented' English and had a German-origin surname by marriage. For some, then, it might be possible to avoid ethnic difference being noticed. Sometimes this might simply be a matter of presentation:

> Even when I would have conversations with people at work and we would talk about what we had for dinner, I would make up what I had for dinner because what I really did have was beans and rice and something that, you know, was ethnically appropriate, versus what everybody else was talking about, steak, potatoes.
>
> *(Hite 2007: 27)*

For many, however, their ethnicity is a central aspect of their identity: 'My culture is my way of living. It is part of who I am. It is not a thing I can hang in the closet and then put it on. It's who I am' (Hite 2007: 28). For many in ethnically diverse cultural contexts, such as those of Britain and the United States, there is likely to be a recognition that the individual straddles two cultural contexts. In such a situation it might be understandable if the individual has a dual cultural identity: 'It's who I am. It's not that I think about it. It's just who I am. I am part of two cultures and it just can't be one without the other. It's like it's one culture' (Hite 2007: 28). This comment that 'It's like it's one culture' is interesting. It suggests a high level of integration of the two cultures. Equally, however, another strategy is to see them as separate and to move between them – being Hispanic at home and with Hispanic friends and more 'American' at work, perhaps. Gordon (2007) refers to this as bicultural competence. But how and whether one negotiates such cultural diversity as someone who might have dual allegiances – have a 'pull' of identification to two different ethnicities – is an important issue for the individual and for others in both cultures. This might be examined further using two examples from Essers et al.'s (2010) study of Muslim immigrant businesswomen in the Netherlands.

Fatna is a young (25 years old) woman who still lives with her family and under the influence of a father who is described as authoritarian. She defies his expectations and wishes in running a business, but she is cautious in the way she pursues this. She defines herself in ethnic terms – she feels Turkish first, rather than Dutch. She runs a greengrocery and wholesale business with her two sisters. She dresses conservatively and appears willing to conform to Turkish cultural norms for young single women, such as not going out on Saturday nights. In business dealings she emphasizes behaving with care and making sure her father can trust her and that she does not bring shame to her family. She seems willing to adjust to the cultural norms of the Turkish community in Holland (while noting that these may be rather more restrictive for women than in modern Turkey itself). Fatna's way of largely conforming to the cultural norms of her community, while carefully pushing at its boundaries (in engaging in entrepreneurial activities traditionally associated with men) seems very different to that of another woman, Leila, also of Turkish origin.

Leila is 41 and runs her own television production company. She identifies primarily with women rather than with her ethnic identity and her documentaries deal with women's oppression. She sees herself as neither Dutch nor Turkish but a 'citizen of the world' (Essers et al. 2010: 334). However, she does not so much deny her Turkish identity as create a hybrid with a more Westernized one. She is described as wearing Turkish dress but Western jewellery. Her story is interpreted by Essers et al. as one of emphasizing autonomy and agency in the construction of a hybridized identity – 'transcending the limitations stemming from the intersectionality of gender and ethnicity', as they put it (Essers et al.: 334). If Fatna is rather cautious and prepared to live within a set of ethnically imposed constraints, Leila seems more adventurous – willing to pick and choose and defy convention, if necessary. Fatna is not without agency – she makes choices, she is active in constructing her identity as a business-woman. But she seems more willing to position herself as conforming to a certain ethnic positioning and one that reproduces a sense of ethnic identity, more willing to accept a position that is ascribed to her by others, by the culture she finds herself in.

Note, though, that Essers et al. (2010) often construe gender and ethnicity in terms of limitations. Perhaps a more neutral way of putting it would be in terms of possibilities – both Fatna and Leila seem aware of different possibilities – they simply make different choices within a range of alternatives. Moreover, in the account provided by Essers et al., two contingent factors seem to be relevant to how the individuals construct their identities. One is common to both – their position within a social context that is at once Western and 'Dutch' and 'Turkish'. The other is the rather contrasting behaviours of their fathers – with Fatna's described as authoritarian and Leila's seemingly more supportive of her unconventional behaviour (in Turkish ethnic terms). Agency and autonomy are not necessarily simply the product of strong characters or purely personal choice – they may themselves be context dependent. In accepting or transcending a particular ethnic identity one makes choices that are not in conditions of one's own choosing. The die might be loaded in favour of one decision or another, depending on power relations and actions of others. Furthermore, the cases of Fatna and Leila suggest that acceptance of particular ethnic identities might be a matter of degree: one might be more or less 'Turkish' in a Dutch context. This could also vary over time and location, depending on interaction with others: with Granny, you might be more Turkish – with a Dutch supplier, more 'Dutch'.

Conclusion

Racial or ethnic identification is a chronic feature of working life in multiracial/ cultural Britain, as it is elsewhere. We are often positioned and position ourselves in racialized or ethnicized ways through the push and pull of identification.

We are not usually able freely to choose our ethnicity or race yet to some extent we can choose how to act on the basis of our ethnicized or racialized position – and trying to ignore it is one form of action. We can, as members of a particular racialized and ethnic group, influence how that group is defined by others and defines itself – but always within a network of power relations in which certain speech acts and actions may be silenced, ignored or suppressed in various ways. There are personal and political choices to be made as to how to act. To what extent we challenge perceived injustice or seek to make visible and challenge their underlying roots is a political question. To what extent we celebrate and valorize particular cultural, ethnic and racial features is a political question. How you or I answer these questions will depend on our values which, in turn, are influenced by our position in a social world that is racialized and ethnicized. However, our actions, thoughts and feelings are not necessarily tied to those of the dominant culture, or the culture into which we are born or pushed towards. Personally, I am attracted to the values of modesty, respect and prioritizing of the group that characterized Maōri culture – and although I am not Maōri I would find it easy to support what they are doing and how they are doing it. The opportunity to show solidarity with them is rather limited, however: I am at the other side of the world and our working lives do not bring us together. Perhaps in some small ways my knowledge and sympathy might make me act in different ways – perhaps challenge what I see as dominant cultural norms here in the UK where I live and work. This might put me at odds with standard English cultural norms, but we can cross borders, look across borders and have productive cultural interchanges that may help redefine our own ethnicity.

BOX 5.4 AT THE MOVIES: ETHNICITY AND RACE

Some movies relevant to the themes of the chapter are:

My Beautiful Launderette (1985, director Stephen Frears)
The Help (2011, director Tate Taylor)
12 Years a Slave (2013, director Steve McQueen)
The Butler (2013, director Lee Daniels)

References

Acas (2015) 'HSO7: Framework monitoring form', at http://www.acas.org.uk/index.aspx?articleid=4701&q=ethnic+monitoring (accessed 11 December 2015).

Alcoff, L. (2006) *Visible Identities: Race, Gender, and the Self.* Oxford: Oxford University Press.

Anthias, F. and Yuval-Davis, N. (1992) *Racialized Boundaries: Race, Nation, Gender, Colour and Class and the Anti-Racist*, in association with Harriet Cain. London: Routledge.

Atewologun, D. and Singh, V. (2010) 'Challenging ethnic and gender identities: An exploration of UK black professionals' identity construction', *Equality, Diversity and Inclusion: An International Journal*, 29(4): 332–347.

Atewologun, D., Sealy, R. and Vinnicombe, S. (2015) 'Revealing intersectional dynamics in organizations: Introducing "intersectional identity work"', *Gender, Work and Organization*, doi: 10.1111/gwao.12082.

Bradley, H. and Healy, G. (2008) *Ethnicity and Gender at Work: Inequalities, Careers and Employment Relations*. Basingstoke: Palgrave Macmillan.

Carmichael, S. and Hamilton, C. V. (1969) *Black Power*. Harmondsworth: Penguin Books.

Childs, P. and Williams, R. J. P. (1997) *An Introduction to Post-Colonial Theory*. London: Prentice Hall Harvester Wheatsheaf.

Cochrane, L. (2009) 'Senegalese weavers' ethnic identities, in discourse and in craft', *African Identities*, 7(1): 3–15.

EHRC (2015) 'Glossary of terms', at http://www.equalityhumanrights.com/advice-and-guidance/public-sector-equality-duty/guidance-on-the-public-sector-equality-duty-draft/glossary (accessed 11 December 2015).

Essed, P. and Trienekens, S. (2008) '"Who wants to feel white?" Race, Dutch culture and contested identities', *Ethnic and Racial Studies*, 31(1): 52–72.

Essers, C., Benschop, Y. and Doorewaard, H. (2010) 'Female ethnicity: Understanding Muslim immigrant businesswomen in the Netherlands', *Gender, Work and Organization*, 17(3): 320–339.

Fanon, F. (1970) *Black Skin White Masks*, trans. Charles Lam Markmann. London: Paladin.

Gandhi, L. (1998) *Postcolonial Theory: A Critical Introduction*. Sydney: Allen and Unwin.

Gordon, G. (2007) *Towards Bicultural Competence: Beyond Black and White*. Stoke on Trent: Trentham.

Guardian (2014) 'Police officer Carol Howard v the Met: "I was absolutely humiliated"', at http://www.theguardian.com/uk-news/2014/sep/09/carol-howard-black-female-police-officer-discrimination-met-tribual-victory (accessed 20 December 2015).

Healy, G. and Oikelome, F. (eds) (2011) *Diversity, Ethnicity, Migration and Work: International Perspectives*. Basingstoke: Palgrave Macmillan.

Heath, A. and Cheung, S. Y. (2006) 'Ethnic penalties in the labour market: Employers and discrimination' in *Research Report Department for Work and Pensions*. London: DWP.

Hite, L. M. (1996) 'Black women managers and administrators: Experiences and implications', *Women in Management Review*, 11(6): 11–17.

Hite, L. M. (2007) 'Hispanic women managers and professionals: Reflections on life and work', *Gender, Work and Organization*, 14(1): 20–36.

Holdsworth, M. (2002) *Foreign Devils: Expatriates in Hong Kong*. Oxford: Oxford University Press.

Holvino, E. (2000) 'Hispanics in the workplace: Assessing the "best" and "worst" companies', *Diversity Factor*, 8(4): 12–16.

Jenkins, R. (2004) *Social Identity*. London: Routledge.

Jenkins, R. (2008) *Rethinking Ethnicity*. London: Sage.

Kenny, E. J. and Briner, R. B. (2013) 'Increases in salience of ethnic identity at work: The roles of ethnic assignation and ethnic identification', *Human Relations*, 66(5): 725–748.

Law, I. (2010) *Racism and Ethnicity: Global Debates, Dilemmas, Directions*. Harlow: Longman.

Len-Rios, M. E. (2002) 'Latino professionals in public relations', *Public Relations Quarterly*, 47(1): 22–26.

Leonard, P. (2010) 'Organizing whiteness: Gender, nationality and subjectivity in postcolonial Hong Kong', *Gender, Work and Organization*, 17(3): 340–358.

McDermott, M. (2006) *Working-Class White: The Making and Unmaking of Race Relations*. Berkeley, CA; London: University of California Press.

MacPherson of Cluny, W. (1999) *The Stephen Lawrence Inquiry*. London: Stationery Office.

Marra, M. and Holmes, J. (2008) 'Constructing ethnicity in New Zealand workplace stories', *Text and Talk*, 28(3): 397–419.

May, R. and Cohen, R. (1974) 'The interaction between race and colonialism: A case study of the Liverpool race riots of 1919', *Race and Class*, 16(2): 111–126.

Medina, J. (2003) 'Identity trouble: Disidentification and the problem of difference', *Philosophy and Social Criticism*, 29(6): 655–680.

Ministry of Justice (2015) 'ET and EAT annual tables', at https://www.gov.uk/government/statistics/tribunals-and-gender-recognition-certificate-statistics-quarterly-april-to-june-2015 (accessed 11 December 2015).

Pompper, D. (2007) 'The gender-ethnicity construct in public relations organizations: Using feminist standpoint theory to discover Latinas' realities', *Howard Journal of Communications*, 18(4): 291–311.

Poster, W. R. (2007) 'Who's on the line? Indian call center agents pose as Americans for U.S.-outsourced firms', *Industrial Relations*, 46(2): 271–304.

Ram, M. (1992) 'Coping with racism: Asian employers in the inner city', *Work, Employment and Society*, 6(4): 601–618.

Said, E. W. (1978) *Orientalism*. London: Routledge and Kegan Paul.

Telegraph (2015) 'Rachel Dolezal admits she was "born white to white parents"', at http://www.telegraph.co.uk/news/worldnews/northamerica/usa/11971254/Rachel-Dolezal-admits-she-was-born-white-to-white-parents.html (accessed 20 December 2015).

Zerbinos, E. and Clanton, G. A. (1993) 'Minority practitioners: Career influences, job satisfaction, and discrimination', *Public Relations Review*, 19(1): 75–91.

6

GENDER

Introduction

Gender matters. From birth, if not before, we are all gendered. But how does this affect work and relations in the workplace? This chapter starts with what might seem unnecessary – a consideration of what we mean by gender, before moving on to consider gender inequality at work and then the doing and undoing of gender in the workplace.

But what is gender? One answer is a biological one. At birth we are labelled 'male' or 'female', depending on certain (usually) obvious physiological differences that we are culturally disposed to attend to. This suggests 'gender' is a binary system, consisting of male and female, although this can be challenged with reference to a third sex, or a wider range of possibilities (see for example Herdt 1994). Gender, though, is not reducible to biological differences and can be seen as socially constructed (e.g. see Marshall 2003). The way this is done is through particular social processes and identifications. An apparently trivial example of this is the way we might come to associate pink with girls and blue with boys. This is an arbitrary assignment (and culturally specific) but it might lead girls and boys to identify strongly, in some cases, with 'their' colour. It becomes an expression of 'their' self-identity, as well as a marker of collective identity – 'girls' or 'boys'.

In a binary gender system there is a strong emphasis on difference which creates tensions with equality. Under the UK Equality Act (2010) it is illegal to discriminate on grounds of sex and there is, as in many cultures, a formal commitment to gender equality. This sits uneasily with the recognition and persistence of gender difference, however.

Gender difference and inequality at work

The pattern of gender differences at work in countries like the United Kingdom is well known. Women earn less than men, on average, and are less likely to be found in higher-level jobs. There are also gender differences in the kinds of jobs people do. I will briefly explore these differences before considering their origin and prospects for change.

While in the UK there is a legal requirement to pay men and women equally where they are doing the same work, or work of equal value, on average women continue to be paid less than men. In 2014, according to the UK Office of National Statistics (2015a), the gender pay gap among full-time employees was 9.4 per cent, based on rates of pay per hour. The difference for full-time and part-time employees combined was much higher at 19.1 per cent. This pay gap seems to be related principally to three factors: firstly, a tendency for part-time jobs to be paid at low rates, and women are disproportionately found in such jobs; secondly, a tendency for men and women to do different kinds of jobs, with women concentrated in lower-paid occupations; and thirdly, a tendency for women to fail to advance in their occupations to the same extent as men – often referred to as the 'glass ceiling effect'. I will examine each of these, briefly, in turn.

In 2012 44 per cent of women in the UK were estimated to work part time but only 13 per cent of men (Equalities and Human Rights Commission 2013). To a large extent this seems to be related to childcare being a predominantly female role in the UK, as in many other cultures (although whether this is inevitable and natural or socially constructed is an issue that can be debated). The same source states that in 2011 82 per cent of men with dependent children compared to 30 per cent of women with dependent children were working full time. Only 6 per cent of fathers with dependent children compared to 37 per cent of mothers were working part time. This is related to gendered expectations about who has primary responsibility for childcare as well as for domestic labour (see Chapter 2 and also Glover and Kirton 2006). There are some signs that this is changing somewhat, with more men with dependent children beginning to work part time (Equalities and Human Rights Commission 2013), something that does point to the socially constructed nature of such differences, but there is a long way to go to achieve equity. Where a mixed-gender couple both work full time, it is usually still women who look after the children as childminders, nannies or nursery assistants with men in these positions being a very small minority (Cameron et al. 1999).

The second major factor explaining the gender pay gap is that of occupational differences according to gender. Certain occupations are made up predominantly of either men or women. According to the UK's Office of National Statistics Labour Force Survey (2015b), 100 per cent of butchers, for example, were men, while 100 per cent of nursery nurses and assistants were women (no doubt there are exceptions to this, but too rare to be picked up by this large-scale survey). Among civil engineers 88 per cent were men, while among human resource and industrial relations officers 60 per cent were women. Such differences reflect gendered attitudes to different kinds of work, different choices of subject at school and university and a channelling of expectations from teachers, parents, media representation of occupations and peers (for example, see Powell et al. 2012; Siann and Callaghan 2001). But such differences are not fixed forever. There are examples of occupations changing towards a more equal gender balance (doctors, for example), where previously they were male dominated. There are also continuing attempts to change the gender balance in occupations including science, engineering and construction, and this is often done through attempts to mobilize women's networks (e.g. the Wise campaign – see Wise 2015).

If some occupations are dominated by one or other gender, why is this? One explanation might be that it reflects existing differences between the genders, perhaps even 'natural' or biologically given differences (such as strength). However, I find sociological explanations more convincing. Jobs such as butchering and civil engineering are not essentially unsuitable for women, but they may conflict with prevailing social expectations and norms. Conversely, some jobs might be deemed more suitable for women and they may lead them to be favoured in selection decisions, whether through conscious or unconscious bias. As Acker (2006: 45) has put it: 'The ideal worker for many jobs is a woman, particularly a woman who, employers believe, is compliant, who will accept orders and low wages.' In the UK in 2015, according to the Labour Force Survey (Office of National Statistics 2015b), 93 per cent of receptionists were women. Is this because they are seen as more likely to be a positive, welcoming and attractive face to predominantly male visitors in business?

An interesting study to consider in thinking about this issue is Leidner's (1991) US study of two occupations – food servers in McDonalds and insurance sales agents. Neither job seems to be 'essentially' suited to either men or women and yet the first set of jobs was observed to be predominantly held by women and the second by men. This can of course vary over time and in place to place (he points out that in Japan insurance sales is a woman's job), but these were his observations in the cases he examined. What he argues is that the men and women doing these jobs found ways of interpreting them that were aligned to their gender. The job of serving food, he suggests, might be seen as in line with cultural expectations of feminine behaviour: being deferential, smiling at customers, being slow to react aggressively to customers who may be difficult or abusive. However, insurance sales requires some similar attributes, as well as social skills in establishing and maintaining rapport and displaying interest in the other that is, in US and UK culture, coded feminine. The male insurance agents instead emphasized how their work involved determination, aggressiveness, persistence and stoicism – traits more congruent with masculinity. This suggests that occupations are only contingently 'masculine' or 'feminine' – they might be interpreted in different ways. Identity work may go into reconciling a gendered self-identity with the job (see also Grunert and Bodner 2011), but this draws on culturally available norms. This may also come to reproduce a gendered structuring of occupations as they come to be seen as congruent with stereotyped notions of men and women. This need not be fixed for all time – if it is socially constructed it is also susceptible to social challenge and change through the operation of a number of forces, including but not exclusively the agency of people who might want to promote change.

The third major factor explaining the gender pay gap is that of differential rates of advancement, culminating in what is often referred to as a 'glass ceiling' whereby invisible barriers prevent women advancing to senior positions. Perhaps a better metaphor is the 'labyrinth' (Huyt 2013). There are examples of women advancing to very senior positions (even, in the UK, to prime minister), but these seem rare – as if women have a more difficult time in navigating to the top. What can explain this? One explanation lies in the conscious or unconscious bias against women that might affect decision makers when it comes to promotion. Some of this might be related not to the gender of the person as such but to the status of the woman as a mother, where this is known. King (2008), in a study of academics in the US for example (people you might expect to be relatively free from gender bias), suggests that senior academics were biased against mothers, in that they expected them to be less involved in their work (in line with role expectations that they will put a higher priority on their domestic roles than men) and also less flexible in their use of time or in relocating. In fact, according to this study, on all measures the relatively junior academic mothers either matched or exceeded fathers in the scores for role involvement, flexibility and commitment, suggesting a gap between actual behaviour and the stereotype. It is possible that the fact that women scored higher in measures of role involvement and continuance commitment (expressing a wish to stay with the organization) reflects their trying to overcome negative stereotypes. King's study suggests, however, that there is no basis for thinking that motherhood should affect promotion, based on attitudes of women towards employment, yet this bias against mothers might still be prevalent. More-over, it may be shared by women as well as men, but while men are numerically dominant in most senior roles it is mainly men who are the ones who are in a position to act on it, leading to something of a 'maternal wall' (Crosby et al. 2004) as a barrier to promotion.

Men may also continue to practise behaviours associated with the 'old boys' network' which favours, consciously or unconsciously, men. It may be difficult for women to break into what is something of a closed circle, based on common norms and patterns of interaction (including things as mundane as conversations about football) that may serve to exclude women, when men favour those who are like them and 'fit in' with prevailing norms. This can be described as homosociality (see Collinson and Hearn 1996; Marshall 1995). Those women who do advance may feel they have to behave like men and play the game by men's rules (see Wajcman 1998). But it would be understandable if many were reluctant or unable to do so. Indeed, Marshall's (1995) study suggests that this is a major reason for women deciding to 'move on' out of managerial roles.

Even if women remain in full-time employment and return to work quickly after the birth of a child, they may still experience a break in their career that hampers their advancement. A controversial argument by Hakim (2002, but see also Broadbridge 2010; McRae 2003; Man Yee 2007 for alternative views) emphasizes women's choices, including, sometimes, prioritizing motherhood over professional or occupational advancement. But choices are made under certain conditions: prevailing norms, company and national policies regarding benefits, maternity leave entitlement and childcare, as well as negotiations with partners and the experience or expectation of barriers may well affect certain 'choices'. They may not always be positive ones, based on the valorization of motherhood and a willingness to prioritize the domestic sphere, they may be reluctantly made or women may feel ambivalent about them (see also Glover 2006; Hollway and Featherstone 1997).

Walsh (2012), in focusing on lawyers, shows how even women with strong career aspirations can internalize the idea that they will assume the major responsibility for household work and childcare and be likely to experience significant work/family/life tensions as a result, largely due to the time-intensive expectations of professional commitment. In Walsh's study the experiences of women who had children were consistent with this outcome. Her work could be seen as an example of the operation of 'inequality regimes', which Acker (2006: 443) defined as 'loosely interrelated practices, processes, actions, and meanings that result in and maintain class, gender, and racial inequalities within particular organizations'. She points out that:

> In general, work is organized on the image of a white man who is totally dedicated to the work and who has no responsibilities for children or family demands other than earning a living. Eight hours of continuous work away from the living space, arrival on time, total attention to the work, and long hours if requested are all expectations that incorporate the image of the unencumbered worker.
>
> *(Acker 2006: 448)*

Acker also points to routine practices in recruitment, wage setting and informal interaction that serve to reproduce inequality.

BOX 6.1 IN THE NEWS: SURVEY OF WOMEN ARCHITECTS

In January 2015 results of the *Architects' Journal* survey of women in architecture were widely reported. The survey had 1,104 responses (20 per cent of them men). 76 per cent of women reported facing discrimination in their career and 62 per cent of the women in the survey said they had suffered discrimination in their practice. One commented that 'I've experienced less discrimination from builders on site than from any other section of the industry. The worst experiences have been from clients and colleagues.' The survey found that women were paid less than men at all levels. Almost 90 per cent of female respondents believed that having children put women at a disadvantage in the architecture profession while only 50 per cent of male respondents did so.

Source: *Architects' Journal* 2015

These gender differences in pay, promotion and type of occupation are stark and seem to fit uneasily with manifest commitments to gender equality. Of course it should be acknowledged that this status of women in the workplace in the United Kingdom today is very different from that of 50 or 100 years ago. It was not so long ago that women could not study for a degree but now over 50 per cent of graduates are women. It was not so long ago that in many occupations women were required to stop work once they were married in the expectation that their primary role was to look after their husband, children and household (particularly through shopping, cooking and cleaning). And yet in 2015 in the United Kingdom 68.8 per cent of women aged from 16 to 64 were in work, compared with 78.3 per cent of men (Office of National Statistics 2015c). It was not so long ago that all managers were men and it made sense that Whyte's (1960) classic study of managers could be called The Organization Man, without any sense that this was a partial view. So one can draw a picture of women's advancement in the course of the last 200 years and conclude that they are now less unequal than they were.

A large measure of the advance of women has been due to their mobilization as women in women's movement activity (see Barry et al. 2012). From the actions of the first-wave feminists in the suffragette movement fighting for the vote to second-wave feminism in the 1960s (which could be seen as a movement against the confinement of women to a household role), to third-wave feminism and what some would see as fourth-wave feminism, including battling everyday sexism (Everyday Sexism 2015), women have been active in fighting against the kind of structural inequalities that I have pointed to. Some of this has occurred within particular organizations, occupations and professions and also, significantly, within trade unions (see, for the latter, Kirton and Healy 2013; Glover and Kirton 2006).

The relative improvement in women's position in employment that has occurred in the 20th and 21st centuries may not be entirely due to their mobilization as a collective movement for change, however. Capitalism's voracious appetite for labour at certain times in the economic cycle sucks people into the labour process who might otherwise be excluded. Women in the 1960s and 1970s were a source of labour to be exploited at a time when capitalism also fed the desire for higher levels of consumption in the household and when there were inflationary pressures, including those associated with housing costs, which put pressure on households to find ways of increasing their household income. In such circumstances even women who have no identification with feminism might become more willing to enter the workforce. Moreover, as social norms change, such tendencies become self-reinforcing.

Doing and undoing gender

Much of the work on gender in the workplace was inspired by second-wave and third-wave feminism and focused on the position of women, while a smaller but important body of work also focused on men (Collinson and Hearn 1996; Kimmel et al. 2005). The literature on gender from the 1970s through to the 1990s often focused on gender difference. However, an important trend in the literature, prompted in part by Judith Butler's work (Butler 2011; Lloyd 2013), was to shift the focus away from gender difference based on fixed categories and relatively stable structural positions of male and female, men and women, and instead to look at the process of gendering: of how 'gender' is done and undone. This may shift attention away from the inequalities between men and women as distinct and stable groupings and towards the way in which gender is produced, reproduced and challenged. This also tends to see gender in terms of the operation of multiple signifiers of gender, and how they are utilized. This in turn might lead us to focus on ideas of masculinity and femininity, including the idea that these are not always tied to people in a straightforward way; that men and women might behave in ways that subvert gender expectations as well as reinforce them, and that the performance of gender is complex. There are many ways of being masculine or feminine that are culturally and situationally specific and can be drawn on in the course of interaction. We can also play with expectations, as in the performance of drag artists. Here I want to illustrate such positions with reference to a variety of studies.

One obvious way people 'do' (and sometime undo) gender is in how they dress. Haynes' (2012) study of lawyers shows how this may work in a professional context to the disadvantage of some women. She quotes a partner in a law firm describing a recruitment situation as follows:

> The two men were dressed in suits and the two women had a kind of a pant suit and a skirt type suit on but then one of them had gigantic shoes on and it was kind of like, 'Okay, you were almost there honey, I almost would have taken you seriously'... I never saw her again (Partner A, law firm).
>
> *(Haynes 2012: 497)*

I find this a fascinating comment. It says a lot about gender relations. Consider the decisions these applicants made in dressing. One can imagine the men had no problems in deciding whether or not to wear a suit: they knew what was expected and acted upon it – perhaps they had internalized the norm to the extent it was what they felt best expressed their professional selves. But the women? Did the woman who chose 'gigantic' shoes act on a whim? Perhaps not, perhaps she saw this as 'power dressing', as making her look more authoritative. Or was it that she was following fashion and reference groups outside the legal profession? Was it possibly even an act of resistance: an attempt to stand out and be different from the norm? Whatever the explanation it seems to have been a bad decision as far as getting the job was concerned. And this illustrates the different kinds of identity work taking place. For the man the identity work seems easy, for the woman there is a far more difficult set of choices to make. She may be aware of such difficulties and navigate them successfully, she may even enjoy the sense of agency this invokes, but it is hard work and might carry costs.

Another way in which we do and undo gender is in how we speak. Again Haynes' (2012) study shows some of the difficulties that women face and that may explain the 'labyrinth'. On the one hand promotion committees and recruiters are looking for people who have impact, but when women speak authoritatively it seems to be construed as overbearing. One respondent described a discussion over hiring as follows:

> We disagreed with the hiring partner on a candidate… his reaction… to the way
> that she was speaking, because she does have this very authoritative manner of
> speaking, is that she was strident and he couldn't get past that and listen to what
> she was saying because she was so strident and he felt attacked (Associate lawyer A).
>
> *(Haynes 2012: 498)*

Women who seem to adopt the kinds of behaviour seen as normal in the law
profession are subject to negative characterizations:

> If a man had made the same arguments, in the same manner, in the same way
> as a woman, you know they were just protecting their clients' interests or
> whatever, but if a woman does it, she is a bitch. That is one of the things for
> women, at least in litigation, it is more of a problem for women to be taking
> strong positions and arguing forcefully and striking that balance. If you do it too
> much you are a bitch, that is how you would be characterized and you know,
> with some people, if you do it at all you are a bitch (Partner A, law firm).
>
> *(Haynes 2012: 499)*

This suggests that there are different criteria for men and women when judging
performance and that the position of women is confounded by gendered stereotypes
of the 'bitch' – even if the behaviours associated with it are also those associated
with the norm for men in the same situation. As Haynes puts it: 'what is regarded as
professional for a man may be regarded as too masculine for a woman' (2012: 499).

These examples suggest that people actively position themselves but do so under
conditions in which they are only partially in control – the expectations and responses
of others are crucial and these are institutionalized and culturally specific (see Alcoff
1988). Some positions are uncomfortable and prompt either exit, accommodation or
resistance, others are more comfortable and congruent. The way employers and
employees interpret jobs often does have a gendered element. Our jobs may reflect
our gender, but sometimes the reflection is distorted. Sometimes we might need to do
a considerable amount of work to reconcile job and gender, and sometimes this work
will be too arduous or unrewarding. But equally we human beings do have a capacity,
often, to make the best of a bad job, to somehow find even in the humblest or most
gruelling situations some redeeming feature that makes it tolerable. Culturally specific
ideas about gender provide resources to do this. To see the job of butchering as a
manly exhibition of toughness, or caring work as an exhibition of feminine concern
for others, is to perform identity work. Sometimes gender structures reinforce occupational structures – but these are also dynamic and subject to disturbance. While
people may reconcile themselves with uncomfortable situations they can also sometimes resist and rebel, fired by a sense of injustice. It is this that can fuel a social
movement for change – but it depends on collective action as well as individual action.

Grünenfelder's (2013) study of women development workers in Pakistan shows
some of the complexity of negotiating gendered relations. These women faced
restrictions on travelling alone through fear of sexual harassment. They also had to

counter suspicion of men who fear these women are agents of a Western attempt to destabilize the traditional gender order:

> Villagers do not like foreigners and NGOs. Villagers think that these people would provoke their women (Office attendant, social organization office, 23 July 2008).
> The problem is that the NGOs have motivated the women against their husbands (Male social organizer, 23 July 2008).
>
> *(Grünenfelder 2013: 606)*

Faced with such fears and suspicions the women make a variety of adjustments. Some ensure their husbands accompany them on their way to work, or avoid interactions with male team mates to present themselves as 'modest and decent Muslim women' (Grünenfelder 2013: 608). Others seek to draw a distinction between their own identities as educated, urban women who have broken away from rural traditions and the 'jungly others' (Grünenfelder 2013: 609) and favour more equal gender relations. The position of one woman emphasizes temperament and personal experience as part of this othering and her explanation for her position in formal employment that challenges traditional gender norms:

> [F]rom the very beginning my character was like… was controlling things, like an administrator. Even at home, when I was a child, in my absence – later on I came to know – my father used to call me: 'Where is the magistrate?' So when I became a magistrate people were laughing. I said: 'What has happened? You are laughing'. They said: 'What your father used to say now proved true'. So this was my temperament (Female manager of a governmental development project, 22 July 2008).
>
> *(Grünenfelder 2013: 610)*

This is an example of identity work that draws on the personal to legitimate and explain a challenge to traditional gender norms.

Another example of women challenging traditional norms is found in Ainsworth et al.'s (2014) study of women firefighters in Australia. These women have to negotiate what she describes as 'problematic masculinity'. For example, the standard uniforms made urination difficult for women and a lack of toilet facilities meant that women often had to urinate behind a tree or truck which was considered embarrassing. Some female firefighters restricted their fluid intake to avoid this, risking dehydration: 'When I have to go to the toilet it makes the blokes laugh… They think it's hysterical that there will only be one tree in a paddock and they all go behind it… It's not hysterical… it's horrible' (Ainsworth et al. 2014: 48). But they also describe these women expressing 'preferred femininity'. The women sometimes presented themselves as able to recognize their own feelings and identify with the feelings of others, thus being able to provide more effective assistance to those affected: 'Women are much better when say you get to a house fire and there is a woman or children all upset… We are just able to offer support… A man would have no idea let alone even think about doing that' (Ainsworth et al. 2014: 49). However, the author also identifies 'problematic femininity', too, with some women distancing themselves from feminism:

> A lot of women's libbers have made it so hard for us because they have been the equivalent of the male chest beaters… they have made it so bloody hard for us girls that just want to get out there and train to the best of our ability and practise what we have been taught to do.
>
> *(Ainsworth et al. 2014: 50)*

There was also a distancing from being 'bitchy':

> There are not many women there, but some of them can be quite revolting… They are so bitchy… Just about who turns out and who is better than who… Women can gossip, and they go about talking to all their other mates in the brigade. If you are out, you are out… Women can be nasty pieces of work to each other.
>
> *(Ainsworth et al. 2014: 51)*

Ainsworth et al.'s work suggests not so much a dissolution of gender norms as negotiation around them. These women are positioned as women and to a large extent define themselves as women, seeking to find the best way of accommodating their gender to the situation.

Another study that explores similar themes is that of McDonald's (2013) study of nurses in the US. Nursing is a predominantly female role, but McDonald looks at the views of both women and men nurses. He recognizes that: 'a universal list of characteristics associated with masculinity and femininity does not exist since all definitions of masculinity and femininity are applicable only in specific socio-historical and cultural circumstances' (McDonald 2013: 562), but he shows how men and women student nurses do think of characteristics in gendered ways in this context. For instance, Claudia, an undergraduate student at a community college, states:

> Well, I think, like I said, just being compassionate and trying to be under-standing of how the patient is feeling. Just being more in touch with that. How are people feeling instead of putting out what they say is the normal masculine. Well, you just don't talk about your feelings, you are a guy, you don't talk about your feelings. But in nursing you have to know how your patient is feeling so that you can care for him better.

This quotation shows assumptions of what is 'normal masculine' and associates com-passion with femininity. McDonald shows how one male student – Bill – incorporates 'feminine' characteristics into what he takes to be required for him to be a good nurse while another woman student emphasizes the importance of knowledge, science and efficiency in nursing, and McDonald sees this as 'reconstructing the professional iden-tity of a nurse in ways that move beyond the stereotypical feminine traits that tend to be associated with the nursing profession, most notably its nurturing component' (McDonald 2013: 573). He also describes a situation in which a female nurse stands up to a male doctor and sees this as acting against the submissive female stereotype and using direct and confrontational language, 'which is culturally coded as masculine' (McDonald 2013: 575) in telling the doctor to shut up.

McDonald provides a powerful case for seeing these students as doing identity work in which they sometimes weave characteristics associated with other genders into their own occupational identities. However, while I am sympathetic to such work I think we need to be cautious about identifying masculinity as the antithesis of femininity as sometimes suggested by McDonald. Certainly one could easily come up with a list that demonstrates this: how to be 'tough' is masculine and 'tender' is feminine, to be 'hard' is masculine and 'soft' is feminine and so on. But often the differences that are claimed might not he antithetical. Within nursing McDonald's respondents discuss the importance of compassion and caring as coded feminine. This is compelling, but the opposite of compassion and caring is not the use of scientific knowledge and the pursuit of efficiency – it is a lack of care or cruelty. The point is that even in binary conceptions of gender, assumptions about gender differences can be based on different qualities rather than on opposites. In Gilligan's (1982) influential work on gender differences in ethical development she argues that women and men tend to develop in different ways, with women developing an ethics of care and men an ethic of justice. This suggests, however, not the development of opposite ethical principles but differences, both of which might have merit. This is often a better way to think of gender difference.

However, as soon as we recognize difference there is a tendency to judge one as superior to the other. It is precisely this that feminists such as de Beauvoir – for example, in her book *The Second Sex* (de Beauvoir 1993) – have argued against, since it often is to women's disadvantage. It is precisely this that Gilligan is arguing against, as do those who argue for women's knowledge being based on different principles to men (Harding 1996). Certainly, I think it is important to question the assumed inferiority of characteristics associated with women. However, we also need to be cautious about reifying and exaggerating differences or assuming a homogeneity regarding the 'feminine' or 'masculine' characteristics of men and women. Instrumentality, rationality and competitiveness have all been associated with masculinity (e.g. see Davies and Thomas 2002), but the extent to which these can and should be associated with masculinity and coded in a gendered way is questionable. Certainly those who favour an approach that emphasizes the doing and undoing of gender would not assume that these characteristics are associated with one sex alone. Moreover, even as men and women 'do' gender they may do so in many different ways. The literature on masculinity, for example, distinguishes different types of masculinity, emphasizing that it can take different forms. Differences according to class and ethnicity might render the meaning and content of masculinity very different. The masculinity of the working-class boys in Willis' (1977) classic study is very different from that of the men managers portrayed in Collinson and Hearn's book (1996), the former more unruly and rough than the latter. Connell (2005, see also Kimmel et al. 2005) emphasizes this multiplicity of masculinities but also suggests that they are organized and have a relationship to one another. The concept of hegemonic masculinity refers to the form that is dominant in any one culture and might render, say, the effeminate male police officer a problematic figure (see Chapter 7). Connell emphasizes, however, that 'hegemony is a historically mobile relation' (Connell 2005: 77) – there is no fixed definition of the masculine and the same applies to the feminine.

Conclusion

While we might deconstruct gender and seek to move beyond binary systems that render one gender, or the characteristics associated with it, inferior, we must also recognize gender inequality. Can there be gender difference without inequality? This would require different voices to be seen as simply different, rather than one being superior to the other. But we should not exaggerate difference; we might expect that women and men are able to do the same things, and might not always do things differently. Connell (2005: 21) points out how decades of research into sex differences in a range of mental abilities, emotions, attitudes, personality traits and so on have produced a remarkably consistent picture of either non-existent or small differences. But still the differences are seen as important, indeed are important, as this chapter has shown. In the contemporary workplace things are often structured around male norms and men dominate the higher circles, if not the whole occupation or organization. To break this down requires gender politics. It requires a movement for change in which some sympathetic men might be supporters rather than opponents or passive bystanders (Barry et al. 2012). It may require a valorization of the feminine, as well as everyday feminisms that challenge the domination by men and their associated masculinities. It requires political action at all levels and in all places – in the home, school, trade union or workplace. The forward march of women in the 20th century is pronounced. It is also inclusive, with women recognizing that gender, ethnicity, disability, class and age are interrelated, as we shall see in other chapters. The challenge is to recognize that while such differences may divide women, as well as divide women and men, there is also the potential for solidarity across differences and across genders.

BOX 6.2 AT THE MOVIES: GENDER

Some movies relevant to the themes of the chapter are:

Patton (1970, director Franklin J. Schaffner)
Alien (1979, director Ridley Scott)
Working Girl (1988, director Mike Nichols)
Mrs Doubtfire (1993, director Chris Columbus)
Fight Club (1999, director Chuck Palahniuk)
Made in Dagenham (2010, director Nigel Cole)

References

Acker, J. (2006) 'Inequality regimes: Gender, class, and race in organizations', *Gender and Society*, 20(4): 441–464.

Ainsworth, S., Batty, A. and Burchielli, R. (2014) 'Women constructing masculinity in voluntary firefighting', *Gender, Work and Organization*, 21(1): 37–56.

Alcoff, L. (1988) 'Cultural feminism versus post-structuralism: The identity crisis in feminist theory', *Signs*, 13: 405–436.

Architects' Journal (2015) 'Results of AJ Women in Architecture Survey revealed', at http://www.architectsjournal.co.uk/news/results-of-the-aj-women-in-architecture-survey-revealed/8676351.fullarticle (accessed 12 December 2015).

Barry, J., Berg, E. and Chandler, J. (2012) 'Movement and coalition in contention: Gender, management and academe in England and Sweden', *Gender, Work and Organization*, 19(1): 52–70.

Broadbridge, A. (2010) 'Choice or constraint? Tensions in female retail executives' career narratives', *Gender in Management: An International Journal*, 25(3): 244–260.

Butler, J. (2011) *Gender Trouble: Feminism and the Subversion of Identity*. Hoboken: Taylor and Francis.

Cameron, C., Moss, P. and Owen, C. (1999) *Men in the Nursery: Gender and Caring Work*. London: Paul Chapman.

Collinson, D. L. and Hearn, J. (eds) (1996) *Men as Managers, Managers as Men: Critical Perspectives on Men, Masculinities and Managements*. London: Sage.

Connell, R. (2005) *Masculinities*, 2nd edition. Cambridge: Polity Press.

Crosby, F. J., Williams, J. C. and Biernat, M. (2004) 'The maternal wall', *Journal of Social Issues*, 60(4): 675–682.

Davies, A. and Thomas, R. (2002) 'Gendering and gender in public service organizations: Changing professional identities under new public management', *Public Management Review*, 4(4): 461–484.

de Beauvoir, S. (1993) *The Second Sex*, trans. and ed. H. M. Parshley. London: D. Campbell.

Equalities and Human Rights Commission (2013) 'Women, men and part-time work', at http://www.equalityhumanrights.com/about-us/devolved-authorities/commission-scotland/legal-work-scotland/articles/women-men-and-part-time-work (accessed 15 March 2016).

Everyday Sexism (2015) 'The Everyday Sexism Project', at http://everydaysexism.com (accessed 3 December 2015).

Gilligan, C. (1982) *In a Different Voice: Psychological Theory and Women's Development*. London: Harvard University Press.

Glover, J. and Kirton, G. (2006) *Women, Employment and Organizations*. London: Routledge.

Grünenfelder, J. (2013) 'Negotiating gender relations: Muslim women and formal employment in Pakistan's rural development sector', *Gender, Work and Organization*, 20(6): 599–615.

Grunert, M. L. and Bodner, G. M. (2011) 'Underneath it all: Gender role identification and women chemists' career choices', *Science Education International*, 22(4): 292–301.

Hakim, C. (2002) 'Lifestyle preferences as determinants of women's differentiated labor market careers', *Work and Occupations*, 29(4): 428–459.

Harding, S. (1996) 'Gendered ways of knowing and the "epistemological crisis" of the west' in Goldberger, N., Tarule, J., Clinchy, B. and Belenky, M. (eds), *Knowledge, Difference and Power: Essays Inspired by Women's Ways of Knowing*. New York: Basic Books.

Haynes, K. (2012) 'Body beautiful? Gender, identity and the body in professional services firms', *Gender, Work and Organization*, 19(5): 489–507.

Herdt, G. (ed.) (1994) *Third Sex, Third Gender: Beyond Sexual Dimorphism in Culture and History*. London: MIT Press.

Hollway, W. and Featherstone, B. (eds) (1997) *Mothering and Ambivalence.* London: Routledge.

Huyt, K. (2013) 'Women and leadership' in Northouse, P. G. (ed.), *Leadership: Theory and practice*, 6th edition. London: Sage: 349–379.

Kimmel, M., Hearn, J. and Connell, R. (eds) (2005) *Handbook of Studies on Men and Masculinities.* London: Sage Publications.

King, E. B. (2008) 'The effect of bias on the advancement of working mothers: Disentangling legitimate concerns from inaccurate stereotypes as predictors of advancement in academe', *Human Relations*, 61(12): 1677–1711.

Kirton, G. and Healy, G. (2013) *Gender and Leadership in Unions.* Abingdon: Routledge.

Leidner, R. (1991) 'Serving hamburgers and selling insurance: Gender, work, and identity in interactive service jobs', *Gender and Society*, 5(2): 154–177.

Lloyd, M. (2013) *Judith Butler: From Norms to Politics.* Hoboken: Wiley.

McDonald, J. (2013) 'Conforming to and resisting dominant gender norms: How male and female nursing students do and undo gender', *Gender, Work and Organization*, 20(5): 561–579.

McRae, S. (2003) 'Constraints and choices in mothers' employment careers: A consideration of Hakim's preference theory', *British Journal of Sociology*, 54(3): 317–338.

Man Yee, K. (2007) 'Work orientation and wives' employment careers: An evaluation of Hakim's preference theory', *Work and Occupations*, 34(4): 430–462.

Marshall, J. (1995) *Women Managers Moving On: Exploring Career and Life Choices.* London: Routledge.

Marshall, N. (2003) *The Social Construction of Gender in Childhood and Adolescence.* London: Sage Periodicals Press.

Office of National Statistics (2015a) 'Annual Survey of Hours and Earnings 2014: Gender Pay Gap', at http://www.ons.gov.uk/ons/search/index.html?newquery=gender+pay +gap (accessed 14 October 2015).

Office of National Statistics (2015b) 'Employment by occupation (excel spreadsheet)', at http:// www.ons.gov.uk/ons/search/index.html?pageSize=50&sortBy=none&sortDirection=none& newquery=Labour+force+survey+Employment+by+occupation (accessed 14 October 2015).

Office of National Statistics (2015c) 'Table A05: Labour market by age group: People by economic activity and age (not seasonally adjusted) 11 November 2015 (excel spreadsheet)', at http://www.ons.gov.uk/ons/search/index.html?pageSize=50&sortBy=none& sortDirection=none&newquery=economic+activity (accessed 1 December 2015).

Powell, A., Dainty, A. and Bagilhole, B. (2012) 'Gender stereotypes among women engineering and technology students in the UK: Lessons from career choice narratives', *European Journal of Engineering Education*, 37(6): 541–556.

Siann, G. and Callaghan, M. (2001) 'Choices and barriers: Factors influencing women's choice of higher education in science, engineering and technology', *Journal of Further and Higher Education*, 25(1): 85–95.

Wajcman, J. (1998) *Managing like a Man: Women and Men in Corporate Management.* Cambridge: Polity Press.

Walsh, J. (2012) 'Not worth the sacrifice? Women's aspirations and career progression in law firms', *Gender, Work and Organization*, 19(5): 508–531.

Whyte, W. H. (1960) *The Organization Man.* Harmondsworth: Penguin Books.

Willis, P. E. (1977) *Learning to Labour: How Working Class Kids Get Working Class Jobs.* Farnborough: Saxon House.

Wise (2015) 'Wise campaign', at https://www.wisecampaign.org.uk/ (accessed 5 December 2015).

7

SEXUAL ORIENTATION

Introduction

What is this chapter about? In the literature two terms are used that might be seen as interchangeable: sexuality and sexual orientation. Is there a difference? Skidmore (2004: 231) deals with a notion of sexuality in the workplace that 'relates to the corporeal desires, attractions and erotic behaviour which are sewn into the fabric of everyday working life'. Some might see this as of marginal relevance in the average workplace. For how often does such desire, attraction and erotic behaviour arise? To what extent is it embedded in everyday workplace interactions as opposed to being spontaneous and exceptional or confined to the informal spaces of the organization – flirtations at the office party and the like? To Skidmore (2004, see also Williams et al. 1999), the answer would be to a very large extent. He argues that the work of women, in particular, is often sexualized – subject to sexualized discipline and gaze (see also Fleming 2007). On this view the work of flight attendants, receptionists and those who serve us in banks and restaurants might be sexualized, even when there is no overt sexual activity involved. This view of sexuality in the workplace emphasizes embodiment. As we see another person we may see them as sexually attractive or not. As we experience our body ourselves, we may experience desire for the other or not. This presumably rests largely on visible clues – and not just the visible appearance of the body in question but how the body is positioned, moves and is dressed. However, this view of sexuality in the organization is extremely broad and for the purposes of this chapter I have chosen to focus on what I shall refer to as sexual orientation.

By sexual orientation I mean a set of sexual preferences or gendered identities that may have implications for work (even when no overt sexual activity is involved). In referring to sexual preferences I am thinking in particular of hetero-sexual, gay, lesbian and bisexual orientations but I also consider transsexuality here, which might more accurately be described as an issue of gender identity. Trans-sexuality is included because the literature and the social movement that represents those of diverse sexualities brings them together – often using the acronym of LGBT (Lesbian, Gay, Bisexual and Transgender – or sometimes LGBTQ (Lesbian, Gay, Bisexual, Transsexual and Queer). Because all these distinctions rest on con-ceptions of gender and within-gender or between-gender relations there is an intimate connection between this chapter and that on gender. However, focusing on the issue of gay, lesbian, bisexual as well as heterosexual and transsexual orien-tations in the workplace is to give voice to issues that have been put on the agenda by LGBT people, and is a recognized element in considering diversity in the workplace. Since these issues are big enough in their own right I have decided not to deal with the wider issue of sexuality in the workplace if by that we mean the broad issue of how specifically sexual attraction, desire and behaviour operate in the workplace.

One reason for considering sexual orientation in a book on identity at work is that it can be a profound part of who one considers oneself to be. To be gay, lesbian, bisexual, transsexual or heterosexual goes to the heart of who we are as individuals. Of course, for people whose orientation or gender identity is outside the norm – gay, lesbian, bisexual or transsexual – this can be a profound challenge. Can one be oneself at work when this might be associated with stigma or homophobia, or plain puzzlement? For many gays, lesbians, bisexuals and transsexuals the answer might be to conceal this aspect of themselves – but this itself is interesting and a form of inequality at work that deserves to be considered. And if the person 'comes out' at work, again, this is worthy of attention: how is it done, when is it done, to whom is it done and with what consequences?

All this might suggest that the issue is one of bringing a pre-formed gay, lesbian, bisexual, transsexual or heterosexual identity to the workplace. However, the relevance of the topic might also lie in the workplace as a site for the making of such sexual orientations (and, possibly their remaking). The meanings and evaluations we attach to these terms, and the very emergence of such orientations, might arise in and through workplace interactions. They might arise through the feelings of attraction that arise (consider the film *Brokeback Mountain*), or the experience of discrimination, tolerance or acceptance. The movement of LGBT people for 'libera-tion' that to a large extent followed, and is modelled on, second-wave feminism and the civil rights movement (see Seidman 1997: 139 and Armstrong and Crage 2006) is the inspiration for much of the academic work on the topic, but the topic is, of course, also highly significant for the everyday experience of LGBT people in the workplace. For these reasons it deserves to be considered.

A further reason for considering the issue is that it brings to the fore the rela-tionship between our formal workplace persona – the 'job' – and our private and personal lives and feelings. If we want to understand people at work this, I would suggest, is important. And it is so for those self-identifying as heterosexual as much as for those of other sexual orientations. For this reason I consider here not just gay, lesbian and bisexual orientations but also set these in the context of the dominant heterosexual norm – a norm that is often portrayed as 'natural' and 'normal' but which itself can be seen to be a socially constructed orientation which is not a simple neutral expression of desire but shapes desires and behaviour and can be used to render other orientations abnormal and deviant. The existence of the dominant heterosexual norm, with clear roles for men and women, is often experienced as a difficulty for those who feel differently. Van Zyl (2015: 145), for example, quotes Simone, a lesbian brought up in a religious home: 'For ten years I went through the whole belief that I could change, and the church could change me… until I was 30 when… I thought, actually this is not working. So I accepted myself, and that was possibly the best gift I gave myself.' This example suggests that for the individual there is a 'real' identity that is different from that which is socially given to them. This is what was struggling to find expression, either because of religious beliefs or externally imposed definitions of gender identity. The example also shows someone working on their identity, seeking some readjustment in how they see themselves and others see them – transgressing the heterosexual norm. However, we might also raise the possibility of more radical movements between different statuses: one might not 'be' gay until certain contingencies bring this about – and one might move in either direction between a 'gay' or heterosexual identity, partly on the basis of who one forms a relationship with at the time.

In discussing sexual orientations I want to move beyond a position that deals with a simple binary relationship between the heterosexual norm and the homosexual 'minority'. Instead I want to consider a more complex pattern of difference, for the experience of lesbians is not the same as gay men, or bisexual men. I will not be able to explore these differences in much depth here, but I will at least provide some pointers to them.

The chapter is structured in three sections. The first considers issues of visibility and invisibility, the second inequality and exclusion and the final section considers the idea of 'gay-friendly' organizations.

Visibility and invisibility

In dealing with sexual orientation we are dealing with something that could be seen as a private matter and as invisible. In Weber's classic analysis of bureaucracy, he says:

> Its [i.e. bureaucracy's] specific nature, which is welcomed by capitalism, develops the more perfectly the more the bureaucracy is 'dehumanized,' the more completely it succeeds in eliminating from official business love, hatred, and all purely personal, irrational, and emotional elements which escape calculation.
>
> (Weber 1970: 215–16)

We must remember, too, that Weber saw bureaucracy as a feature of both government and private-sector organizations and as a pervasive feature of modern life, even if bureaucracy has negative connotations today. Its features, as Weber analysed them (the emphasis on rules, hierarchy, instrumental rationality and calculation), are still pervasive. In such circumstances those of us who find ourselves working in bureaucracies might feel our sexual orientations are something for the private sphere and must not intrude at work. Whether we are gay or straight is not something we need to express at work.

However, the issue of the visibility or otherwise of sexual orientations has been raised as a key issue, particularly by people who are not heterosexual. The issue of 'coming out' has been a prominent theme and something that carries both personal and political weight. Coming out as gay, lesbian, bisexual or transgender suggests a process – a process of revelation or disclosure. It is necessary precisely because of the assumption of heterosexuality. You might be presumed to be 'straight' until you announce you are 'queer' – or it is revealed for you by others (when you may have a choice of denial or acceptance). In the literature on the subject this issue is frequently addressed as an important issue in the workplace. For despite Weber's analysis of the 'pure' kind of bureaucracy based on technical rationality and 'dehumanized' work, organizations are made up of people who do interact in human ways. They do discuss their private lives, do form friendships and even stronger relationships and the personal is not so easily separated from the official.

In a study by Colgan and Wright (2011: 562), nearly three quarters (72 per cent) of the men but less than half of the women (47 per cent) said they were out to everyone at work. Nearly half of the women and one fifth of the men said they were out only to 'some people at work'. The gender difference is explained in part by occupation, with more women than men working in schools, social services and housing who seemed reluctant to come out to clients, customers and students (Colgan et al. 2006). Another explanation for the difference in rates of disclosure between men and women might be that women, already facing the possibility of gender discrimination, preferred to hide their sexual orientation, particularly when in a male-dominated workplace. Moreover, black and minority ethnic women might fear the potential for triple prejudice (based on race, gender and sexual orientation) and choose to conceal their sexuality from almost all colleagues (Colgan and Rumens 2015: 114–15):

> I think what happens with sexuality is that it's much easier just for it to be brushed aside because it is something that you can hide. I cannot hide the fact that I'm Chinese; I cannot hide the fact that I am a woman. But the other issue, I can just not address it.

Connell's (2015) study of lesbian and gay teachers in California and Texas shows them adopting a variety of positions on whether to come out to their students. Some did not come out and considered it inappropriate or unnecessary. Some did – and chose to be role models to other students – including, but perhaps not only, gay or lesbian students or those unsure of their sexuality. Connell also emphasizes the existence of 'homonormative' presentations (see also Duggan

2002) – expressions of gay/lesbian identity that 'manage the dissonance between being lesbian/gay and being a teaching professional by highlighting their similarities to their heterosexual counterparts' (2002: 49). One teacher, when asked about the advice he would give to a just 'out' gay and lesbian teacher, replied 'well, it's up to the gay or lesbian teacher to act like a person, and not have bizarre or flamboyant character' (51).

Of course, teachers who do not come out to students might come out to some or all colleagues, perhaps taking into account likely reactions.

Inequality and exclusion

The issue of whether or not to make one's sexual orientation visible to others is made in the context of organizational and working lives that may render non-heterosexual orientations problematic. In describing how they hid their sexual orientation, one US court employee in 1995 said:

> I knew that I would lose work if any of the [bosses] found out that I was gay. I was conscious of having to remain somewhat distant to most people. I did not get close to people because in their natural course of conversation most people talk about their spouses and families. I only spoke about work-related matters, never joined any group of co-workers for a drink, and never went to any firm events except those that were absolutely obligatory, and then I left as soon as possible.
>
> *(Brower 2015: 68)*

Such behaviour might possibly lead the employee to be focused and productive – but it also distances them from many incidental pleasures, reduces the opportunities for friendship and diminishes opportunities for informal networking that are important in building a career.

Keeping quiet about sexuality can also come at a cost, however. Bowring and Brewis (2015: 36) quote Jane, a member of the US military at a time of DADT (Don't ask, don't tell – in force from 1994 until 2011) as saying: 'Keeping quiet, after a while it killed my naturally boisterous personality. I didn't like who I was becoming because I couldn't be me.' This was part of her decision to leave.

Another example is provided by Brower (2015: 60–1):

> An American court employee said 'As a gay employee there is not much that I can say about this delicate subject because I cannot even be myself at my place in employment. I have to lead two different lives. Sometimes my co-workers ask me if I have a girlfriend, if I am married, how many children I have, and I have to answer with a lie. All this makes me feel very unhappy. In addition, sometimes the people that I work with make fun of gay people in front me, and I have to laugh about it and pretend that it does not bother me.'

A useful concept is that of heterosexual normativity, sometimes referred to as heteronormativity (Butler 2011; Lloyd 2013): this inscribes the heterosexual orientation with normative force and renders other orientations as, at best, unusual and, at worst, deviant and undesirable. Other orientations have been (and still are, in some quarters) seen as associated with sin, disease or psychological disorder (Rumens and Kerfoot 2009: 768).

In many cases heteronormativity lies in the taken-for-granted assumption of heterosexuality. Heteronormativity can lead to exclusion or social discomfort of those who do not share a heterosexual orientation in the course of informal workplace interaction and behaviour. Conversations about family life, what one did at the weekend and displays of family photos and the like can all be a source of exclusion and difficulty for those who do not conform to dominant norms. Willis (2009), in an Australian study, provides examples of young men feeling excluded because of their sexual orientation. For example, he quotes Trent, the only gay male with a work team at a chemical warehouse, as saying:

> Sure, as a lot of 'straight' guys do they will spend hours on end talking about women, you try and participate but knowing you can't really, and eventually they will just leave you out, it's easier for them. A female client will walk in and their jaws drop and everyone thinks they are normal but if a guy walks in and I get a twinkle in my eye, then it's 'pathetic'. I think although they [guys at work] don't directly treat me bad it's just not an even playing field.
>
> *(Willis 2009: 636)*

Trent's position seems to reveal how on a day-to-day basis the 'visibility' of the gay man might be negotiated. The comment that 'you try to participate but knowing you can't, really', suggests that there may be failed attempts to participate or decisions not to say anything while expressing a 'twinkle in my eye' may also have to be moderated. In such circumstances it would be understandable if employees decided not to come out, or to come out only to some people they might trust. But if someone is only partly 'out' there is the risk of not being able to control the disclosure – someone else might 'out' the person – either deliberately or not. 'Outing' might also come from some slip-up rather than being a deliberate act as the following example illustrates, in a Turkish context:

> I started dating, and in the heat of first love – this was my first proper gay relationship – I stupidly allowed him to hold my hand briefly on Istiklal Street as we were walking to a gay club. A work colleague and his wife walked past us. I was terrified, and I desperately hoped he didn't see me. From that moment, the night was ruined for me and I kept worrying. Nobody said a word about it when I got to work on Monday. Just as I relaxed, right before lunchtime, my boss took me in his office and told me they didn't need people like me there and asked me to leave the job. I couldn't believe my whole world went

upside down just like that. I hated myself for being so indiscreet; I kept thinking I should've been more careful.

(Öztürk 2011: 1112)

As Öztürk makes clear, being gay in Turkey is less likely to be tolerated than in some other countries, such as the US and the UK, but even here there can be similar reactions:

> GM: When I came out, I was working for a housing association in a hostel for homeless teenagers… My line manager said to me: 'Don't you think it best that you keep your private life private?' And there was someone at the housing association who started to hide his cup so that he wouldn't get AIDS.

(Humphrey 1999: 137)

Coming out can also bring some difficulties, but many might feel it is worth it. This is not a straightforward balancing of the negative and positive consequences, as the following quotation illustrates, it is more complex than that and more unpredictable in its consequences (Humphrey 1999: 138):

> I hate feeling that I'm living a lie; I really hate feeling that other people are making assumptions which I know to be wrong. Honesty and truth are really important to me, really important… And in a situation like a two year [social work training] course, where you're talking about social workers' politics and power relationships – it's such an important part of who I am that I couldn't do that without it coming out – I couldn't even think about it!… Plus there's an element of enjoying it – challenging stereotypes and preconceptions… wanting that debate, that diversity, all kinds of difference… And it makes people think – and it makes them more careful – they actually have to think about what they say, they can't make homophobic jokes or bigoted remarks. Well, they can, but they'll be challenged if they do!

The decision to come out as gay, lesbian, transsexual or bisexual might be experienced either as liberating or as difficult – or as a mixture of both. Bowring and Brewis (2015: 36) cite Trivette (2010: 224), whose respondent is quoted as saying that when he retired and was able to live as a gay man it was as if he had changed from 'a small, 1950s portable black and white' television to a 'wide screen high definition TV'. McCormack et al.'s (2014) study of bisexual men in the US found that those of an older age group (36–42) experienced more negativity in coming out compared to younger bisexual men (25–35). This might reflect changes in social attitudes in the US (and the UK) towards homosexuality in recent years. But the experience might be more complex than a simple 'positive' or 'negative' label might imply – the experience might be different with different people, or be difficult in different ways at different stages of the process. Rumens (2011: 142) refers to a gay man who describes the experience of coming out to his wife and friends as follows:

I was pretty desolate when I moved out of the marital home, having come out to my wife and friends. Most people didn't want to know me… then I started to panic about what my kids would think of their dad being gay, breaking up the family. I just felt like a monster… I felt guilty, regretting my decision, wondering whether it was all worth it, that my kids were the victims of my selfishness to come out. Cathy and some of the other mums didn't start from that position. They approached me with a sympathetic ear, telling me that divorce and being gay was not the end of the world but the start of something new. It took me a while to appreciate this, but then we starting talking about run-of-the-mill stuff like coping with stroppy teenage kids and being single again. They gave me the strength to see that being a dad is really important to me, and that being gay needn't get in the way of that.

A similarly sympathetic reaction is described by Wharton (2014) in his auto-biography in which he describes coming out in the British army – although he did also experience some homophobia and even a physical attack that seems to have been prompted by homophobia (from a person who, from his account, would seem to have suppressed gay sexual feelings). This illustrates that the process of coming out has costs as well as rewards that might not be easily calculated. Those of a non-heterosexual orientation who are not 'out' have a difficult decision to make. They might either overestimate or underestimate negative reactions.

A survey by Day and Schoenrade (2000) in mid-west USA suggested that disclosure was linked to lower work–home conflict and higher commitment to their organization and they also found anti-discrimination policies seemed to have a small but positive relationship with job satisfaction, organizational commitment and lower work–home conflict, as did support from top management (assessed separately). Stonewall (2015a) – the UK-based organization campaigning for LGBT rights – asserts that 'Our members know that people perform better when they can be themselves' (Stonewall 2015a). However, Van Zyl (2015) provides a case that is not so straightforward. A South African transgender train driver found her colleagues were not sympathetic:

My colleagues were very shocked… I am changing from a man to a woman… I am asking for your support. I want you to look at this with open minds. I don't want you to discriminate against me and push me aside. So it happened. People ostracised me. They didn't want to talk to me.

(Van Zyl 2015: 147)

When she told her HR department about transitioning, she was sent for psychological evaluation and prevented from driving trains for three months. However, after invoking a legal process she won her case for a return to driving trains – but only after her CEO had sent an email to all staff emphasizing that no discrimination would be tolerated.

Such a case shows that disclosure is not necessarily either 'positive' or 'negative' – it might be a process full of difficulty but also with potential gains. It also shows how context matters, including in this case the legal context. A further example of this comes from Bowring and Brewis (2015), who found that after changes in legislation in the US one lesbian said, 'I decided I was going to be a poster child. I was senior enough for there to be no repercussions – in this way I could make it easier for others coming behind me.' Asked why she adopted this stance she said: 'Because I'm that much of a feminist' (2015: 37). But she recognized it might be different in different parts of the military (she was in a music section) and also for men coming out as gay, showing again how context matters.

Öztürk's (2011) study of the position of lesbian, gay and bisexual employees in Turkey reveals a range of discriminatory and negative behaviour towards those who were 'out': these included job termination, threats of violence, unwanted jokes and innuendos, and harassment (see also Öztürk and Özbilgin 2015).

One lesbian who was 'out' at work is quoted as saying:

> Turkey is a patriarchal society, so women are like objects. My hyper-heterosexual colleague told me that women are like a car – you don't want a used car, so you always try to get a virgin, and lesbians are like a new or used car which has a permanent factory defect. My colleagues don't panic about me being a lesbian. They just make bizarre jokes and call me names like 'dominant woman', which fits into their idea of lesbianism. I think if I were a gay man though, they might have fired me right away.
>
> *(Öztürk 2011: 1112)*

Öztürk suggests that the extent of homophobia varies by size of company, with harsher treatment and job termination more likely in small or medium-sized firms, while in larger firms the discrimination tended to take the form of unsettling or traumatizing jokes and abusive comments.

Willis (2009: 639) also, in an Australian context, shows how coming out as gay can have strong negative consequences and outright hostility:

> My former boss was a total arsehole! I still don't know how, but someone allegedly told him I was gay and as he is an evangelical [Christian] he made things very difficult. E.g. would not let me leave work, had a 'gay' chair for me and everyone else used a normal office chair... It was truly horrible. I thought about going to the EOC [Equal Opportunity Commission]; however, it was his word against mine and my fellow workers shared his views.

The experience of a hostile working environment might well cause someone to leave the organization if they have the opportunity to do so and while, under UK legislation, they might be able to bring a case of 'constructive dismissal', many employees are likely to want to simply get on with their life elsewhere and not endure the cost and trouble of a legal process with an uncertain outcome.

Rocco and Gallagher (2006) have used Super's career model to outline ways in which heterosexuality confers privilege at every stage of the career. At the first stage, in choosing a career, LGBTQ people may deliberately avoid occupations where it is difficult to pass as heterosexual or where the penalties for disclosure of a gay identity are seen as high, either because of institutional policies or the attitudes of co-workers. While Rocco and Gallagher do not provide examples, Humphrey's (1999) study of gay men and lesbians in the UK public-service context suggest that lesbians may be attracted to the caring professions (childcare, social work, etc.) while gay men might find certain public-service occupations less likely to be homophobic (although certain jobs such as teaching, as we have seen, do pose particular challenges over whether to come out to students or service users). Their study and others (Colgan and Rumens 2015) also show selecting such occupations and sectors is no guarantee of an absence of homophobia.

Rocco and Gallagher (2006) argue that at the later stages of establishing and advancing one's career, LGBTQ people may be at a disadvantage in so far as they are excluded from informal social networks as they navigate a whole host of social situations in which heterosexuality is the perceived norm. At the advancement stage they referred to a study by Ellis and Fox (2001) showing that those who hold heterosexist beliefs help gays and lesbians less than those who are not heterosexist. LGBTQ people may therefore have less access to mentoring and support in their career enhancement – unless they conceal their sexual orientation. Finally, in negotiating their work/life roles they often experience less family support, and colleagues may be less able to offer support to the employee as they have less knowledge of the issues facing LGBTQ people.

However, while Rocco and Gallagher (2006) are no doubt correct in pointing to sources of potential disadvantage, theirs might be a somewhat one-sided view. LGBTQ people who do not have children but are in stable partnerships might be better able to resemble the male breadwinner model and be at a relative advantage in furthering their career. This might lead us to expect that there might even be certain advantages in a departure from the heterosexual norm – perhaps for lesbian women in particular, where they do not have children. Looking at earnings, Arabsheibani et al. (2005) found a mixed pattern of advantage with gay men (defined in this study in the restricted way of living in a household with another man) earning more than non-gay men on average, but less than those in heterosexual households. On the other hand, the study found lesbians (defined in equivalent terms as gay men) appearing to have a marked advantage in pay and other benefits. However, a limitation of this study is that there was no consideration of whether the person was 'out' at work or not, and the definition of gay and lesbian excludes gay and lesbian people not living with a same-sex partner. Nor is there any consideration of the effect of having dependent children or not. Nevertheless, the study does suggest that being gay or lesbian is not necessarily to be set at a disadvantage in every respect.

Gay-friendly organizations?

Willis (2009) draws an analytical distinction between inclusive and exclusive work spaces for gay men and, although this might be too stark a distinction, it does suggest a range of possibilities. It is worth noting the experience of 'inclusion' and acceptance as well as exclusion and discrimination:

> It was a good working environment… my boss he was great, he was really quite accepting, he had a lot of gay friends so there was never any sort of ill sentiment towards anybody who was different who worked in or came to the restaurant, that's what I mean by alternative, it welcomed everybody.
>
> *(2009: 639)*

Broomfield's (2015) study of gay men in the UK police force suggested there had been huge institutional change in a more 'inclusive' direction from what had previously been a hostile environment for gays. This was evinced by recruitment policies (e.g. recruitment at gay pride events). In another sector and country Fleming (2007) deals with an Australian call centre that has a culture of fun and 'being yourself', which attempts to make work less monotonous. This also had a culture in which being gay is tolerated: 'The CEO, James Carr said in the local business press: "We've tried to create a workplace in which people of either sex, gay people and people from other places can come and really enjoy the time they spend with each other and their managers in the environment"' (2007: 248).

David's (2015) study of call centres in the Philippines deals with the employment of transgender people and suggests that many of these organizations do more than tolerate such employees. As one respondent put it:

> There's really no gender issues, because we even hire transvestites, trans-sexuals, drag queens; bakla is our local term. There is a large population of gay people in this business, maybe because they can emulate the accent better, I'm not sure if that's even true. I think their propensity to be involved with the company is higher than, for the lack of a better term, straight people. They have discipline in terms of the work, because they have to save up money for their breast augmentation or anything to do with their physical bodies.
>
> *(David 2015: 181)*

This means that being gay or transgender is not unusual in this organization. As another respondent put it:

> And the good thing about working in a BPO [Business Process Outsourcing organization – offshore call centre] is, they respect each other. Most importantly, if you're within the office, because in BPO there are a lot of gay people, a lot of lesbians, a lot of transgenders. A lot. That's where you can see where your bosses are gay, supervisors are gay.
>
> *(David 2015: 178)*

This is not to suggest that the organization is not without tension. David (2015: 186) also reports very different reactions to two transgender women, seemingly based on personality, with one much more accepted than the other:

Because she's funny. She's that funny! [laughs] And the other one was Evelyn. Oh, my God, she was pretentious, she was a little bit bitchy. So there was a little bit of bias there, and it really pissed Evelyn off so bad, because people were okay with Irene going to the [women's] restroom, but if it was Evelyn, that was the time the complaints came. HR even had to intervene.

BOX 7.1 IN THE NEWS: HOMOPHOBIC ABUSE

In 2013 an employment tribunal heard the case of a London city trader who complained of being the victim of homophobic abuse. Described as married, with two children and straight Barney James claimed that he was the victim of a sustained campaign of harassment on the basis of sexual orientation. He said he was sent hard-core gay porn, called a 'fat homo' and he described how a co-worker called him a 'boring, sad, fat, gay ****', and claimed that sitting next to James would make him gay. The lawyer representing the company in defending the case was reported to have asked James whether the abuse could have been simply banter and said: 'As a 6ft 3in rugby player, who is married with children, that was the joke as you are clearly not gay.' The case was later settled out of court.

Source: *Pink News*, 22 April 2013

Broomfield's (2015) study of gay men in the UK police force also shows the contingent nature of acceptance, but this time based on the field in which they worked. It was argued that effeminate male officers would not be successful in street policing but they might flourish in police station-based units that value 'feminine capital': one constable suggested the value of his own effeminacy, although in a nuanced way: 'I am a man myself remember. I mean, I'm a red blooded male the same as them. But we can offer input in certain situations from almost a female perspective and engage with them in that way, and it works, it does work!' (2015: 83). This is taken further in Simpson's (2015, see also Mills and Helms Mills 2004) study of male cabin crew – men in a job (unlike the pilots) now largely feminized, taking a subordinate, serving role in which effeminacy is not, perhaps, a problem. In such cases we see the possibility that those who depart from the heterosexual norm might have certain advantages, whether that comes from enlivening the working environment or in dealing with customers.

Commenting on the pattern across organizations in a UK context one commentator stated:

I have been involved in lesbian and gay stuff for 15 odd years or more. And there was a time where local authorities were, you know, over here in the scale of being great. It was like the banks and all the other institutions, financial institutions, were bad. It's swung completely the other way; banks are now…

brilliant... But local authorities... I was surprised, actually, how difficult it was for people still in [local authority] to be out (Gay man, local authority).

(Colgan and Wright 2011: 560–1)

However, from Fleming's (2007) study of call centres referred to earlier, we can get a sense of the fragile nature of a 'gay-friendly' organization. He describes an exchange which is reasonably portrayed by Fleming as homophobic:

Mark: People supposedly look at Sunray and see this hip, young, cool crowd.
Jackie: They don't, they see a bunch of pretentious fashion victims.
Mark: You don't even work there.
Jackie: Thank fucking god. [To me] When I go to meet Mark I wait a block down the road because if I wait outside I get looked at by the Sunray people to see what I'm wearing. I hate it; it's like being back at high school. They all must wear stylish clothes to [sarcastically and impersonating a subscriber] 'fit in'.
Mark: But I don't wear them.
Jackie: But you're a guy, it's different.
Mark: There are plenty of guys that get fully dressed up.
Jackie: But they're all gay, Mark. [Laughs uncontrollably]
Mark: That's discrimination! [Laughs] Well, yes there are a number of gay individuals there.

(Fleming 2007: 250)

However, if this is homophobic it is perhaps because of the association of these gay men with a particular kind of representation of the self – not the sexual orientation or sexual activity itself. Nevertheless, it shows the limits of tolerance and the possibility of latent rather than expressed homophobia existing, even in apparently 'gay-friendly' organizations. Indeed, we can see gay and lesbian people themselves negotiating the meaning of these orientations and their expression:

Some of my female friends at work think that, because I'm gay, I'm therefore interested in clothes, male grooming, having a clean and tidy house and all these things. It's a complete stereotype... my house is not a show home, I've got two teenage sons and it's a mess most of the time.

(Rumens 2011: 113)

This seems to be a case of a gay man showing a degree of identification with heterosexual people who share some of the same experiences – having teenage sons and a messy house. While not disidentifying as gay it is a particular way of being gay that emphasizes similarity with the heterosexual norm, rather than difference. Another example of this comes from a man in Rumens and Kerfoot's study (2009: 774):

Twenty years ago, I couldn't have been seen as professional... I would have been seen as a poof... but employment rights, a more liberal society and better protection from my employer has meant that I can be an openly gay professional... I am the new acceptable face of homosexuality... straight acting, a professional who drives an Audi with the partner at home, has holidays abroad, wears nice clothes, and what's wrong with that? Just blending in... rather than being a thorn in the side of society.

This is also emphasized by David (2015: 189): 'While trans women are expected to perform in stereotypical ways, their gender expressions (appearance, conduct, and dress) must also remain within certain limits deemed respectable and workplace-appropriate.' In certain contexts, then, including those involving the professions, occupational norms would seem to set limits on how sexual orientation can be expressed: 'The hospital is not ready... for a camp acting doctor... because it brings sexuality into the public eye, and is the workplace the right place to do that? I think the answer is "no" because it's at the expense of patients' (Rumens and Kerfoot 2009: 776).

Another example of someone negotiating their way through different conceptions of gay and professional identities is provided by Rubens in the case of Tom, an HR manager which Rubens and Kerfoot (2009: 778) describe as follows: 'It's becoming a hard HRM environment, and I sometimes feel that I'm exposing myself to criticism from other managers about being too soft, especially if I come across as being a bit effeminate.'

Another professional addresses the same issue of a professional and gay identity as follows:

I want to look more edgy than the other guys in the office, especially the straight ones. I can do that through clothing... I guess it panders to the stereotype that gay men dress well... I'm okay with that. But you don't want to overdo it... be seen to be a fashion victim that spends more time thinking about what to wear to work rather than on the job in hand.

(Rubens and Kerfoot 2009: 780)

Broomfield (2015) also suggests that while there is more tolerance of gays there is still the persistence of heteronormative masculinity whereby being effeminate or camp becomes a problem: 'Isaac a police constable was signed off work with stress for a time and said: "I am effeminate, and I would not have come up against such homophobia if I'd been seen as a butch gay man"' (Broomfield 2015: 82). Another officer reported: 'a friend of mine, who is that way inclined [effeminate], had quite a hard time, to the point of getting bullied out of the job' (Broomfield 2015: 82). Another comment was that:

Being effeminate would make it more difficult to police the streets. Whilst attitudes have changed, there are a lot of people out there who could give you abuse. With a camp guy… would they be able to do the job as well? What if you've got someone you need to taser? If you need to break up a fight? You gotta [be able] to just jump on them. [In those situations], masculinity… it certainly helps.

(Broomfield 2015: 80)

Rumens (2015) queries the term 'gay-friendly' and points to its homogenizing 'gay' (LGBT) experience and close association with the business case for diversity. He raises the question of whether this can also be a 'process by which gay and lesbian people are folded into normative heterosexual culture' (Rumens 2015: 193). He refers to Williams et al. (2009), who point to people who either were compelled to downplay their homosexuality at work or were constrained by stereotypes about how LGBT people were expected to look, act and work.

Much of what has been said so far suggests individual responses in a context of constraint, but there is also a collective response in and through unions and through social movement activity – LGBT networks and organizations such as Stonewall that campaign and promote change. Colgan and Ledwith's (2002) work shows how LGBT issues have been taken up and promoted in and by trade unions in the UK and elsewhere, with some if limited success. Stonewall has also made a business case for diversity and offered ratings of organizations through the 'workplace equality index' (Stonewall 2015b). Stonewall's Diversity Champions programme has managed to engage a number of employers, tapping into an apparent desire to be seen as progressive, inclusive places to work. Stonewall's 12th workplace conference in London in 2015 was attended by 750 people and Stonewall boasts some 700 organizations who are 'diversity champions' and 'committed to working with Stonewall to improve their workplaces for gay, lesbian and bisexual staff' (Stonewall 2015c).

This might be indicative of an interest in the issue of LGBT issues, with prominent business leaders such as Lord Browne arguing for an inclusive attitude to LGBT people in which they are able to come out and be themselves (Browne 2014). This is also evidence of action by LGBT people and sympathetic supporters, and of a positive move towards diversity.

Before we become too excited about the possibility of the establishment of gay-friendly organizations we must remember that this leaves a lot of organizations that are not diversity champions and we might feel sceptical about the extent to which even these 700 or so organizations truly provide an environment in which every gay, lesbian, bisexual and transsexual person feels accepted and can flourish. Nevertheless, it is evidence of a movement for change and action of a collective, organized nature as well as of individual agency.

Conclusion

As well as bringing out the particular experiences of those with particular kinds of sexual orientation there is much that is in the literature on sexual orientation that is of general interest. On a general level it raises issues of the boundaries between working lives and our private lives and how our inclusion or exclusion in a workplace might be based as much on informal, personal factors as formal ones. It raises issues shared with disability and age as to choices about what to reveal, when to reveal it and to whom. Issues of inclusion and exclusion, visibility and invisibility permeate the discussion. We have seen how heteronormativity may confer advantages on those who conform and create problems for those who do not, but we have also seen that challenging heterosexual norms does not necessarily lead to disadvantage. Much depends on the context. Identity work around sexual orientation involves processes whereby we render visible or invisible our self-identifications in relation to our sexuality. If, at times, those who do not conform to heterosexual norms identify *with* others who share a similar counter-identification against the norm, then this can be the basis of solidarity across any differences that exist between gay, lesbian, bisexual and transsexual categories, as well as within such identity positions.

Attending to differences in sexual orientation has the potential to challenge dominant assumptions about the lives and natures of employees. It might make us more tolerant of difference if we reject the hegemony of heteronormativity. It might make us recognize that our inclusion in workplaces, as social individuals, is based in part on our sharing with others aspects of our private lives. But it also raises the challenge that this might reveal differences and divisions as well as similarities and sources of identification. The chapter reveals something of the experience of those with diverse sexual orientations but it also shows agency both in individual adaptations to the work situation and to collective mobilization for change. In so far as this challenges discrimination and exclusion it raises the possibility of something different and better.

If this chapter raises the prospect of more tolerant, diverse and respectful workplaces it also suggests the possibility of oppressive, discriminatory and hostile forms for those who do not conform to heterosexual norms. The contribution of writers and activists in this field lies partly in queering expectations. Queer theory challenges and subverts existing assumptions and norms and is aligned to the collective movement for change that accepts diversity in sexual orientation and raises the possibility of more fluid and diverse forms of sexuality. Writers and activists on sexual orientation have forced the issue of sexual orientation onto the agenda, in part because of a sense of injustice and dissatisfaction with the oppression of LGBT people. The extent to which such actions have had an impact is variable. In the UK and US, for example, there is evidence of much success in achieving greater equality and acceptance. Turkey is a very different case. The future is uncertain everywhere. One possible future is that of a rather small widening of possibilities so that only some expressions of alternative sexualities are tolerated, leading to continuing pressure on individuals to conform to dominant norms even if they are given some leeway to stray from heterosexuality. But gains can also be lost. These issues are often ones that invoke strong passions. It is by no means certain that those voices favouring tolerance of sexual diversity will prevail. Another possibility is that issues of sexual orientation will become aspects of an increasing diversity among work-places, so that those of a gay, lesbian, bisexual or transsexual orientation may find workplaces where they are valued and included, but others in which they are excluded or not tolerated. This might lead to the segregation of LGBT people in certain occupations and organizations to the detriment of workplace diversity in other occupations and organizations. The individual and collective agency of gay, lesbian, bisexual and transsexual people will be critical, but so too will the responses of those who identify as heterosexual.

BOX 7.2 AT THE MOVIES: SEXUAL ORIENTATION

Some movies relevant to the themes of the chapter are:

Brokeback Mountain (2005, director Ang Lee)
Pride (2014, director Matthew Warchus)
Carol (2015, director Todd Haynes)

References

Arabsheibani, G. R., Marin, A. and Wadsworth, J. (2005) 'Gay pay in the UK', *Economica*, 72: 333–347.

Armstrong, E. A. and Crage, S. M. (2006) 'Movements and memory: The making of the Stonewall myth', *American Sociological Review*, 71: 724–751.

Bowring, M. and Brewis, J. (2015) 'Navigating service and sexuality in the Canadian, UK and US militaries' in Colgan, F. and Rumens, N. (eds), *Sexual Orientation at Work: Contemporary Issues and Perspectives*. New York: Routledge.

Broomfield, J. (2015) 'Gay men in the UK police services' in Colgan, F. and Rumens, N. (eds), *Sexual Orientation at Work: Contemporary Issues and Perspectives*. New York: Routledge.

Brower, T. (2015) 'Courts as workplaces for sexual orientation minorities' in Colgan, F. and Rumens, N. (eds), *Sexual Orientation at Work: Contemporary Issues and Perspectives*. New York: Routledge.

Browne, J. A. (2014) *The Glass Closet: Why Coming Out Is Good Business*. London: W. H. Allen.

Butler, J. (2011) *Gender Trouble: Feminism and the Subversion of Identity*. Hoboken: Taylor and Francis.

Colgan, F. and Ledwith, S. (2002) *Gender, Diversity and Trade Unions: International Perspectives*. London: Routledge.

Colgan, F. and Wright, T. (2011) 'Lesbian, gay and bisexual equality in a modernizing public sector 1997–2010: Opportunities and threats', *Gender, Work and Organization*, 18(5): 548–570.

Colgan, F. and Rumens, N. (2015) *Sexual Orientation at Work: Contemporary Issues and Perspectives*. New York: Routledge.

Colgan, F., Creegan, C., Mckearney, A. and Wright, T. (2006) 'Why a gay-friendly working environment can boost productivity', *People Management*, 12: 80.

Connell, C. (2015) 'Reconsidering the workplace closet: The experiences of lesbian and gay teachers' in Colgan, F. and Rumens, N. (eds), *Sexual Orientation at Work: Contemporary Issues and Perspectives*. New York: Routledge.

David, E. (2015) 'Purple-collar labor: Transgender workers and queer value at global call centers in the Philippines', *Gender and Society*, 29: 169–194.

Day, N. E. and Schoenrade, P. (2000) 'The relationship among reported disclosure of sexual orientation, anti-discrimination policies, top management support and work attitudes of gay and lesbian employees', *Personnel Review*, 29: 346–363.

Duggan, L. (2002) 'The new homonormativity: The sexual politics of neoliberalism' in Castronovo, R. and Nelson, D. (eds), *Materializing Democracy*. Durham, NC: Duke University Press.

Ellis, J. and Fox, P. (2001) 'The effect of self-identified sexual orientation on helping behavior in a British sample: Are lesbians and gay men treated differently?' *Journal of Applied Social Psychology*, 31: 1238–1247.

Fleming, P. (2007) 'Sexuality, power and resistance in the workplace', *Organization Studies*, 28: 239–256.

Humphrey, J. C. (1999) 'Organizing sexualities, organized inequalities: Lesbians and gay men in public service occupations', *Gender, Work and Organization*, 6: 134–151.

Lloyd, M. (2013) *Judith Butler: From Norms to Politics*. Hoboken: Wiley.

McCormack, M., Anderson, E. and Adams, A. (2014) 'A cohort effect on the coming out experiences of bisexual men', *Sociology*, 48: 1207.

Mills, A. and Helms Mills, J. (2004) 'When plausibility fails: A critical sensemaking lens on resistance' in Thomas, R., Mills, A. J. and Helms Mills, J. (eds), *Identity Politics at Work: Resisting Gender, Gendering Resistance*. London: Routledge.

Öztürk, M. B. (2011) 'Sexual orientation discrimination: Exploring the experiences of lesbian, gay and bisexual employees in Turkey', *Human Relations*, 64: 1099–1118.

Öztürk, M. B. and Özbilgin, M. (2015) 'From cradle to grave: The lifecycle of compulsory heterosexuality in Turkey' in Colgan, F. and Rumens, N. (eds), *Sexual Orientation at Work: Contemporary Issues and Perspectives*. New York: Routledge.

Pink News (2013) 'Straight, married city trader suffered years of "heartbreaking" homophobic abuse', at http://www.pinknews.co.uk/2013/04/23/straight-married-city-tra der-subjected-to-years-of-heartbreaking-homophobic-abuse/ (accessed 13 December 2015).

Rocco, T. S. and Gallagher, S. J. (2006) 'Straight privilege and moral/izing: Issues in career development', *New Directions for Adult and Continuing Education*: 29–39.

Rumens, N. (2011) *Queer Company: The Role and Meaning of Friendship in Gay Men's Work Lives*. Farnham: Ashgate Publishing.

Rumens, N. (2015) 'Is your workplace "gay-friendly"? Current issues and controversies' in Colgan, F. and Rumens, N. (eds), *Sexual Orientation at Work: Contemporary Issues and Perspectives*. New York: Routledge.

Rumens, N. and Kerfoot, D. (2009) 'Gay men at work: (Re)constructing the self as professional', *Human Relations*, 62: 763–786.

Seidman, S. (1997) *Difference Troubles: Queering Social Theory and Sexual Politics*. Cambridge: Cambridge University Press.

Simpson, R. (2015) 'Sexual spaces and gendered dynamics: The experiences of male cabin crew' in Colgan, F. and Rumens, N. (eds), *Sexual Orientation at Work: Contemporary Issues and Perspectives*. New York: Routledge.

Skidmore, P. (2004) 'A legal perspective on sexuality and organization: A lesbian and gay case study', *Gender, Work and Organization*, 11(3): 229–253.

Stonewall (2015a) 'Diversity Champions Programme', at http://www.stonewall.org.uk/at_ work/diversity_champions_programme/default.asp (accessed 23 April 2014).

Stonewall (2015b) 'Workplace equality index', at http://www.stonewall.org.uk/get-in volved/workplace/workplace-equality-index (accessed 1 December 2015).

Stonewall (2015c) 'Stonewall workplace conference', at http://www.stonewall.org.uk/employer/stonewall-workplace-conference-attended-record-number-business (accessed 1 December 2015).

Trivette, S. (2010) 'Secret handshakes and decoder rings: The queer space of don't ask don't tell', *Sexuality Research and Social Policy*, 7(3): 214–228.

Van Zyl, M. (2015) 'Working the margins: Belonging and the workplace for LGBTI in post-apartheid South Africa' in Colgan, F. and Rumens, N. (eds), *Sexual Orientation at Work: Contemporary Issues and Perspectives*. New York: Routledge.

Weber, M. (1970) *From Max Weber: Essays in Sociology*, trans. and ed. H. H. Gerth and C. W. Mills. London: Routledge and Kegan Paul.

Wharton, J. (2014) *Out in the Army*. London: Biteback.

Williams, C. L., Giuffre, P. A. and Dellinger, K. (1999) 'Sexuality in the workplace: Organizational control, sexual harassment, and the pursuit of pleasure', *Annual Review of Sociology*, 25: 73–93.

Williams, C. L., Giuffre, P. A. and Dellinger, K. (2009) 'The gay-friendly closet', *Sexuality Research and Social Policy: A Journal of the NSRC*, 6: 29–45.

Willis, P. (2009) 'From exclusion to inclusion: Young queer workers' negotiations of sexually exclusive and inclusive spaces in Australian workplaces', *Journal of Youth Studies*, 12: 629–651.

8

DISABILITY

Introduction

Are you disabled? Yes or no? This is a question you may be asked in the course of applying for a job in the UK. Why? It might be to help ensure the employer can make reasonable adjustments that will help a person with a disability to meet the demands of the job. But what is disability? It seems to indicate a lack, an inability to do certain things, an impairment. However, as Strauss (2013: 461) has pointed out, many psychiatric disorders seem to be an excessive version of some trait that is considered socially desirable – e.g. ADHD is excessive energy, obsession is excessive focus, autism is excessive individualist autonomy and self-reliance. The excess seems to turn something positive into an impairment – or at least it is seen as such. But by whom? Is it seen as such by the person who 'has' it? By a doctor or psychiatrist who diagnoses it? By other people who see the person as atypical and 'impaired'? Or by some combination and interaction between all three?

For those of us who do not identify ourselves as disabled, disability might seem a marginal issue – particularly in the workplace. One to be dealt with in the relatively rare cases we come into contact with someone who we identify as disabled (unless, of course, we work with or for the disabled). However, the issue of disability deserves wider attention and, arguably, enables us to think about how we deal with difference in the workplace that might have relevance beyond the issue of disability as such. The issue of disability forces us to think through many issues that are shared with other identities considered in this book, but in complex ways. The issue of disability, it seems to me, sheds interesting light on organizations and work. It brings into sharp relief, and makes us question, what is assumed to be 'normal'. Moreover, in these neoliberal times, when organizations strive to be 'high-performing' organizations, it may not even be enough to be normal – one must strive for 'excellence', strive towards an abstract, ideal model of an employee that may not exist on this earth.

Approaches to disability

It is common in the literature on disability to distinguish between the social and medical models of disability (e.g. see Barnes and Mercer 2010). The medical model is how many would currently see disability – as something residing in the individual and synonymous with specific physical or mental impairment; to be addressed, if possible, as a medical problem, with drugs, surgery, prosthetics or other medical interventions as the solution. This is echoed in the UK Equality Act (2010) definition: a person has a disability if s/he has a physical or mental impairment which has a substantial and long-term adverse effect on that person's ability to carry out normal day-to-day activities (Equality and Human Rights Commission 2015). This seems to conflate the impairment with the disability. A radically different approach is to define disability as socially created – as the process by which people with impairments are excluded and oppressed. This is the 'social' model of disability. Thus the British organization, the Union of Physically Impaired against Segregation (UPIAS) in 1976 took the view that: 'it is society which disables people. Disability is something imposed on top of our impairments, by the way we are unnecessarily isolated and excluded from full participation in society' (UPIAS 1976: 4). A flavour of this approach is to be found in Oliver's (1990, cited in Barnes et al. 1999: 29) reformulation of questions used by a survey by the Office of Population Censuses and Surveys (OPCS) designed to assess 'disability' in the 1980s:

OPCS: 'Can you tell me what is wrong with you?'
Oliver: 'Can you tell me what is wrong with society?'
OPCS: 'What complaint causes your difficulty in holding, gripping or turning things?'
Oliver: 'What defects in the design of everyday equipment like jars, bottles and tins causes you difficulty in holding, gripping or turning them?'

Thus the medical problem identifies the problem as residing in the individual, the social model sees it residing in society – in how society deals with particular bodily or mental differences. Perhaps, though, these two views need to be integrated (rather than conflated) and, arguably, the definition currently favoured by the World Health Organization (WHO) does this, using the International Classification of Functioning, Disability and Health, whereby disability is: 'an umbrella term for impairments, activity limitations, and participation restrictions, denoting the negative aspects of the interaction between an individual (with a health condition) and that individual's contextual factors (environmental and personal factors)' (WHO 2011: 303). Notice, however, that this definition revolves around a 'health condition'. And even the social model of disability rests on a notion of impairment that seems to be an unproblematic, objective condition residing in the body, even if it is in the brain. Focusing on 'health conditions' raises the issue of medical discourse that distinguishes the 'normal' and 'healthy' from the abnormal, the aberrant. Again, in everyday life we take this kind of thinking for granted but it is a socially constructed process and can be denaturalized and destabilized.

In what follows I hope to illustrate something of the complexity of life for someone 'with' an impairment. If sometimes I appear to equate disability with the impairment, it is because the author I am referring to does so.

The variability of disability and impairment

The wheelchair might serve as a visible sign of impairment, but we do not see the impairment itself, which might be muscular, or neurological. Similarly, we might not recognize that a person is blind if they do not have a white stick, or deaf if we do not see the hearing aid. Indeed, these implements might be as useful for indicating impairment as they are in dealing with the impairment as such. Where the person in a wheelchair encounters situations that the wheelchair does not cope with (for example, a set of stairs) this provides an example of how society might impose mobility constraints on a person with certain impairments. Much effort has gone into making modern buildings wheelchair-'friendly' – but transport and buildings often present challenges and make mobility a problem.

Many forms of impairment are not clearly visible at all. Various forms of mental health conditions or learning difficulties might count as disabilities on a common-sense basis, and certainly count as conditions that are highly medicalized, but they might not be immediately obvious to anyone who does not know the person. And, indeed, the person who 'has' such a condition might not want to reveal them for fear of stigmatization. When and how someone is identified as 'disabled' – and when and how they come to identify themselves as disabled is, then, more complex than might be assumed.

The kinds of adjustment required to deal with particular impairments are highly variable, too. Ramps might aid mobility for a paraplegic, a desk chair of a particular design might help with fatigue for someone with mild arthritis, large print might aid the visually impaired; but adjustments might be subtle, too: for someone with Asperger syndrome it has been suggested that it might be useful to provide clear instructions in writing, rather than orally (see Worton and Binks 2008: 77).

Another way in which 'disability' is highly variable lies in how and when the impairment arises. Some people are born with an impairment, but many impairments are acquired – perhaps through an accident but often through disease. Some are progressive, others relatively stable, while still others fluctuate considerably. As someone with epilepsy put it 'some days you're fine and you could work all day and another day when you get up in the morning you just know you're not going to be able to do anything that day' (Riach and Loretto 2009: 109). Some impairments are mild, some severe; some are treatable or even curable, many are not. Duff and Ferguson (2012: 86), for example, refer to an accountant with Ehlers-Danlos syndrome (EDS) that creates loose, unstable joints and highly flexible fingers and toes. The nature of EDS means that her 'problems can sort of change from one week to the next'. The gradual onset of some conditions also makes the notion of a binary 'disabled/non-disabled' categorization problematic, but it also raises questions about identification and self-identification – when does one become disabled in such circumstances?

The variability of the category raises the question of whether disability is an 'identity'. While people might see themselves as disabled, or others as disabled, often those with particular impairments might be slow to recognize it, or deny it, or cover it up or identify themselves as 'disabled to a certain degree' (Riach and Loretto 2009: 109), suggesting that it is a continuum rather than a binary. Carol Thomas, for example, was born with no left hand but, while eschewing artificial or cosmetic hands, she often hid her condition by putting her left 'hand' in a pocket, for fear of an adverse reaction (Thomas 1999: 54–5). However, she does self-identify as disabled and draws attention to the psychological and emotional costs of such impairments, which might range from mild embarrassment to painful feelings of rejection (1999: 48–55).

This example may suggest that the issue of disability is also strongly associated with stigma and stigmatization (Brown 2013). Goffman (1968), in his classic study of the 'management of spoilt identity', describes stigma as an 'attribute that is deeply discrediting' (13). Goffman makes clear the social, rather than the 'natural' origins of such stigmas. As he puts it: 'We lean on... anticipations that we have, transforming them into normative expectations, into righteously presented demands' (12). The issue raised by impairment is the nature and extent of the stigma attached to it. Stigma always involves a negative evaluation, loaded with affective responses such as dislike, revulsion, disgust and, as Brown (2013) makes clear, fear. Those who champion disability rights and seek to self-identify as disabled have to fight such stigmatization.

Disability and inequality

In the UK those classified as disabled are more likely to be unemployed (Hoque et al. 2014: 431) and only 51 per cent of those with disability were found to be economically active, compared with 85 per cent of those not classified as disabled (ONS 2015). They are also more likely to be found in low-skilled and low-status jobs, suggesting discrimination and channelling into such positions. For example, Riach and Loretto (2009: 113) refer to the account of one disabled person:

> I went to a disability advisor [in the job centre] and they said that now you've got a slight disability as well there's no way you will expect to earn what you used to earn, you're going to have to downgrade. She actually suggested training to go and work as a care assistant... I was so insulted.

While another commented: 'They seem to have a blinkered view that disabled people are just wanting to operate computers for the rest of their days' (2009: 112). According to these authors (112), disabled and older workers are likely to be stereotyped as suited to low-paid, low-skilled jobs, and not considered on the basis of the skills developed during their career.

Brisenden (1989) provides a young disabled person's perspective in an article entitled 'young, gifted and disabled' – a title that consciously echoes the expression 'young, gifted and black'. He argues that, like black people, the disabled often face prejudice – but also low expectations. Employers tend, he argues, to focus on the problems and are full of 'doubts and hesitations' (1989: 219), rather than focusing on the talents and abilities the disabled person might bring. In the light of such perceptions – or in the anticipation of them – it is not surprising to learn that many people with impairments prefer not to disclose them when applying for jobs, although in doing so some recognize that there are risks associated with such a strategy – risks associated with the information being uncovered (Riach and Loretto 2009: 109–10).

Exclusion because of impairment can, of course, happen at any time in one's life and Shier et al. (2009: 70) describe how one person who had an accident gave up work because they felt they had no energy and became depressed. The study illustrates prejudice towards people with an impairment – an ignoring of the human capital the person does possess – as well as the psychological response to the situation that makes continued employment in the role difficult.

Even when the disabled do manage to secure employment, or maintain it in the face of acquired disability, they often face difficulties. Wilson-Kovacs et al. (2008) explore the barriers to career advancement of disabled professionals, based on qualitative in-depth interviews with 14 UK participants in various professional positions (including senior civil servants, managers, medicine, law, education, IT consultancy and university lecturers). They had various types of physical impairment, including congenital, acquired and deteriorating conditions (2008: 708). The barriers they experienced included lack of opportunity to take on challenging roles and responsibilities that might lead to learning. As one of them put it (709): 'You are not necessarily given the cutting edge stuff, you're often given safer pieces of work rather than cutting edge so you're not stretching and therefore because you're not stretching you're not necessarily learning.'

Another study by Duff and Ferguson (2012) refers to accountants with visible disabilities being steered away from client-facing roles. Perhaps here the problem is the manager's or colleague's assumptions about what is appropriate or possible – but these might often, from the disabled person's viewpoint, be wrong. Indeed, this perhaps shows the strength of the 'social' model of disability in that it is the attitudes towards impairment that cause the problem rather than the impairment itself.

BOX 8.1 IN THE NEWS: HIDING DISABILITY

Riam Dean was reported as having been awarded £8,000 by an employment tribunal who found against Abercrombie and Fitch who employed her. Riam Dean has a prosthetic arm which she covered with a cardigan. The company made her work in the stockroom as it felt she did not have the right 'look' for the Saville Row store in central London.

The tribunal found that while Riam Dean was the victim of harassment, she did not suffer disability discrimination. The ruling stated:

'The tribunal is satisfied the reason for the claimant's dismissal was her breach of the look policy in wearing a cardigan. Whilst the tribunal is satisfied the claimant's dismissal was a consequence of her unlawful harassment, it can not be characterised direct disability discrimination.'

Source: BBC, 13 August 2009

Another perceived barrier identified by Wilson-Kovacs et al. (2008) was that of lack of knowledge, time or other resources that would enable the disabled person to achieve more. Sometimes this might be due to the perceived cost or difficulty of providing these adjustments but often it seems to be a lack of imagination or thoughtfulness. They provide an example of someone who had difficulty fitting their disability scooter into a lift. A bigger lift was available but it took six months before someone mentioned it.

Such barriers might require a lot of determination to overcome:

The only way you really get things as an individual is to argue in a reasonable way about what you want, and battle it out until the resources are provided, and in some cases it ends up in court, and if you're lucky you'll manage to have a good compelling argument up front and you eventually get it. It's not diplomatic and it's not quick.

(Wilson-Kovacs et al. 2008: 711)

The solution here seems to hinge on interpretations of what is 'reasonable' – something that might well be open to diverse interpretations.

Another barrier identified in the same study is the lack of organizational and peer support. One example provided was that of a university lecturer who, as his polio-related condition worsened, found more difficulty in mobility as well as in carrying teaching materials and with tiredness. As he said:

The more physical problems you have in mobility, in getting around, in doing things, the more complicated that makes trying to hold down a job. In my instance, initial reactions from my employer were all-or-nothing. This is the job, you can either do it and if you can't do it, then you should retire... But when you talk to people like Access to Work, who actually try and encourage people like myself to stay in work, they have a very different point of view.

(Wilson-Kovacs 2008: 712)

The same person also thought peers were not always supportive: 'There are other colleagues who are not at all helpful, who consider that my capability to do less means more [work] for them, which they don't appreciate... so they don't go out of their way to be helpful' (2008: 713). If such reactions of peers appear harsh, what this account does not provide is the view of the colleagues themselves. One can imagine that they may be sympathetic towards their impaired colleague but feel unable to help due to other pressures. In such cases it might be easier to avoid the colleague than to face them and refuse to help. This example also points to the ways in which even non-manual positions, such as those of a university lecturer, involve embodiment and particular normative expectations of the bodies in motion. When these are not met, problems emerge, leading to difficult adjustments for the individual and those around. To what extent individuals have the ability and time to make these adjustments is highly context-dependent but in high-paced environments, which might include the contemporary university, these might be difficult to make.

Moreover, the problems of impairment might not just be in the performance of the duties associated with the job as in a broader range of associated performances. Naraine and Lindsay (2011) emphasize the barriers to full social inclusion in their study of blind and low-vision employees in Canada. Problems included getting to social events outside the workplace (which sometimes stopped them going) and difficulties at the event location if they were able to attend, including social difficulties such as people not identifying themselves. At large events such as conferences it is obviously difficult for the visually impaired to identify the people they might want to talk to, so networking becomes difficult. Situations such as sharing holiday photos also becomes difficult, as does the ability to read body language. Reliance on others was identified as sometimes rendering social interaction difficult – they were put in dependent mode and often treated charitably but not engaged with as people. However, being dependent could undermine self-esteem. Also, there can be problems with people acting on the basis of assumptions about need, not need itself, while disabled people might understandably be reluctant or unable to articulate their needs in a given situation, for a variety of reasons – they may assume it is obvious or it is the other person's role to find out, or they may find it embarrassing to do so.

Bullying can also be a problem for those with impairments. Foster (2007) gives the account of a primary school teacher who was initially absent from work due to a physical impairment and who was pressured to return to work by the head teacher. She subsequently had more sick leave and experienced depression. The head teacher called a special meeting of school governors and parents and organized a letter of no confidence in the teacher, and when she requested a job share she said:

> [The school] really wanted to make it difficult. They said I could start work immediately because I was fit to return to work. But they couldn't effect the job share until half term so I'd have to go back to work on a full-time basis for at least a month, and boy, did they try to break me in that month. It was a concerted effort by everyone.
>
> (Foster 2007: 74)

She found other teachers had been told not to cooperate with her and she was allocated work that a junior staff member would normally do. Another case of bullying is the Australian flight attendant with multiple sclerosis whom Vickers

(2009) describes as being the subject of victimization and heightened surveillance even in the early stages of the condition when it was not interfering with her performance.

Brisenden (1989) points out that the disabled are often treated not with hostility but with a patronizing attitude, manifesting in kindness and concern and an assumption that the disabled person cannot look after themselves and is in need of special treatment. Even kindness can be seen as oppressive by a disabled person who just wants to be treated the same as others. Basas (2010), for example, describes how, as a law student at Harvard, she found fellow students waiting patiently 50 yards ahead to push the automatic button on a door. She writes that she wished they had just slammed the door in her face as they did for other students (33). She wanted to be treated the same as other students, rather than differently in this respect.

Responses

Basas (2010: 59–60) goes on to describe three forms of self-accommodation for women disabled attorneys in the USA: firstly by acquiring adaptive equipment or making physical space changes themselves, secondly by selecting jobs that were disabled-friendly and flexible (often dealing with disability issues) and thirdly by becoming their own bosses through entrepreneurialism.

An example of the second type of adaptation included a lawyer who opted to work as a government attorney and was given time off for counselling (Basas 2010: 64). She thought private employers probably would not have been so accommodating of her mental health issues, although she thought they might have if she had a condition such as diabetes (suggesting variability in the degree of stigma associated with different conditions). Another example is of a lawyer who avoided courtroom trial work due to her age and hearing issues. Instead she worked in appellate law, doing criminal appeals for the state. This allowed her to write and research in a cubicle or at home, 'then have my fifteen-minute argument with three appellate judges in a quiet courtroom with no interference, no noise, few people. It worked very well with my hearing issues' (Basas 2010: 64).

Becoming one's own boss is another way of adapting to the disability imposed by hostile organizations or forms of work. Another lawyer with impairments that included rheumatoid arthritis set up her own practice so that she could avoid a situation that demanded billing for a high number of hours and a large volume of work: 'I have been lucky that I can manage my own schedule and workload depending on my health at any given time. I created a strong administrative support team' (Basas 2010: 68).

These forms of self-accommodation can be seen as active strategies in which the disabled person seeks to overcome disadvantage imposed by the norms of the profession. Basas also reveals cases where agency takes a more negative form – what she refers to as 'covering' disability. This can take the form of concealment – sometimes selectively from certain people or at certain times, such as when applying for a job – or by ensuring that, if visible it is not seen as interfering with performance. As an example of the latter Basas (2010: 76) quotes one woman as saying:

> My very obvious disability compels me to make an excellent first impression and set just the right note to make those coming in contact with me comfortable. Similarly, I feel that any work must be above standard and promptly completed in order to assuage any uncertainties about my ability to compete with other attorneys. One has to demonstrate that disability is irrelevant to competence and thereby cultivate confidence in clients, employers and coworkers in order to succeed.

Such covering might, of course, be quite difficult to maintain and Basas suggests this might lead to exhaustion, burn-out and frustration (96).

Covering can also be done prior to employment by failing to disclose a disability. Shier et al. (2009: 67) refer to one wheelchair user who said he did not let employers know: ''Cause I find that if I do it might scare them or it might give them a reason to say "don't bother coming in".' Notice here the assumption that this might 'scare them' – the candidate then has to deal with any adverse reaction.

Covering, of course, is not without its risks. Hiding disability might create problems where and when it is revealed or discovered. Or the successful covering of a particular disability by one person might make it difficult for those who come after, who may want to adopt a different strategy. Basas (2010: 62), for example, refers to one woman who had chosen not to make use of accommodations such as speech-recognition software as a law student and who said:

> A few years later [after law school], I met a woman with a learning disability who was attending the same law school. She reported having a much more difficult time with accommodations because the staff kept pointing to the fact that I had not sought X or Y. Not exactly the kind of legacy I should have left those who were sure to follow.

What Basas calls 'covering' might not be a deliberate strategy. Watson (2002), in interviews with 28 disabled people (14 men and 14 women), argued that these people often did not self-identify as disabled. They saw themselves as 'normal' (without denying they had an impairment). Watson also raises the issue of how what I would call self-identity relates to collective identity. He argues that they did not see themselves as part of a collective identity, a 'community' of disabled people. Such positionings might shift over time, and even with context, of course. Vallantine (2008: 150) provides the perspective of someone with Asperger syndrome who describes how initially in his career he tended not to disclose his condition to employers and colleagues. 'I only thought of myself as Stuart'. However, he came to realize that what he saw as normal was far removed from other people's definition: 'I thought nothing of being upset and throwing a tantrum if a pen was moved a foot away, despite engaging in conversation about a recent football match a few minutes earlier' (Vallantine 150). He later came to disclose his condition to the employer and colleagues and says 'I feel that I have succeeded in raising awareness of autism spectrum disorders to my fellow colleagues. This has resulted in greater rapport with and respect from my immediate colleagues' (Vallantine 151).

What can be done?

If the disabled are excluded from employment, or from particular types of more financially or intrinsically rewarding roles, this is a grave disadvantage. For disabled people, as for anyone else, employment can offer financial security and enhanced opportunities for consumption as well as independence, status, social relationships; and a chance to use abilities rather than be defined by disability. Employment might thus be seen as doubly important for many disabled people, as an opportunity to escape from dependence and prove their value to society. There is also the motivation to avoid being *thought* of as dependent and perhaps even as someone who exploits the social security system at the expense of the taxpayer (see Smits 2004, cited in Duff and Ferguson 2012). To what extent is such exclusion justified? To what extent is it enforced on disabled people by unjust or uncaring social arrangements? These seem important questions to consider, not just when the issue arises when a particular person with a particular impairment comes along, but in general. To what extent do we want to create organizations and forms of work that allow for a high degree of human variability in abilities and impairment – and if we do want to design inclusive forms of organization and work, how do we do so?

In the UK, as in many other countries, there have been attempts to prevent unwarranted discrimination against those with impairment in employment and policies to encourage inclusion through making 'reasonable adjustments' (or 'accommodations' in US parlance). The issue of what constitutes reasonable adjustment is potentially contentious and the employer and the disabled person might well make different arguments here. Consider, for example, the epileptic who is fine some days and not others. How many working days of good performance would be acceptable?

Asperger syndrome and other neurological conditions pose particular problems for the negotiation of disability since diagnosis can be delayed and there are also various degrees of the condition, which makes some people question whether it should be seen as an impairment at all, rather than part of natural human variability (Strauss 2013: 467). Moreover, even if the employee does find it possible to adjust to work demands the general social demands associated with the workplace might be another matter. Those with autism spectrum disorders might find everyday socializing and social events after work difficult, for example. An adjustment that might suit one person, such as favouring a quieter bar for social events rather than a busier one, might be unpopular with others. How far adjustments are made and what adjustments are made can be difficult decisions to make. Furthermore, there is often an absence of conversation that might result in a negotiated settlement that

all parties are happy with: it is easy for the person with Aspergers simply to refuse
the offer to go to a bar after work, and it is easy for those offering to ignore the
issues that might arise for the person with Aspergers, deafness or other disorders. It
is also easy for both parties to make assumptions that limit inclusion: the colleague
does not invite Stuart, who is known to 'have' Aspergers, to the bar after work
because he assumes he will not want to go, while Stuart does not express a preference
for a quiet bar because he assumes colleagues like it noisy.

Attempts to encourage organizations to be more inclusive of disability have, in
the UK, included the national 'two ticks' initiative. Many organizations display the
two ticks logo on employment advertisements and company promotional material
along with the slogan 'positive about disability'. The two ticks award is made after
an accreditation process which requires employers to demonstrate adherence to five
commitments (Recruitment and Disabled People 2015):

1.   to interview all disabled applicants who meet the minimum criteria for a job
      vacancy and to consider them on their abilities;
2.   to discuss with disabled employees, at any time but at least once a year, what
      you can both do to make sure they can develop and use their abilities;
3.   to make every effort when employees become disabled to make sure they stay
      in employment;
4.   to take action to ensure that all employees develop the appropriate level of
      disability awareness needed to make these commitments work;
5.   to review these commitments every year and assess what has been achieved,
      plan ways to improve on them and let employees and Jobcentre Plus know
      about progress and future plans.

However, Hoque et al.'s (2014) study suggests that there is little evidence that
employers who achieve the two ticks award are any better at dealing with disability
than those without, and that processes of exclusion such as those identified in this
chapter are still pervasive in such organizations.

This suggests that it is often left to the individual person with an impairment to
negotiate their own position – although they may do so with varying degrees of
success. Using strategies of self-accommodation or covering, such as those Basas
(2010) identifies, those with impairments may find more or less satisfactory or sus-
tainable ways of coping in employment. Of course some employers and managers
can be supportive – but according to Foster (2007: 78) this often means simply
devolving matters of adjustment to the disabled person: 'This could either be
viewed as empowering the employee and acknowledging they are best placed to
know the type of adjustment they require, or as an abdication of responsibility,
however benevolent, on the part of the manager.'

There is also the possibility of collective action by those identified or self-identified
as disabled. Indeed, legislation making discrimination against those with disability
unlawful and that imposes certain duties on employers to support inclusiveness, as
well as initiatives such as the two ticks initiative, can be seen as successes for the

disability rights movement, even if these laws and policies are limited in their effect. Watson (2002) argued that for many of the people with disability he studied, however, identification with a collective 'disabled' identity was limited. Their self-identity was not founded on a recognition of difference. 'The question could also be asked as to who is being the more radical; those who reject disability as an identifier or those who embrace it?' (2002: 522); and Watson argues against those who see disability as the basis of identity politics. However, his own research suggests that it is not 'either/or' – it could be both. A disability rights movement can be discerned in the UK, as well as elsewhere, and if membership of the movement might, in individual cases, be disputed this is typical of social movements generally. Activists come and go, and activism takes many forms, not all very visible. Watson (2002: 522) recounts the views of Stella:

> If I am, if anyone is, denied access because of bad planning, bad design, through no fault of your own, inevitably you come away with – well, I come away with two things: I come away with a disappointment and a view of myself in one dimension as being lesser – in other words I have lesser access to certain things and therefore I must be a lesser person mustn't I? But the other thing that does for me because of the relationships I have, is to actually stimulate and challenge and say 'Let's change this'… But what I would then do with that fact is to share it with other disabled people and do something about it.

This willingness to join with others to 'do something about it' I see as a defining feature of social movement activity and it does suggest identification with others who share particular characteristics. In so far as we can discern a disability movement as a social movement it is a remarkable thing, as it is based on solidarity working across so many differences – differences in the type and severity of impairment as well as differences of age, gender, class, ethnicity and so on. It has its academic arm in disability studies (e.g. see Davis 2013) and its visible manifestation in organizations such as Disability Rights UK and demonstrations against changes in government policies that adversely affect those with impairments (e.g. BBC 2012). However, as with any social movement, its politics also take subtle, subterranean forms, in the micro politics of resistance in organizations and civil society (Melucci 1988). Perhaps in this the disability rights movement might be seen as an example of a progressive form of politics that is based on difference but also transcends differences. Perhaps, too, as Basas (2010) suggests, out of the networking of those fighting for the rights and inclusion of those with impairment there is:

> the potential for coalition-building. The more disabled attorneys are perceived by their classmates, colleagues, and supervisors as members of a cultural minority group, the better chances they have at connecting with other groups experiencing stigma and discrimination… These kinds of ideological and activist bridges are untapped resources for changing workplaces for all groups involved.
>
> (Basas 2010: 108)

Conclusion

Disability raises important issues of what is 'normal', what is valued, what is seen as an 'impairment' and what are 'reasonable' adjustments in work and organizational life that facilitate inclusion and positive regard. It also raises profound questions of how we deal with difference; of when we are silent and the same, of when we are loud and proud to be different; of how we interact across differences. Most disability studies deal with disability from the point of view of those with an impairment. Viewed from the point of view of those identifying themselves as disabled the story is largely one of exclusion, or of difficult accommodations. Even where legislation supports inclusion and legislates against discrimination, and even where employers have formal policies or practices meant to provide 'equality', there is evidence to suggest little knowledge and understanding of these in practice. If the disability movement has made some gains, there is still much to be done, but there is a need to act at many different levels. At the individual level there is much that those with impairment can do, but there is also, through empathy and conversation, much that what Goffman (1968), I think ironically, calls 'us normals' can do. This would involve individual and collective action producing solidarity across differences and designed to make organizations and work more tolerant, inclusive places. I think we need to act with optimism but also be conscious that, in such actions, we are swimming against the tide of conformity to norms that seek ever higher levels of performance, with less and less time for conversation and caring.

BOX 8.2 AT THE MOVIES: DISABILITY

Some movies relevant to the themes of the chapter are:

Rear Window (1954, director Alfred Hitchcock)
Still Alice (2014, directors Richard Glatzer and Wash Westmoreland)
The Theory of Everything (2014, director James Marsh)

References

Barnes, C. and Mercer, G. (2010) *Exploring Disability*, 2nd edition. Cambridge: Polity Press.

Barnes, C., Mercer, G. and Shakespeare, T. (eds) (1999) *Exploring Disability: A Sociological Introduction*. Oxford: Polity Press.

Basas, C. G. (2010) 'The new boys: Women with disabilities and the legal profession', *Berkeley Journal of Gender, Law and Justice*, 25(1): 32–124.

BBC (2009) 'Woman wins clothes store tribunal', at http://news.bbc.co.uk/1/hi/8200140.stm (accessed 12 December 2015).

BBC (2012) 'Disability protests', at http://www.bbc.co.uk/news/uk-england-london-19437785 (accessed 15 November 2015).

Brisenden, S. (1989) 'Young, gifted and disabled: Entering the employment market', *Disability, Handicap and Society*, 4(3): 217–220.

Brown, L. C. (2013) 'Stigma: An enigma demystified' in L. J. Davis (ed.), *The Disability Studies Reader*. London: Routledge.

Davis, L. (ed.) (2013) *The Disability Studies Reader*, 4th edition. London: Routledge.

Duff, A. and Ferguson, J. (2012) 'Disability and the professional accountant: Insights from oral histories', *Accounting, Auditing and Accountability Journal*, 25(1): 71–101.

Equality and Human Rights Commission (2015) 'Glossary of terms', at http://www.equa lityhumanrights.com/private-and-public-sector-guidance/guidance-all/glossary-terms#d (accessed 1 December 2015).

Foster, D. (2007) 'Legal obligation or personal lottery? Employee experiences of disability and the negotiation of adjustments in the public sector workplace', *Work, Employment and Society*, 21(1): 67–84.

Goffman, E. (1968) *Stigma: Notes on the Management of Spoiled Identity*. Harmondsworth: Penguin.

Hoque, K., Bacon, N. and Parr, D. (2014) 'Employer disability practice in Britain: Assessing the impact of the Positive About Disabled People "Two Ticks" symbol', *Work, Employment and Society*, 28(3): 430–451.

Melucci, A. (1988) *Nomads of the Present: Social Movements and Individual Needs in Contemporary Society*. London: Raduis.

Naraine, M. D. and Lindsay, P. H. (2011) 'Social inclusion of employees who are blind or low vision', *Disability and Society*, 26(4): 389–403.

ONS (Office of National Statistics) (2015) 'Labour market status of disabled people', 11 November, at http://www.ons.gov.uk/ons/search/index.html?newquery=Disability+ unemployment (accessed 12 December 2015).

Recruitment and Disabled People (2015) https://www.gov.uk/recruitment-disabled-peop le/encouraging-applications (accessed 1 December 2015).

Riach, K. and Loretto, W. (2009) 'Identity work and the "unemployed" worker: Age, dis ability and the lived experience of the older unemployed', *Work, Employment and Society*, 23(1): 102–119.

Shier, M., Graham, J. R. and Jones, M. E. (2009) 'Barriers to employment as experienced by disabled people: A qualitative analysis in Calgary and Regina, Canada', *Disability and Society*, 24(1): 63–75.

Smits, S. J. (2004), 'Disability and employment in the USA: The quest for best practices', *Disability and Society*, 19(6): 647–662.

Strauss, J. (2013) 'Autism as culture' in Davis, L. J. (ed.), *The Disability Studies Reader*. London: Routledge.

Thomas, C. (1999) *Female Forms: Experiencing and Understanding Disability*. Buckingham: Open University Press.

UPIAS (1976) *The Union of the Physically Impaired against Segregation and the Disability Alliance Discuss Fundamental Principles of Disability: Being a Summary of the Discussion Held on 22nd November, 1975 and Containing Commentaries from Each Organisation*. London: UPIAS.

Vallantine, S. (2008) 'Surviving the workplace: Asperger syndrome at work' in Edmonds, G. and Beardon, L. (eds), *Asperger Syndrome and Employment: Adults Speak out about Asperger Syndrome*. London: Jessica Kingsley.

Vickers, M. H. (2009) 'Bullying, disability and work: A case study of workplace bullying', *Qualitative Research in Organizations and Management*, 4(3): 255–272.

Watson, N. (2002) '"Well, I know this is going to sound very strange to you, but I don't see myself as a disabled person: Identity and disability"', *Disability and Society*, 17(5): 509–527.

WHO (2011) *World Report on Disability*. Geneva: World Health Organization.

Wilson-Kovacs, D., Ryan, M. K., Haslam, S. A. and Rabinovich, A. (2008) '"Just because you can get a wheelchair in the building doesn't necessarily mean that you can still participate": Barriers to the career advancement of disabled professionals', *Disability and Society*, 23(7): 705–717.

Worton, D. and Binks, P. (2008) 'Case study by an employee with Asperger syndrome and his line manager' in Edmonds, G. and Beardon, L. (eds), *Asperger Syndrome and Employment: Adults Speak Out about Asperger Syndrome*. London: Jessica Kingsley.

9

AGE

Introduction

How old are you? Does it matter at work?

Self-identity is intimately related to age and ageing. We often use date of birth as part of our personal identification and we track the progress of our lives chronologically: we 'have' a certain age. At any one time we might also identify ourselves as young, old or middle-aged. Of course we might also disidentify ourselves in relation to certain ages – 'I'm not old' – with various degrees of vehemence. Who we are is also closely bound up with our life course and the experience it gives us. Ricœur (1992) refers to narrative identity – we can all tell a story of our lives and, to a large extent, this story is who we conceive ourselves to be. And yet this person is also someone who is changing over time. Even more than the other identities considered here, such as 'race', ethnicity and gender, age represents a shifting identity, requiring renegotiation and shifting identifications with others.

As Bodily (1994) has argued, we use the concept of age in one of three directions: inward toward ourselves, outward towards those older than ourselves or outward towards those younger than ourselves. To this I would add a fourth orientation – outward towards those of a similar age. This latter type might well form the basis of identification *with* these others. In this chapter the issue of age and ageing is explored, dealing first with the issue of inequality. This is followed by a consideration of generations and then of the life course.

Inequality and age

As with other social identities considered in this book, age can be associated with inequality but it is also one of the protected characteristics in the UK Equality Act (2010) which seeks to address the problem of discrimination on the grounds of age.

Ageism might be seen as based on negative stereotypes although, as Bodily (1994) points out, ageism might involve positive as well as negative assumptions. For Bodily, ageism is associated with the assumption that 'time itself has causal force' (187). That is, we see it as somehow natural to associate certain attributes with age. We might explain reckless behaviour as caused by youthfulness or forgetful behaviour caused by old age.

Clearly there are similarities between ageism and racism or sexism in that they can all be associated with negative stereotyping (although see Bytheway and Johnson 1990 for further discussion). One key difference between ageism and racism, or sexism, however, is that people rarely change race or sex but we all age. At any stage we might feel we are positioned at the 'wrong' age – being either too old or too young. And at any age we might be at a relative disadvantage or advantage compared to those of other ages – either in material rewards or in power and status. Relative advantage or disadvantage is not distributed randomly, however – it is rooted in occupational and cultural norms and in particular organizational and historical conjunctures.

If we take participation in the labour market as a sign of social inclusion and enhanced opportunities for consumption, then those over 50 or so would seem to be a disadvantaged group in the UK today. The proportion of those in the UK's 35–49 age group who were economically active in 2014 was 86 per cent, while for the 50–64 age group it was only 72 per cent (Office of National Statistics 2015). The older worker is often the one chosen for, or opting for, redundancy or early retirement (McGoldrick and Cooper 1988), or, if unemployed, looked over for recruitment (Sargeant 2011). This is complicated by the question of how far the older worker chooses to exit the labour market or is forced to do so. McGoldrick and Cooper's (1988) study of early retirement in Britain in the 1980s, as well as Clarke's (2005) more recent study of 'voluntary' redundancy among white-collar Australian workers aged between 30 and 54, both show how so-called voluntary redundancy is something many experience as a choice made under conditions of constraint. As one person rather graphically put it: 'I guess I don't want to say it was entirely voluntary, but it was all a matter of timing. If you are driving along in a train that is going to go over a cliff is it voluntary that you jump out of the train? (Kevin)' (Clarke 2005: 247). Clearly for some, redundancy or early retirement might be an attractive option – an escape from stress or drudgery. However, exclusion from economic activity often brings a deterioration in financial well-being as well as greater isolation (Vincent 1995), so there is likely to be a range of experiences among the retired and economically inactive, including the highly positive or highly negative (see also Chapter 2 and Feldman and Turnley 1995; Fineman 2011; Künemund and Kolland 2007; McGoldrick and Cooper 1988; Parker 1982; Riach and Loretto 2009; Schuller 1989).

Of course there are cultural differences in how different ages are viewed. In the West a high value is placed on youthful appearance and energy. In other cultures there may be more value placed on elders who have more experience, or who control valued resources such as land or other property (see Bond et al. 2007).

Vincent (1995: 35–8), for example, provides the example of the Tiwi aboriginal society in which elderly men have the most power and status. They control marriage in their favour – taking younger women as wives and preventing younger men from doing so in a variety of ways. There is of course no intrinsic reason why the old should be viewed as inferior and the experience of ageing is, culturally, highly diverse (see Bond et al. 2007; Lamb 2014; Vincent 1995). It is our interpretation of particular ages that matters. Moreover, the way we portray particular ages can be complex and multifaceted. The young can be seen as enthusiastic and energetic – or reckless and troublesome. Similarly, there can be both negative and positive attributes associated with the older person (Hummert 2011). Also, who is categorized as 'old' or 'young' can vary with occupation. As Riach (2011: 56) has pointed out, an IT professional might be considered old at 30 while among surgeons someone in their 40s might be seen as 'junior'.

If old age is often viewed negatively in contemporary Western society it may be because it is associated with decline and impairment. To be young, or appear young, is to be desired, to be old is to be past it (Pompper 2011, but see also Featherstone and Hepworth 1989; Fineman 2011). If we have to get old we want to look young and feel young. Cosmetic surgery and products such as hair dyes are all part of the repertoire to hold back the tide of ageing for those past their 'prime'. This suggests a masking of ageing, making it invisible or disguising it. As Lamb (2014) has put it, successful ageing in the North American context (and, we might add, the European context) is not really ageing at all in late life, but rather maintaining the self of one's earlier years. This might be seen as a process of identification with 'youth' and disidentification with old age.

Paul and Townsend (1993), in the American context, argued against what they see as the myths associated with the older worker, including the myths of declining performance, increasing absenteeism due to ill health and difficulties with or reluctance to train and learn new things. They present arguments and evidence against each myth. Such arguments seem particularly important in the context of an ageing society and the limits of employment seem to be a key public policy issue and, not surprisingly, the subject of much research and debate (e.g. see Birren 2006; Field et al. 2013; Hedge and Borman 2012). The consensus among researchers in the field seems to be that popular attitudes are often out of kilter with the capabilities of older workers in an age when life expectancy is rising and the health of people in their 60s and 70s is improving. In such an era the arguments for longer 'working' lives seem powerful (see Wise 2010). Such work can be used to promote disidentification – seeking to remove the negative connotations and stereotypes associated with ageing. However, it may also be seen as a strategy of minimizing differences – a form of emulation in which the older worker says 'really I am just like you – young at heart'. And yet ageist attitudes persist or, and this may be equally significant, are assumed to exist by older workers, making them anxious or motivated to disguise their age. This might be interpreted as a sign of intergenerational competition, as an older generation feels under threat from a younger generation – and it is to the consideration of generations that we now turn.

The generations

The idea of a 'generation' is an important one. We commonly think of life as a succession of generations as we succeed our parents and our children and grandchildren come after us. If age is also to be seen as a collective identity, it is often because we see ourselves as similar to others of 'our' age or generation.

A commonly used categorization of the generations, as they relate to the workplace, distinguishes between the 'traditional' generation (sometimes called the silent generation) and the baby boomers, followed by generation X, Y and Z (e.g. see Egri and Ralston 2004). As Smola and Sutton (2002) point out, however, there is no agreement on the dates for defining these generations with the 'baby boomer' generation variously described as starting in 1940 to 1946 and ending in 1960 to 1964, generation X coming after from the late 1960s to the late 1970s or early 1980s, and with the 'millenials' or generation Z following them from the 1980s through to the early 2000s.

There are obvious problems in defining where one such 'generation' begins and ends, and any division must be somewhat arbitrary. But however you divide them, one common assumption is that these generations have different values and attitudes to work and that this can cause misunderstanding and conflict (e.g. see Flynn 1996 and Schullery 2013). This may be a plausible hypothesis, given the likelihood of different experiences of the different generations, but what experience matters is open to question. Is it significant, for example, whether one watched Happy Days as a child or Teletubbies, to give references to TV shows mentioned by Smola and Sutton (2002) in their discussion of generational differences? However, they also mention economic changes such as differential rates of unemployment – might these be more significant? Might this result in the work ethic of later generations being less than previous generations, for example?

Egri and Ralston (2004: 213) characterize the successive generations in the US as follows:

> Silent generation members are viewed as hard-working, dependable, and supportive of conservative values that emphasize the importance of loyalty, duty, conformity, and security... Baby Boomers have been described as very individualistic, competitive free agents with high interest in self-fulfillment through personal growth... They have demonstrated a strong work ethic and high job involvement, which has led to economic security and career success, although often at the expense of their personal lives... Generation Xers learned to be highly individualistic, financially self-reliant, and entrepreneurial risk takers... [and] place less importance on job security and status, but more on personal freedom and challenging work, which allows for a balanced work-personal life style... While supportive of social liberalism and environmentalism, they hold more conservative political and family values than Baby Boomers.

The methodological challenges of comparing generations are numerous (e.g. see Parry 2014) and most relevant studies are cross-sectional; they compare generations at one point in time which may skate over changes within a generation over time. Moreover, studies seem inconsistent in their portrayal of intergenerational differences and often seem to find relatively little difference at all (e.g. see Cennamo and Gardner 2008) – they certainly do not suggest that they are the basis for major intergenerational conflict and it is probably best not to exaggerate the differences between generations or to hold stereotypical views of them. A major problem with existing studies of generational difference is a tendency to generalize about an entire generation, regardless of class, gender, ethnicity and occupation. This makes the capacity for differences within a generation enormous and renders generalizations about them at best oversimplified. Moreover, any differences between generations that do exist at any one time might be based on their position in the life course. It seems likely, for example, that younger people will be preoccupied with building their careers while older workers might be preoccupied with the transition out of employment. Any differences between generations regarding the 'work ethic' might, then, be connected to their position in the life course at the point of comparison, rather than some long-lasting difference in values. We thus need to attend to the changes occurring as each generation ages, while remaining alert to the possibility that the experience of people of a given class, ethnicity and gender, etc. in each generation, as they age, may not be identical. If we might identify with people of 'our' generation this might be largely because we share a similar place in the life course and the concept of life course might be a more fruitful way of discussing age-related identifications.

The life course

A feature of ageing is that although it is a continuous process we often experience it as a sequence of more or less dramatic shifts in status. Representations of the life course as a series of stages abound. Shakespeare (in *As You Like It*, act II, scene 7) portrayed the seven ages of man starting from the 'mewling and puking' infant to the final stage 'sans teeth, sans eyes, sans taste, sans everything'. This and other similar portrayals of the life course suggest a pattern of ascent followed by decline. We expect physical and intellectual prowess to increase over time as the person develops into their 'mature' years, but we also expect these powers to decline with old age – although the point at which decline starts might be delayed. In the workplace, getting older is associated with a career and often this is expected to be a story of progression to higher levels of pay and responsibility, with any decline associated with retirement and exit.

Featherstone and Hepworth (1989) make a number of useful points about the life course. First they emphasize the complexity and flexibility of the life course in contemporary society – rather than fixed 'stages' of life, implied by the life-cycle concept, they use the life course to 'suggest more flexible biographical patterns within a continually changing social system' (Featherstone and Hepworth 1989: 154). Secondly, while recognizing and drawing attention to cultural factors in the meaning of age and ageing (and changes in its meaning), they point to the need not to neglect the 'unavoidable biological aspects of existence' (Featherstone and

Hepworth 1989: 147). Thirdly, they suggest a need to consider the degree of control (cognitive, emotional and bodily) as variables that might change over the course of one's life, as well as reciprocity – meaning the extent to which the individual is engaged in reciprocal exchanges with the community, rather than dependence. Finally, they argue for a view of old age to be understood in relational terms; that is in relation to:

> a) a discussion of the grounds for accounting for other stages of life, b) a discussion of the previous life of the old people which acts as a background and context for their expectations and experience of old age; and c) the relation of old people to the other generations following behind who may have their own cultural priorities which point towards either a 'caring' or a 'stigmatising' attitude towards the old.
>
> (Featherstone and Hepworth 1989: 155)

The life-course idea is similar to the idea of a career. Super (1957) established an influential developmental theory of careers in which he distinguished five stages: growth, exploration, establishment, maintenance and disengagement. Attending to the life course draws attention to the importance of experience over the course of one's life, but it need not play into an individualized conception of the person at work. In one's life one's choices, including career and employment choices, are not entirely individual but made under certain social, economic and historical conditions. At a macro level these include gendered social norms and social policies – towards 'normal' retirement age, for example – as well as economic conditions that offer varying levels of opportunity for economic activity. And at a micro level they include negotiation at a household level with partners as well as being subject to the influence of friends, teachers and acquaintances (see Loretto et al. 2013).

In general terms probably most people in the West would expect to enter employment in their late teens or early 20s and to retire sometime in their 60s or 70s (the exact endpoint expected to increase over time). Indeed, it has been argued that the life course in modern societies is more tightly scheduled than in many traditional societies. In particular, there is a fairly rigid division of the life course into the stages of pre-work, work and post-work or retirement (Kohli 1990, 1991, cited in Vincent 1995: 57). However, there is also evidence that the life course is becoming less predictable. Using data from a nationally representative sample of high school graduation cohorts of 1960 and 1980, Buchmann (1989), in the USA, found greater variety in the timing and sequencing of educational, occupational and family transitions in the early adult lives of the 1980 cohort. This unpredictability also affects retirement from employment or self-employment that renders the individual 'economically active'. We may expect to work for 40 years but ill health or redundancy may cut short our working life. Equally, changes in pension or retirement policies may require people to extend their working life beyond that which was expected. Writing in 1989, Schuller refers to the degree of ambiguity in later life as people move rather unpredictably between work and retirement and where the transition can be less than clear cut. Today things seem even more ambiguous as people often work beyond retirement age, or beyond the point at which they qualify for pensions. We now have both early and late retirement (Sargent et al. 2013).

The phenomenon of mass retirement on the grounds of age is, in historical terms, a relatively recent one and associated with the development of pensions in the early 20th century (although the British civil service introduced a 'superannuation' fund in 1810 – see Parker 1982). For much of the 20th century retirement ages were reducing – sometimes with an explicit aim of tackling unemployment. Retirement policies and pension arrangements at that time created what Wise (2010) portrayed as incentives to retire early. Organizational restructuring in times of recession or business downturn, or through mergers and acquisitions, often prompted rounds of redundancy, voluntary or otherwise, that often meant older workers left employment. McGoldrick and Cooper's (1988) study of early retirement in late-1980s Britain revealed a range of responses. As one man put it: 'It was a real mental shock, after being employed for 48 years to become suddenly unemployed at the age of 62. It has left a void, a feeling of now being "unwanted", a "bit of a nuisance", "on the scrap-heap" or just a "pensioner"' (1988: 52). Another man: 'I didn't tell her [his wife] for days. I couldn't bring myself to it, and I could tell she knew there was something wrong. When I did, it was the worst moment of my life' (53). This reaction might suggest a commitment to the male breadwinner model – the man felt shame and emasculation as his 'proper' role in the relationship was disrupted. However, loss of status associated with 'retirement' is not felt only by men. A few years earlier Parker (1982) refers to one woman commenting that: 'They assume you are deaf, dull witted, and so on, not because you're 60 but because you are retired. It seems like they treat older people in a childlike way' (49). Retirement, it would seem, is linked to ageism.

However, retirement could and can also be viewed in a positive light. McGoldrick and Cooper (1988: 55) also reported a man saying: 'I was glad to be on the list [for redundancy]… The company had been running down for ages and it was a relief to be finishing. Besides, there was a severance payment, and if I could get a part-time job it would give me more time for my hobbies.' Another mentioned redundancy offering more time with his wife and grandchildren. If this illustrates the attractions of life beyond employment others emphasized the 'push' factors coming from dissatisfaction with the job itself: 'After 39 years the job was not as interesting as when I started and the department seemed very different. Although the changes took place rather slowly, they got to the stage where I was bored with the job' (1988: 87). The play of push and pull factors can also provoke ambivalence. Another man in McGoldrick and Cooper's study who volunteered for redundancy also expressed some ambivalence: 'Actually, I didn't object since I had further plans, but it does get you down to be singled out by being over 50' (58).

Policies and arguments that promote early retirement are now being challenged: partly in the face of what is seen as a fiscally unsustainable policy of supporting dependency for a rising number and proportion of older people (Wise 2010).

Mortality rates have improved dramatically in the West in recent decades, so that in the UK, for example, in 2007 people aged 72 had the same mortality rate of those aged 65 in 1960 (2010: 133). Given these changes it might seem reasonable to expect people to work longer and clearly there are some who would like to do so, but for others the retirement years are the golden years. We might, for example, remember a case described by Parker (1982) of Norman, a retired senior manager. He became dissatisfied with hassles of his job and took early retirement. He recognized a loss of status – 'Nobody is interested in a retired person's view' (45), but he liked retirement. He played golf, worked on the computer (programming) and travelled with his wife: 'After a very satisfactory career, I reached a point where work was becoming a burden. So I side-stepped the situation and retired… The basis of life changes, and in my case it has definitely changed for the better' (46).

Of course, this is a person for whom there did not seem to be financial worries – presumably his pension was sufficient to pay for the golf club fees and travel, as well as day-to-day living expenses. It is not so easy for some, for whom continued paid employment in some capacity might be desirable on financial grounds. For many, retirement is associated with low income and isolation (Vincent 1995). The distribution of 'winners' and 'losers' in the retirement game is not, of course, random, but is affected by occupation, class, gender, ethnicity and disability (see Victor 1989 and Cameron et al. 1989).

Of course the idea of a career is often associated with an upward trajectory. Thus for Pahl and Pahl (1971), in their study of managers and their wives in England in the 1960s, the career was seen as moving up: 'life is a hierarchy and success means moving up in it. Marking time and staying in the same position is interpreted as dropping out' (259). While such views might still be found today they are con-tingent on the prospects for advancement. In the harsher corporate and economic climate of the early 1990s, Goffee (1992), based on a study of managers in six large British organizations, argued that organizational restructuring led to a reconsidera-tion of job aspirations. For some the changes seemed to cause great disappointment and frustration but for others, particularly, they suggest, male managers, this led to a psychological withdrawal from the career – or at least a reprioritization:

> I suppose in some ways I've opted out of the rat race. I must admit my work enables me to live and to provide a proper education and upbringing for the children. It's certainly not one hundred percent work… I don't shut home life out at all. I mean… you get to a stage in your career when you think you've gone far enough and you've achieved enough – and it's not promotion at all costs. Some people have the drive to go right to the very top and others don't. I'm one of those who don't and I'm quite happy with what I've achieved. It gives us a reasonable standard of living, able to provide the children with more than enough. I'm quite happy (Male, early 40s, Engineering and Maintenance).

> *(Goffee 1992: 363)*

Of course, retirement might not necessarily spell the end of one's working life or career. Elite athletes 'retire' early – typically by the age of 20 for gymnasts (Kerr and Dacyshyn 2000). Given the investment of time and effort in these activities it would be surprising if 'retirement' did not present problems of readjustment and difficulties of making a transition to other activities. However, the literature also seems to show plenty of cases of successful transitioning and the development of new working lives, often in fields far removed from the athlete's former sport (Coakley 1983). This suggests that we might think of retirement not as a permanent cessation of 'work' but simply a change of working status – with full-time employment, part-time employment, self-employment or unpaid work all being part of a restructuring of our self-identity over time.

The new thinking on careers (Arthur et al. 1999; Hall 2001) suggests that they are much more fluid and unpredictable than the mid-20th-century models that Super and others suggested. Arthur et al. (1999) suggest that careers are becoming 'boundaryless' in that they transcend the boundaries of one organization and exhibit either physical or psychological mobility – or both. Others suggest a similar idea of a 'protean' career that it involves a self-directed and/or values-driven career and in which personal agency (rather than corporate career planning) is at the core (see Briscoe and Hall 2006 for a comparison and clarification of concepts). Similarly, in a discussion of careers that raises the issue of gender differences in career patterns (with women tending to have less 'linear' careers than men), Mainiero and Sullivan (2005) suggest the idea of 'kaleidoscopic' careers for women in which the career is not a simple movement upwards, as this woman's experience illustrates:

> I left college for a great career opportunity at a local phone company. I worked as a marketing manager for a while, starting off as a staff assistant and moving up to the manager's spot. I loved my work and did it well. But over time I realized there was no way I was going to be president of that company and started to think about other options. My husband had taken a job up in Hartford, CT, and I was pregnant – finally. I struggled getting pregnant and did not want to take any chances with this baby. So I left the dream job and stayed home while raising my three children, at least while they were young. I figured I would go back to work after the first one, and I did, part-time for a while, but that didn't work out. Then I returned to work, helping my husband in his consulting practice for a while. I even took client assignments. But we got on each other's nerves and the work wasn't fulfilling enough. I needed a job where I could be home for the bus in the afternoon and still have a challenge. I found employment in my town as a Museum Curator – who would have thought. The job is not challenging but I can be close to home and available to my children. I am thinking of starting my own antique shop in town, because I love antiques, and that would be more fulfilling for me.

(Mainiero and Sullivan 2005: 109)

Such kaleidoscopic careers and rebalancing of priorities over time is not something specific to women, of course. Bown-Wilson (2011) suggests that late careers often involve a rebalancing of priorities and refers to Sturges (1999), who argued the emphasis might shift from material criteria for success to those of influence and autonomy.

In considering careers and the life course of the worker, then, we might not necessarily expect an easy pattern of a steady rise until they fall off the 'cliff' of retirement, and not even a smooth curve of ascent and decline, but a rather more variegated and unpredictable pattern.

However, through every stage in one's life course the possibility of marginalization on the grounds of age might be commonplace, in ways that are often too subtle for anti-discrimination legislation to pick up. Consider, for example, Angouri's (2012) sociolinguistic study in which she presents the case of a young woman in a small business. Sometimes she was reluctant to speak, marginalized or treated in a condescending way – something she interpreted as arising because of her perceived youthfulness and inexperience. 'We talk "work" I say something and he will say "yes the child is right and we are wrong"'. She does not like such responses: she feels that colleagues and customers treat her with less credibility; she feels that their identification of her is unreasonable. She is often silenced by it, made to feel uncomfortable or undervalued by it (see also Archer 2008). But while ageing might be sufficient to resolve such problems for younger workers (if they can stay around long enough), becoming older can bring other challenges as well as solutions to problems.

At the other end of the age spectrum in the workplace, Pompper (2011: 476), for example, refers to a senior feature writer for a daily newspaper consciously avoiding talking about her grandchildren at work for fear of being stigmatized. The fact that this was an African American woman in the US may also be relevant: she may not have wanted age to be added to other aspects of her identity that might lead to disadvantage, but perhaps age was the one that might, at least at this point, have been most easily masked. The women in Pompper's study also reported a variety of conditions including 'loss of energy and mobility, achy joints, loss of vision, and sometimes dizziness' (2011: 478). These point to the prevalence of bodily changes associated with ageing that might well provide some basis for negative stereotyping, but what is striking is that these were often masked by those concerned. Consider, too, this quotation from a performance artist:

> I am entering a new stage in my life. My age is catching up to me. I feel some pressure from my environment to adapt to middle-aged conformations. Not from my friends, who are in the same boat as me but... from general society. I'm considerably heavier than I was ten years ago. I'm trying to analyse my feelings about all this and come up with some kind of resolution but it's quite hard.
>
> (Holland 2004: 120)

This illustrates how we might feel about ageing. We feel age 'catching up' to us, unsettling us. If once we were too young now we are too old to be doing what we did before, or in the way we did it. We have to adjust to others' expectations of us. But it can be hard to adjust. Becoming older can also bring marginalization, just as being young can. In their study of two 'olderpreneurs' (older entrepreneurs) Mallett and Wapshott (2015) describe how one of their entrepreneurs, Thomas, felt he was marginalized as a man in his 50s:

> On one occasion Thomas talked in subdued terms about his experience at his last employer where he felt marginalised and was, as he saw it, 'set up to fail'. He felt ostracised from his employer due to his relatively advanced age within the firm and had the impression that 'the world no longer sees me as the 40-year-old who is going places [b]ut as the 50-something-year-old who is making up the numbers'. Thomas elaborated... again a touch of the age thing. There was a couple of occasions, particularly from younger women, before I had even opened my mouth an assumption that they knew what I was going to say and that I was kind of old school. You know 'would you like to make the coffee little girl' kind of stuff and that is so far from where I have led most of my career.
>
> (Mallett and Wapshott 2015: 9–10)

His reaction was to set up his own business, seemingly his 'last chance of really pulling it all together and doing something significant' (10). As one ages, one can become more conscious of one's mortality, but at any age one might also be mindful of the financial needs of one's self and family. The authors described the views of the other olderpreneur, Edward, as follows:

> The risks associated with outright business failure were persistent concerns. Nearing his planned retirement, Edward deliberately avoided exposure to financial liabilities that could not be easily covered if the business had to close while, at the same time, admonishing himself for electing to run a small business profitably rather than pursuing significant growth.
>
> (Mallett and Wapshott 2015: 12)

These cases point to exit as associated with the experience of ageing – exit from particular work situations, or exit from economic activity itself. They also illustrate that age can present identity troubles at both a young, old and middle age.

Gender and ageing

Gender, of course, may be a significant factor in the experience and attitudes towards ageing. Sontag (1972) argued that there was a double standard in American society in which the qualities most highly valued in men – competence, autonomy and earnings potential – increase over the middle decades of life while those most highly valued in women – physical attractiveness and sexual availability to men – decline with age. Bernard et al. also argue that there is a glass ceiling of age for women. As one manager put it: 'women hit their peak younger than men' and 'women get where they are going by the age of 35' (Bernard et al. 1995: 61). However, as Bernard et al. also argue, women are often never at the right age, being considered either too young and inexperienced or too old and past it. This might be contrasted with the idea of the flexible female. Ainsworth (2002) examined documents relating to an Australian public enquiry on the problems of the older (over-45) worker seeking employment, and found that in the final report the older woman had disappeared. The paper deals with the construction of the 'flexible female', who does not appear in the report as they are seen to be 'advantaged' in the labour market on account of flexibility.

BOX 9.1 IN THE NEWS: GENDERED AGEISM AT THE BBC?

Olenka Frenkiel, a journalist at the BBC for many years, claimed that she was forced out by ageism. She wrote: most of my contemporaries – women reporters of my generation – had gone by the time I reached my mid-50s a few years ago. In Current Affairs, I was the last one standing – and yes, in the end I did want to go but only because they had made it so unpleasant. I'm not speaking of 'presenters', often hired for their good looks and on-screen charm. I'm talking about reporters, who appear on screen in the course of their journalism. I'd had 30 great years. But now, while I could see the guys of my age thriving, the women were gone. And I too, I realized, was being rubbed out. No more films were being commissioned from me. It was a struggle to get any assignments. HR had no record of me and my managers had omitted to appraise me for three years. My salary was still paid but apart from that, I was treated as though I wasn't there. For a while I fought back – hawked myself around other departments and persuaded them to commission the stories my own had rejected. These won some more awards and bought me another few years. But it was unpleasant. This is how it's done. Not just to me but routinely when they decide it's time for you to go. They starve you of work – then point out your low productivity and the fights you've had to get your reports on air. Now you're not just unproductive, you're also difficult.

Source: *Guardian*, 7 November 2015

Gordon et al. (2002: 333) provide an example of one US professional woman's negotiation of her work identity at the age of 37:

> So I would say at about age 37 I decided I had done what I wanted. I had become a partner and I had had absolutely no life of my own… Everything that was personal time had gone… So now I tend to do most anything. I volunteer at both my kids' classes. I work for school overrides. I try to be a real part of their life at home too. And what does it is it really reduces the number of hours I can work which reduces the amount of money that I can make, but I make plenty of money.

This case also illustrates how, with hindsight, such changes might be viewed favourably, as the 'right' decision, even if they are difficult decisions at the time.

Golembiewski (1978) has referred to mid-life transitions that can affect men and women, although sometimes at different stages of career and for different reasons. He pointed to the transitions for men often revolving around the gap between aspirations and achievement, as well as a growing sense of mortality and pressures from spouses and adolescent children. As he puts it, the mid-life transition 'fishes in deep and dark waters' (1978: 216), suggesting the capacity for personal crisis and ontological insecurity. Such crises are not merely personal but are negotiated, as Edward's case illustrates, in the context of personal relationships in households where there might be complex interdependencies. While Erikson (1997) sees the life course as a succession of 'crises', Gordon et al. (2002) suggest it is more a restructuring and rebalancing. Mid-life can be presented as a period of full 'maturity' and personal growth, but much depends on one's assessment of one's achievements and whether they meet, exceed or fall short of expectations. Gordon et al. (2002) cite Levinson (1977) as suggesting men who judge themselves as falling short may reframe success in terms of personal happiness rather than accomplishments.

Moore (2009: 662) provides an example of how ethnicity, gender and age intersect, but also shows a person reluctant to concede too much to dominant social norms. She reports a 52-year-old unemployed Pakistani woman who wanted a job in retail saying:

> I personally think from what I'm experiencing is that it's very difficult when you're old to find a job. Everybody it seems to me is looking for a younger person. I think that people of 50 plus face discrimination... being a woman you are always... always... do you know what I mean? You get these feelings; do you know what I mean? But sometimes the people on the street are more racist to you; from my background, the way I dress, perhaps the way I talk, perhaps even the way I look. So yes, you are discriminated all the time. It's just that sometimes it's hurtful, sometimes it's scary and sometimes you don't care... like for the certain jobs that I've put applications in, I feel like an older woman. I have asked for a job in a shop as a sales assistant, I've asked for a job on the stalls and things like that. They look at you and 'Oh, I don't think you can do that job'... being an older woman, maybe a woman and also physical appearances like, you know, they want a younger person who shows more cleavage – I don't cover fully and all that, but I do wear a scarf.

Another woman quoted by Moore (2009: 665–6) said:

> The ideal worker shape is a hard one to fit into if you're older, if you're less enthusiastic by now, you're less willing to work late because you've got other things you'd like to be getting on with, if you find it harder to get up stairs, if you're the wrong shape physically, if you're fat or crumpled in some way,

because I look at all these sort of fit, young eager women at [employers' name] and I think, yes, they're all of a kind, a few years out of university. Obviously, individually they have a hell of a lot to offer, but they fit this ideal worker shape which I think an older person doesn't because as you get older you become more yourself and more formed and less malleable.

These respondents are pointing to the power of the employer to define expectations and to identify these women as less than 'ideal'. There is a process of counter-identification with an alternative to the employer's ideal – the 'older woman'. Other women might, of course, seek to conform to the ideal and might go to considerable lengths to do so: through zumba classes (Pompper 2011: 476), weight loss programmes and the like. In occupations requiring interaction with customers and clients, youthful appearance is all part of looking and sounding right that is increasingly valued in the service economy depending on aesthetic labour (Nixon 2009). But ageing is also relevant in those jobs that may not require aesthetic labour but are physically demanding jobs. Marchant's (2013) study illustrates how a group of male construction workers in Australia adjusted to ageing. For them chronological age seemed less important than physical capacity and they pointed to people at relatively young ages (in their 30s) who needed to leave the trade. The workers she interviewed were still working and seemed to view their chances of continued employment favourably. They were conscious of the wear and tear their work imposed on their bodies, however. One of her respondents put it like this:

Because when they get to 40 and then their knees start going and their sciatic starts going and their legs start going and they've got a sore back… maybe they've lost an eye because they ran into steel or they've got cuts and scars all over them and… like cancer from the sun… by the time you get to 50 you're blown out, you're worn out. It's like too physical, you're worn out.

(Marchant 2013: 851)

Another commented that:

You can't work hard all day you just can't put in five huge days like you did when you were 30… you're knackered the next day if you're doing drainage three or four days in a row, it just knocks you around, getting in and out of the trenches (Plumber, 52).

(Marchant 2013: 852)

One theme that emerged in this study was having the capacity to keep going as long as one could keep fit enough to work. The workers stressed how doing the work kept you fit as well as wearing you out and they adopted various strategies to help them keep working, ranging from cortisone injections and steroids to yoga and aerobic exercises. There were also tools they could use, or work adjustments to make: 'I just got to be careful about how I sort of move the body a bit. I use a bucket now to sit on, I've got to position my posture… and the physio made a big difference (Plumber/air conditioning installer, 41)' (852). They also adjusted the work they did, or accepted:

> One thing I don't do now which I refuse to do and that's dig holes, made that choice a few years ago and said, that's it, no more, never again. I'll get a machine in and pay a couple of hundreds of dollars rather than do it myself (Builder, 53).
>
> *(Marchant 2013: 853)*

All this might be equated with the way people with impairments negotiate 'reasonable adjustments' or accommodations – although it is unlikely that these men would see themselves as disabled. Marchant positions these workers, theoretically, in relation to hegemonic masculinity (2013: 846) where traits may include physical strength and endurance, independence, control, being the breadwinner, striving at work and executing skills-based activity. As Marchant puts it:

> These tradesmen negotiate ageing by emphasizing hegemonic masculine traits such as keeping fit, continuing to work, maintaining a work identity and continuing to earn an income. The paradox associated with attempting to maintain hegemonic masculinity in the face of physical decline was evident. Given that most of the tradesmen were still working and had managed to keep going they were asserting hegemonic masculinity while still acknowledging the transition to different but not necessarily subordinated masculinity.
>
> Being old and therefore possibly being subordinated in terms of masculinity was related to loss of bodily function.
>
> *(Marchant 2013: 856)*

Loss of bodily function is not only a problem for those in obviously 'manual' labour. A primary school teacher may begin to find it difficult to kneel down and clerical workers might develop a range of musculoskeletal disorders. There are also changes in attitudes to high-paced work that might be related to position in the life course. As a salesman in McGoldrick and Cooper's (1988: 88) study put it: 'At 55 you can't be as alert as at 35. I was "on the road" five days a week, overnights in hotels for two. The sales targets went up and up, and I was competing with younger men who didn't mind speeding. My wife worried a lot.' Harper (2011) points out a variety of changes associated with ageing – response times and dynamic visual acuity decline with age (the latter after about 45). She distinguishes between manual work, office work and work which has long hours, shift work and intrinsically stressful work. All these forms of work can cause some deterioration in functioning and health over time to greater or lesser degrees. Air traffic controllers typically retire at about the age of 45, and this is associated with the well-established decline of dynamic visual acuity. If this, however, has some valid basis in cognitive functioning, its application to individuals would not justify a simplistic chronological cut-off. Just as some builders might be 'old' at 30, presumably some air traffic controllers might be old at 35 or young at 45.

All work is embodied, although this is more obvious in some jobs than others. The work of a dancer, athlete or bricklayer is obviously embodied and we can expect their work to alter with the effects of age – becoming slower, and less agile and flexible. But the work of a TV presenter, hairdresser or teacher is also embodied and they, too, might suffer from the effects of ageing, even if it is only from the reactions of others. How the ageing body is viewed is of course open to inter-pretation. We might view an older dancer as charming and their experience might enrich the interpretation of the dance, even if they lack some of the flexibility associated with the younger body. However, those who accept the identity of the 'older' worker might, in the contemporary workplace of Europe and the US, be taking a position that puts them on a route towards exit. According to Desmette and Gaillard (2008), based on a Belgium survey of those aged 50–9, the self-categorization as an 'older' worker 'is related to negative attitudes towards work (stronger desire to retire early, stronger inclination towards intergenerational competition) while the perception that the organization does not use age as a criterion for distinguishing between workers supports positive attitudes towards work (e.g. higher value placed on work)' (168). This study suggests that the self-categorization is to some extent an act of agency – although it is not agency without the constraints of the person's own body and of social norms and actions of others (see also Róin 2014). But while social norms and attitudes might have some basis in the reality of bodily functioning, they are often crude categorizations which pay scant attention to individual differences. They can also become a self-fulfilling prophecy in leading to the removal or more or less voluntary withdrawal of the older person from opportunities for cognitive stimulation and training (Rizzuto et al. 2012): our ageing is organized and shaped, but sometimes in ways that might seem perverse if it 'retires' people at the expense of contributions that they might make and against their will and best interests.

Conclusion

While age might sometimes be a latent identity, this chapter has shown that it is often manifest in the workplace. Age shares with other identities considered in this book the characteristic that it can be the basis for inequality; but it differs in its complexity and fluidity. If we live long enough we might, in the course of our life, come across ageism in different ways and to different degrees. We might experience relative advantage and disadvantage. Age is a more fluid basis of identity and identification than other identities with which it intersects, but it shares the same features – the operation of stereotyping, disadvantage, negotiation. As with other identities we may feel age is not salient at a particular point in time, and we might switch between an emphasis on age and other identities such as gender and ethnicity in accounting for our experience.

Ageing is not something confined to those who are 60 or more – we are all ageing all the time. Or ageing is woven together with our other identities (of ethnicity or gender, for example), in the narratives of our lives. In considering age there can be identification or disidentification ('I'm not old'). There can also be problematic identification as in Moore's respondent quoted earlier who says, 'I feel like an older woman' and in doing so suggests she is not what the employer wants.

The life course can be seen as lived experience. It unfolds over time, but is also experienced in prospect and in retrospect. We have expectations and aspirations; we have disappointments and a sense of fulfilment. However, in retrospect and in prospect we are conscious of our younger and older selves – of our career. We see ourselves, as it were, at a distance, as an out-of-body experience – something to be reflected upon. Our former selves might be looked at with envy, amusement or bewilderment; our future selves with trepidation or hope. But such reflections might inform what we do in the present and might shape how we respond to others who are younger, older or the same age as ourselves.

Ageing is a process in which cultural values, personal interpretations and the recalcitrant materiality of the body intersect. We position ourselves in relation to others and might identify with others of a similar age (or disidentify with them). If we may act in concert with those of a similar age this suggests that the idea of the 'generation' is important – but not in the stereotyped way that suggests all baby boomers are the same and all different from 'millennials'.

Ageing, in so far as we all experience it, might provide an experiential basis for understanding inequality and exclusion on the basis of other identities. It might also provide an experiential basis for solidarity across the different kinds of identity dealt with in this book, based on empathy with the experience of disadvantage and marginalization, as well as for solidarity within a particular age group. The extent to which it does so will be variable, of course: one can easily experience ageism as personal rather than political, or experience it largely as a latent rather than manifest identity. Perhaps, however, age is worthy of more attention than it receives and its consideration should not be confined to the study of the older worker, but is potentially relevant at all points in the life course.

BOX 9.2 AT THE MOVIES: AGE

Some movies relevant to the themes of the chapter are:

Wild Stawberries (1957, director Ingmar Bergman)
About Schmidt (2002, director Alexander Payne)
Begin Again (2013, director John Carney)
Brooklyn (2015, director Lenny Abrahamson)

References

Ainsworth, S. (2002) 'The "feminine advantage": A discursive analysis of the invisibility of older women workers', *Gender, Work and Organization*, 9(5): 579–601.

Angouri, J. (2012) '"The older I get the less I trust people": Constructing age identities in the workplace', *Pragmatics*, 22(2): 255–277.

Archer, L. (2008) 'Younger academics' constructions of "authenticity", "success" and professional identity', *Studies in Higher Education*, 33(4): 385–403.

Arthur, M. B., Inkson, K. and Pringle, J. K. (1999) *The New Careers: Individual Action and Economic Change*. London: Sage.

Bernard, M., Itzin, C., Phillipson, C. and Skucha, J. (1995) 'Gendered work, gendered retirement' in Arber, S. and Ginn, J. (eds), *Connecting Gender and Ageing: A Sociological Approach*. Buckingham: Open University Press: 56–68.

Birren, J. E., Schaie, K. W., Abeles, R. P., Gatz, M. and Salthouse, T. A. (eds) (2006) *Handbook of the Psychology of Aging*, 6th edition. Boston, MA: Elsevier Academic Press.

Bodily, C. L. (1994) 'Ageism and the deployments of "age": A constructionist view' in Sarbin, T. R. and Kitsuse, J. I. (eds), *Constructing the Social*. London: Sage.

Bond, J., Coleman, P. G. and Peace, S. M. (2007) *Ageing in Society: European Perspectives on Gerontology*, 3rd edition. London: Sage.

Bown-Wilson, D. (2011) 'The role of age in career progression: Motivation and barriers to fulfilment in older employees' in Parry, E. and Tyson, S. (eds), *Managing an Age-Diverse Workforce*. Basingstoke: Palgrave Macmillan.

Briscoe, J. P. and Hall, D. T. (2006) 'The interplay of boundaryless and protean careers: Combinations and implications', *Journal of Vocational Behavior*, 69(1): 4–18.

Buchmann, M. (1989) *The Script of Life in Modern Society: Entry into Adulthood in a Changing World*. Chicago: University of Chicago Press.

Bytheway, B. and Johnson, J. (eds) (1990) *Welfare and the Ageing Experience: A Multidisciplinary Analysis: Conference Papers*. Avebury: British Society of Gerontology.

Cameron, E., Evers, H., Badger, F. and Atkin, K. (1989) 'Black old women, disability, and health carers' in Jefferys, M. (ed.) (1989) *Growing Old in the Twentieth Century*. London: Routledge.

Cennamo, L. and Gardner, D. (2008) 'Generational differences in work values, outcomes and person-organisation values fit', *Journal of Managerial Psychology*, 23(8): 891–906.

Clarke, M. (2005) 'The voluntary redundancy option: Carrot or stick?', *British Journal of Management*, 16(3): 245–251.

Coakley, J. J. (1983) 'Leaving competitive sport: Retirement or rebirth?', *Quest*, 35(1): 1–11.

Desmette, D. and Gaillard, M. (2008) 'When a "worker" becomes an "older worker": The effects of age-related social identity on attitudes towards retirement and work', *Career Development International*, 13(2): 168–185.

Egri, C. P. and Ralston, D. A. (2004) 'Generation cohorts and personal values: A comparison of China and the United States', *Organization Science*, 15(2): 210–220.

Erikson, E. H. (1997) *The Life Cycle Completed*, extended version. New York: W. W. Norton.

Featherstone, M. and Hepworth, M. (1989) 'Ageing and old age: Reflections on the post-modern life course' in Blytheway, B., Keil, T., Allatt, P. and Bryman, A. (eds), *Becoming and Being Old: Sociological Approaches to Later Life*. London: Sage.

Feldman, D. C. and Turnley, W. H. (1995) 'Factors influencing intentions to retire: An empirical test of theoretical propositions', *Management Research News*, 18(6/7): 28–45.

Field, J., Burke, R. J. and Cooper, C. L. (eds) (2013) *The SAGE Handbook of Aging, Work and Society*. London: Sage.

Fineman, S. (2011) *Organizing Age*. Oxford: Oxford University Press.

Flynn, G. (1996) 'Xers vs. boomers: Teamwork or trouble?', *Personnel Journal*, 75(11): 86–90.

Goffee, R. (1992) 'Organizational change and the corporate career: The restructuring of managers' job aspirations', *Human Relations*, 45(4): 363–385.

Golembiewski, R. T. (1978) 'Mid-life transition and mid-career crisis: A special case for individual development', *Public Administration Review*, 38(3): 215–222.

Gordon, J. R., Beatty, J. E. and Whelan Berry, K. S. (2002) 'The midlife transition of professional women with children', *Women in Management Review*, 17(7): 328–341.

Guardian (2015) 'Olenka Frenkiel: "I realised I was being rubbed out by the BBC"', at http://www.theguardian.com/media/2014/nov/07/olenka-frenkiel-bbc-older-women-ageism (accessed 12 December 2015).

Hall, D. T. (2001) *Careers in and out of Organizations*. Thousand Oaks, CA: Sage Publications.

Harper, D. (2011) 'Health and well-being in older workers: Capacity change with age' in Parry, E. and Tyson, S. (eds), *Managing an Age-Diverse Workforce*. Basingstoke: Palgrave Macmillan: 206–221.

Hedge, J. W. and Borman, W. C. (eds) (2012) *The Oxford Handbook of Work and Aging*. Oxford: Oxford University Press.

Holland, S. (2004) *Alternative Femininities: Body, Age and Identity*. Oxford: Berg.

Hummert, M. L. (2011) 'Age stereotypes and aging' in Schaie, W. and Willis, S. L. (eds), *Handbook of the Psychology of Aging*, 7th edition. London: Academic Press.

Kerr, G. and Dacyshyn, A. (2000) 'The retirement experiences of elite, female gymnasts', *Journal of Applied Sport Psychology*, 12(2): 115–133.

Kohli, M. (1990) *Plenary Address to Second International Conference on the Adult Life Course*. Leeuwenhorst, Netherlands, July.

Kohli, M. (1991) 'Retirement and the moral economy: An historical interpretation of the German case' in Minkler, M. and Estes, C. (eds), *Critical Perspectives on Aging: Political and Moral Economy of Growing Old*. Amityville, NY: Barywoon.

Künemund, H. and Kolland, F. (2007) 'Work and retirement' in Bond, J. Peace, S., Dittman-Kohli, F. and Westerhof, G. J. (eds), *Ageing in Society: European Perspectives on Gerontology*. London: Sage.

Lamb, S. (2014) 'Permanent personhood or meaningful decline? Toward a critical anthropology of successful aging', *Journal of Aging Studies*, 29: 41–52.

Levinson, D. J. (1977) 'The mid-life transition: A period in adult psycho-social development', *Psychiatry*, 40: 99–112.

Loretto, W., Lain, D., Vickerstaff, S. and Beck, V. (2013) 'Employers' use of older workers in the recession', *Employee Relations*, 35(3): 257–271.

McGoldrick, A. E. and Cooper, C. L. (1988) *Early Retirement*. Aldershot: Gower.

Mainiero, L. A. and Sullivan, S. E. (2005) 'Kaleidoscope careers: An alternate explanation for the "opt-out" revolution', *Academy of Management Executive*, 19(1): 106–123.

Mallett, O. and Wapshott, R. (2015) 'Making sense of self-employment in late career: Understanding the identity work of olderpreneurs', *Work, Employment and Society*, 29(2): 250–266.

Marchant, T. (2013) 'Keep going: Career perspectives on ageing and masculinity of self-employed tradesmen in Australia', *Construction Management and Economics*, 31(8): 845–860.

Moore, S. (2009) '"No matter what I did I would still end up in the same position": Age as a factor defining older women's experience of labour market participation', *Work, Employment and Society*, 23(4): 655–671.

Nixon, D. (2009) '"I can't put a smiley face on": Working-class masculinity, emotional labour and service work in the "new economy"', *Gender, Work and Organization*, 16(3): 300–322.

Office of National Statistics (2015) 'Employment, unemployment and economic inactivity by age grou', November, at http://www.ons.gov.uk/ons/datasets-and-tables/index.html?pageSize=50&sortBy=none&sortDirection=none&newquery=Economic+activity&content-type=Reference+table&content-type=Dataset (accessed 27 November 2015).

Pahl, R. E. and Pahl, J. M. (1971) *Managers and Their Wives: A Study of Career and Family Relationships in the Middle Class*. Harmondsworth: Penguin.

Parker, S. (1982) *Work and Retirement*. London: Allen and Unwin.

Parry, E. (2014) *Generational Diversity at Work: New Research Perspectives*. Abingdon: Routledge.

Paul, R. J. and Townsend, J. B. (1993) 'Managing the older worker: Don't just rinse away the gray', *Academy of Management Executive*, 7(3): 67–74.

Pompper, D. (2011) 'Fifty years later: Mid-career women of color against the glass ceiling in communications organizations', *Journal of Organizational Change Management*, 24(4): 464–486.

Riach, K. (2011) 'Situating age (in)equality within the paradigms and practices of diversity management' in Parry, E. and Tyson, S. (eds), *Managing an Age Diverse Workforce*. Basingstoke: Palgrave Macmillan: 43–58.

Riach, K. and Loretto, W. (2009) 'Identity work and the "unemployed" worker: Age, disability and the lived experience of the older unemployed', *Work, Employment and Society*, 23(1): 102–119.

Ricœur, P. (1992) *Oneself as Another*, trans. Kathleen Blamey. Chicago: University of Chicago Press.

Rizzuto, T. E., Cherry, K. E. and Le Doux, J. A. (2012) 'The aging process and cognitive abilities' in Hedge, J. W. and Borman, W. C. (eds), *The Oxford Handbook of Work and Aging*. Oxford: Oxford University Press.

Róin, Á. (2014) 'Embodied ageing and categorisation work amongst retirees in the Faroe Islands', *Journal of Aging Studies*, 31: 83–92.

Sargeant, M. (2011) *Age Discrimination and Diversity: Multiple Discrimination from an Age Perspective*. Cambridge: Cambridge University Press.

Sargent, L. D., Lee, M. D., Martin, B. and Zikic, J. (2013) 'Reinventing retirement: New pathways, new arrangements, new meanings', *Human Relations*, 66(1): 3–21.

Schuller, T. (1989) 'Work-ending: Employment and ambiguity in later life' in Blytheway, B., Keil, T., Allatt, P. and Bryman, A. (eds), *Becoming and Being Old: Sociological Approaches to Later Life*. London: Sage.

Schullery, N. M. (2013) 'Workplace engagement and generational differences in values', *Business Communication Quarterly*, 76(2): 252–265.

Smola, K. W. and Sutton, C. D. (2002) 'Generational differences: Revisiting generational work values for the new millennium', *Journal of Organizational Behavior*, 23(4): 363–382.

Sontag, S. (1972) 'The double standard of aging', *Saturday Review*, 23 September: 29–38.

Sturges, J. (1999) 'What it means to succeed: Personal conceptions of career success held by male and female managers at different ages', *British Journal of Management*, 10: 239–252.

Super, D. E. (1957) *The Psychology of Careers: An Introduction to Vocational Development*. New York: Harper and Bros.

Victor, C. R. (1989) 'Income inequality in later life', in Jefferys, M. (ed.), *Growing Old in the Twentieth Century*. London: Routledge.

Vincent, J. A. (1995) *Inequality and Old Age*. London: UCL Press.

Wise, D. A. (2010) 'Facilitating longer working lives: International evidence on why and how', *Demography*, 47: S131–149.

10

CONCLUSIONS

Introduction

Previous chapters in this book have considered a wide range of literature, albeit necessarily providing a selective coverage of the various chapter themes. In this concluding chapter I want to reflect on this content and consider issues that seem to me to be central to the issue of identity at work, as well as to consider how we might respond to the situation described in the various chapters. The two issues I want to consider in greatest detail here are those of intersectionality and solidarity. The first of these relates to the relationship between the various identity categories identified in previous chapters, while the second is relevant to the question of what is being done and what can be done – it goes to the politics of the matter. Before considering these two issues, however, I want to draw out some key themes that seem to me to run through the various chapters, the themes of identification and related terms.

Identification (*of* and *with*) – disidentification – latent identities

Identity (whether self-identity or collective identity) involves processes of identification – something emphasized by many writers (e.g. Ashforth et al. 2008; Jenkins 2004; Erikson 1980; Ricoeur 1994). I find it useful to think about two modes of identification, however: *identification-of* and *identification-with*. If we follow Ricoeur (1994) and say that identification *of* oneself can be seen as involving attestation we can also, by extension, see something similar occurring at the level of collective identity. This is sometimes formalized – in statements of professional standards, for example – but much of it rests on tacit knowledge and discursive practices. If, then, we can identify particular 'collective identities' such as English, manager, sociologist, feminist, etc. this involves some sense of what it is that this stands for, some ways of saying 'here we (or they) stand' that distinguishes 'our' (or 'their') collective identity from others. Identification of this form is not merely a matter of thought as opposed to feeling, however; as Ashforth et al. (2008) emphasize one can think, feel or act oneself into identification. The feelings explored in the chapters on disability, ethnicity or class, for example, include embarrassment and anger and these can be powerful drivers towards identification. Identification always implies attention to difference, though. As Hall (1996: 17) put it:

> Above all... identities are constructed through, not outside difference. This entails the radically disturbing recognition that it is only through the relation to the Other, the relation to what it is not, to precisely what it lacks... that the 'positive' meaning of any term – and thus its identity – can be constructed.

In exploring issues of identification *with* it may be useful to remind ourselves of some of the pioneering work on 'identity', even if this is largely neglected today – the work of Eric Erikson.

Erikson (1980: 25) says at one point:

> A child has quite a number of opportunities to identify himself [sic], more or less experimentally, with real or fictitious people of either sex, with habits, traits, occupations and ideas. Certain crises force him to make radical selections. However, the historical era in which he lives offers only a limited number of socially meaningful models for workable combinations or identification fragments.

What Erikson points to here is a process of selection but what is also notable is the range of objects he considers the child may identify *with*. These include people (real or fictitious) but also habits, traits, occupations and ideas. Identification *with* is not reduced to belonging to a particular social category (or even aspiring to belong).

There are aspects of Erikson's approach I would wish to retain and which are reflected in the preceding chapters: a concern with the dynamics of identity and the tensions and crises which go on within the individual (as well as within the collectivities with which various collective identities are associated). Thus we have seen how people represented in the preceding chapters have identified *with* certain occupations, ethnicities, sexual orientations, etc. Identification-*with* often seems to be a precursor to identification-*of* – as in the child that Erikson considers who, through a process of selection, gradually comes to 'be' a certain character.

The process of identifying *with* others is often based on similarity – I identify with those of my nation, ethnicity, class, occupation, gender, etc. However, I think it is worth thinking about the potential for it cutting across differences. When we march together, metaphorically or literally, we are never all the same, we are showing solidarity across whatever differences exist. 'Je suis Charlie Hebdo', chanted the marchers in Paris, those of many faiths, ethnicities, classes – although not by any means a representative cross-section of the population. When we identify *with* those who are weak or vulnerable, or who are suffering, it is not always because we share their condition but because we empathize with it.

What exploring *identification-with* leads to, potentially, is an uncovering of the connections that are made and the value they have to the person making them. On the other hand, an exploration of *identification-of* allows us to explore how the person accounts for themselves. And this need not be in fixed terms but in processual, dialogical terms. I am a manager but what kind of a manager have I been and what kind of a manager am I becoming? (See the example of a manager in Chapter 3.)

We have also seen instances of *disidentification*, of cases where people are uncomfortable with either the self they seem to have become or the social category or self to which they are assigned: 'I'm not his wife' (see Chapter 2) or 'I'm not old' (Chapter 9).

The idea of *latent* identities is supported by some of the literature reported in previous chapters. This is a concept first introduced by Gouldner (1957: 284 and see also Chapter 4 in this book). However, I would propose defining latent identities in a somewhat different way to Gouldner, who identified them as identities 'which group members define as being irrelevant, inappropriate to consider, or illegitimate to take into account'. I would propose, instead, to consider latent identities as those that are currently inactive or are hidden. In the chapters on sexual orientation and disability, for example, we have seen how the identities of disabled or gay people *as* gay or disabled people are sometimes hidden from the view of others and might even be irrelevant in particular interactions. This concept of latent identities is very similar to that of Bradley's (2016: 44) passive identities. However, she says about these that passive identities are potential identities that are not acted upon and individuals 'are not particularly conscious of... and do not normally define themselves by them unless events occur which bring those particular relationships to the fore'. I think this is to go too far in suggesting enduring inactivity and we might consider more regular switching between passive and active identities than this implies. Identity work to some extent involves decisions about when to make particular identity categories relevant or not ('the hospital is not ready for a camp acting doctor' − quoted in Chapter 7). In other words, what is foregrounded or hidden is dependent on context and it might vary with context and in the process of interaction. Identity work often involves a transition from a latent to a manifest identification (or, in Bradley's terms, between passive and active) − as in the example of the black prison officer referred to in Chapter 5 who was assumed to be with the prisoner's family rather than an official, even though they were wearing a prison officer's uniform. This might be seen as *identity switching*, in so far as particular identity categories come to be seen as relevant in a certain context and at a certain time or not. But identity work need not just involve switching between identities: sometimes multiple identity categories operate simultaneously, something I will consider further under the heading of intersectionality.

This discussion of identification can easily come to be seen as occurring at an individual level, as related to self-identity, but I would want to argue that it is often relevant to consider collective behaviour and collective identity, too. These terms of identification *of* and *with*, of *disidentification* and *latent identification*, can be applied to collectivities, and always take place in a social context – a context of interaction and discourse. While identification may be the result of an internal conversation (Archer 2003), it can also be profoundly public and political – as debates in and around the women's movements, the LGBT movement and disability movement make clear. However, I see the politics of such identification as so ubiquitous that I do not want to follow Bradley (2016: 44–45) in drawing a distinction between active and politicized identities.

Difference, similarity, managing diversity

Identification certainly involves difference – and differentiation as a set of social practices. Such differences are not static, however, in two senses. Firstly, the nature of such differences can change over time (for example the dress of women and men might change), but also the relationships between 'self' and 'other' or 'them' and 'us' can change over time (consider class relations or gender relations, for example – Chapters 3 and 6 provide ample evidence of change over time). We might also add that identities are not only constructed with reference to the Other, as Hall (1996: 17) puts it, but perhaps to a number of relevant others. I think we need to be careful not to think always in binaries. Class is not the only category where it may be useful to distinguish more than two cases. Moreover, sometimes there may be ambiguous or ambivalent positioning (see Chapters 2, 3 and 6). Even when we do think in binaries, we need to be careful about assuming that one is the opposite of the other. Difference might be formed through different combinations of traits, or from different traits. Woman as non-man is not simply a negation. Language often pushes us into suggesting difference as opposites and difference as relations of superiority and inferiority – but other possibilities exist.

We have seen that identity is predicated on both similarity and difference. But the notion of similarity is not as simple as all that. Similarity is a quality of sameness but what counts as the 'same'? In everyday English we often distinguish between something that is 'similar' and something that is 'identical', but how 'similar' do we have to be for this to count as a 'similar' case? One solution to this is in terms of family resemblance. For Medina (2003), drawing on Wittgenstein's approach to categorization, the construction of identity is the assertion of connectedness of difference – a 'familial view of identity' (660). We need not expect all women to be identical to use the category of woman. What is needed is some socially accepted (and ultimately mutable) way of distinguishing women from those who are not women. This is facilitated by processes of self-identification in which women come to define themselves as women, and then show the signs of this in ways that differentiate themselves from men (wearing different kinds of clothes, for example). Such a familial view both emphasizes the differences that exist within the identity and the instability of it, since connections can change over time and other connections appear. This leads Medina to pose the two questions of 'how does one become a member of these families; and how are these families related to one another?' (2003: 661). To Medina, this seems to involve a kind of selective blindness: seeing some similarities and differences and ignoring others. Another way of seeing this is that it is a way of reaching out in certain directions and not in others. But such 'reaching out' must always come from a certain social position in which there are those who are nearer or further away from us, physically, or in other ways (perhaps in thought, behaviour, feelings). This also occurs in a situation where particular others may or may not be reaching out to us. This is to say that *social positioning* is important (Alcoff 1988).

This 'reaching out' (or not) might, of course, occur at an organizational level and much has been written in recent years about managing diversity (e.g. Kandola and Fullerton 1998; Kirton 2013). While the difficulties of so doing are often recognized (e.g. see van Knippenberg and Haslam 2003), the business case for diversity is often made with the supposed benefits including greater creativity, as well as greater use of a wider pool of talent and the avoidance of problems associated with discrimination (see, for example, Kandola and Fullerton 1998). It might also be seen as essential since diversity is an inevitable feature of life in an era of globalization (see Özbilgin and Tatli 2008; Syed and Özbilgin 2015). However, managing diversity is obviously a managerial approach and it is tied to the business case. While it may be part of a social responsibility agenda, or aimed at attracting a diverse set of customers, ultimately it is pursued because it is assumed to be congenial to the organizational good. In the private sector case this is associated with profit. While many of the policies associated with managing diversity, such as providing greater flexibility in working patterns (see Kirton 2013), are to be welcomed, they are unlikely decisively to counter the divisions, inequalities and discomforts of working lives portrayed in the previous chapters; indeed, I would argue that it is the very nature of capitalism to utilize difference for the pursuit of profit and organizational ends, and this is often to perpetuate and even exacerbate differences (see also Fletcher and Gapasin 2009).

Fragmentation

To the extent that identity invokes difference we might expect an emphasis on fragmentation in the literature. Hall (1996) refers to the fragmented subject while Bradley (2016), in her marvellous book, uses the title *Fractured Identities*. The idea of fragmentation is, of course, in opposition to the idea of a unified, solitary identity (perhaps defined in class terms, for example), but it also reflects third-wave feminism's recognition of diversity within the category of women. However, I think the emphasis on fragmentation can be pushed too far. Hall's own work suggests how there can be processes of unification as well as fragmentation occurring in the construction of, for example, national identities. While I think the metaphor of fragmentary identities is a useful one I think it is also useful to consider a kind of dance between fragmentation and unification (see also Brown 2015). At any one time both processes may be occurring and how they play together is a proper subject of analysis. In the preceding chapters I think we can see plenty of evidence of fragmentation, of differentiation, but there is also unification – even unification across the many differences that exist in the category of the 'disabled' or of minority sexualities. I think, too, that to speak of the fragmented subject can be misleading. Rather than use the metaphor of a fragment it might be better to use the metaphor of a 'side' – as in the two sides of a coin or the six sides in a cube. Thus I might have many sides – a male British sociologist, etc. – and these are all part of who I am, with different sides being shown at different times and more *or less* happily integrated in the one person (see also Giddens 1991: 190; Brown 2015). This also fits with the idea of latent identities, identities that are not active at any one time (occasionally I do not think or act as a sociologist – or at least this 'face' is not in play).

Experience

Many theorists of identity emphasize the role of experience as a source of 'identification' – the shaping of particular identities (e.g. Alcoff 1988; de Lauretis 1984). Thus a feminist identity might be based on the experience of being a woman encountering 'everyday sexism' (see Chapter 6). This example suggests that particular instances of behaviour or sets of interactions mould our sense of self as well as our feeling of belonging to or our identification *with* a given collective identity. It may inform who we come to reach out to, who we see ourselves as resembling, which family we are a member of, in Medina's (2003) terms. It is, of course, how such experiences are interpreted and reflected upon that matters, and possibly how they become sedimented into the narrative of our lives (Ricoeur 1994). I recall an incident in my childhood when my sister objected to being asked to do the washing up because I, her brother, was never asked to do it. What I felt then was that she had a point and I now see this as a defining moment in my self-identification with a pro-feminist identity, even if other events and experiences might have been needed to bring this about. (I would also make the point that this representation of my past might be inaccurate. This story might be a myth. I might possibly be remembering a story told by my sister much later, at a time when I had developed a pro-feminist stance and that makes me now construct a false memory that supports my self-identification. But either way the incident serves to illustrate how we form our narratives of identity from particular events.)

But experience need not be seen as simply made up of a series of incidents, somehow remembered or misremembered, reflected upon and interpreted. The translators of the English edition of Gadamer's book *Truth and Knowledge* (Gadamer 1989: xiii) point out that German has two separate words for 'experience': *erlebnis* and *erfahrung*. For Gadamer, *erlebnis* is associated with particular 'experiences' and the translators explain this as the 'enduring residue of moments lived in their full immediacy'. *Erfahrung*, as used by Gadamer, on the other hand:

provides the basis in our actual lives for the specifically hermeneutic way we are related to other persons and to our cultural past, namely, dialogue and especially the dialogue of question and answer. This kind of 'experience' is not the residue of isolated moments, but an ongoing integrative process in which what we encounter widens our horizon, but only be overturning an existing perspective, which we can then perceive was erroneous or at least narrow.

(1989: xiii)

This is related to another of Gadamer's concepts, that of historically effected consciousness. This is consciousness that is both shaped by history and brought into being historically. To Gadamer such consciousness is not the work of an isolated individual mind but the product of dialogue between people over time. I see this as having much in common with Berger and Luckmann's (1967) work in *The Social Construction of Reality*, although Gadamer gives more emphasis to differences in view and the dynamic nature of knowledge. I would want to emphasize both *erlebnis* and *erfahrung*. My only reservation about this is that it works at the level of consciousness and knowledge and may give too little weight to how, as Ashforth et al. (2008) put it, we can think, feel and act ourselves into identification. The embodied nature of 'experience' should also be emphasized. Experience is not just about what we think and remember; it is what we feel and smell, too, and how these affect what we think and remember. And by 'feel' I mean both the emotional aspect of our experience (joy, anger, disgust) and also the physical sensations (such as the movement of the bowels, sexual arousal, raised pulse rate). Embodied experience is about movement of the body – towards or away, in more or less choreographed or improvized performances (e.g. the signing of the contract or the laugh at a joke). Perhaps in the preceding chapters this is not emphasized enough, but this reflects the heavy reliance placed on methods such as interviews as a source of much of our knowledge of work.

But what kinds of experience matter? We might categorize these, very crudely, as either unsettling or comfortable – our response makes a difference to how we interpret them and what we might think and do in the future. Of course, what we think and feel about experience is itself a matter of our interpretation, shaped by discursive and non-discursive forces. We might be unsettled by 'everyday sexism' or not – but whether we are or not is open to social influences as we come to recognize it, through and after conversation with others. In the preceding chapters there is evidence of a lot of experience that is unsettling, although the extent to which this leads to action orientated to changing conditions is highly variable.

Solidarity

In considering the fragmentation–unification issue, as well as what actions we take on the basis of experience, it is perhaps worth thinking about solidarity as a unifying force. The word perhaps has an old-fashioned ring to it and some might relegate it to 20th-century politics, but I think it still has relevance.

I am inclined to follow Allen (1999), who adopts an Arendtian position in regarding solidarity as 'a kind of power that arises when we make commitments to one another and act in concert' (114). Solidarity is not, therefore, on this view, the pre-condition of action and coordination, but the outcome of it. The attraction of this position, for me as well as for Allen, is that it provides a way of avoiding the positing of an essentialized identity that is prior to solidarity, while still trying to understand 'how oppositional social movements can formulate common goals and strive to achieve them'. Allen and I thus position ourselves away from those such as Butler (1990) who are sceptical about organizing on the basis of an identity category such as 'woman'. It allows us to recognize that there may be differences within a category or between categories but that there may still be the potential for acting in concert. I see the disability movements, the LGBT movements as well as the women's movements as exemplifying this.

Allen (1999) discusses Arendt's accounts of Danish people resisting Nazi policies towards the Jews as evidence of a view of the politics of solidarity that recognizes the possibility of action in common that cuts across differences. Interestingly, in dealing with the same case, Rorty (1989) has argued that the Danes may have acted for parochial reasons, that they may, if questioned, have explained their taking risks to protect a given Jew as arising from the fact that 'this particular Jew was a fellow... Jutlander, or a fellow member of the same union or profession... or a fellow parent of small children' (1989: 190–1). But whether this solidarity was based on parochial reasons or not, I think this view of solidarity has implications for our understanding of what I have called 'identification-*with*'. We need to be alert to two possibilities, firstly that such identification might well be a spur to 'action in concert' that prompts us to make further commitments to one another. Rorty (1989: 190) has argued for solidarity based on the 'imaginative identification with the details of others' lives'. An identification, he emphasizes, that is not based on some universalist principle or common humanity but is always historically and socially contingent. It seems to me that in so far as we may identify *with* the lives of people we encountered in previous chapters this may form a basis for action in concert. But the other possibility is that identification might well arise in the process of 'action in concert' – that as we come to work with others, identification with others might occur. For example, we might find ourselves at a march or in a union or profession where we find ourselves working alongside others who we may not have expected to be there but with whom we come to seek common cause. Fletcher and Gapasin's (2009) account of the recent history of trade unionism in the US provides examples of this, even if it also provides plenty of evidence of division and disunity. This issue of solidarity I also see as related to that of intersectionality, and it is to this I next turn, the final issue I will deal with here.

Intersectionality

In deciding to have separate chapters on issues such as gender, ethnicity and age, I have run the risk of ignoring the relations between these issues. I hope readers of the individual chapters will see, however, that these dimensions are related and that when it comes to age, say, issues of gender are important. In these final pages I would like to address the issue of the relationship between the chapters, or rather the patterns of identification that the chapters consider. To do so I will refer to the literature on intersectionality.

The term intersectionality was coined by Crenshaw in the late 1980s and has been widely used since (e.g. see Anthias 1992; Corlett and Mavin 2014; Hancock 2007; Kerner 2012). Crenshaw's (1889, 1991) initial intervention was focused on the position of black women in the United States. As a legal scholar Crenshaw was concerned that women often could take legal redress against discrimination on one of two grounds – that of racial discrimination or gender – but not both, while often these two seemed to operate simultaneously. In focusing on black women she was, of course, building upon years of scholarship and debates, particularly within the women's movements, around the position of black women and the extent to which their experience and interests were different from those of white women (e.g. Smith 1983; Spelman 1990). It is also worth noting that Crenshaw coined the term explicitly to deal with the condition of marginalized subjects, although since then there are those who would wish to extend it to other groups (Hearn 2014). Since the term was coined, the idea of intersectionality seems to have been very attractive to many feminists seeking to understand the experience and situation of a variety of women in different social positions. The idea easily lends itself to the consideration of many cross-cutting differences, including those of class, disability, sexual orientation and age. It quickly spawned not only a range of empirical studies of intersectional positions but a thriving population of theoretical and methodological studies. However, a cursory look at a number of such studies would show how little agreement there is over how to do intersectionality (Hancock 2007; McCall 2005; Walby et al. 2012). It seems to me that intersectionality is a very fruitful idea, but that is not to say that it cannot come in different forms or be pushed too far. In the next few pages I will discuss some alternative approaches to intersectionality and its relationship to the themes of this book.

The nature of intersections: additionality and beyond

If the simplest case of intersection is considered, that of two lines of difference such as race and gender, then intersectionality could be interpreted as a need to consider both categories, both lines of difference, in an additive way. Thus the condition of black women could be analysed as encountering both racism and sexism, leading to a dual form of discrimination or dual burden. However, theorists of intersectionality, including Crenshaw (1989, 1991), insist that this is not sufficient, that there is something qualitatively different about the experience of, say, black women that renders superimposing one upon the other as insufficient. Shields (2008: 301) suggested that intersectionality involves 'The mutually constitutive relations among social identities', while Holvino (2010) refers to this as 'simultaneity': she wants to consider how the experience of, say, a black woman, is distinctive, precisely because she is a black woman. It is easy to understand this argument in relation to any given individual: a particular black woman's identity cannot be reduced to the summation of her gender and race. Her experience may not be simply a matter of encountering either racial or gender discrimination: sometimes it could be both simultaneously in that the way in which a black woman might be discriminated against might be different from that of a black man. Forms of racism can be gendered, just as gender discrimination can be racialized. As Yuval-Davis (2006: 195) puts it in relation to the argument about the more complex case of the interaction of race, gender and class:

> Our argument against the 'triple oppression' approach was that there is no such thing as suffering from oppression 'as Black', 'as a woman', 'as a working-class person'... Any attempt to essentialize 'Blackness' or 'womanhood' or 'working classness' as specific forms of concrete oppression in additive ways inevitably conflates narratives of identity politics with descriptions of positionality as well as constructing identities within the terms of specific political projects. Such narratives often reflect hegemonic discourses of identity politics that render invisible experiences of the more marginal members of that specific social category and construct an homogenized 'right way' to be its member.

In thinking about how class and gender, for example, are 'mutually constituted', we might use the example referred to by Prins (2006: 284) of a working-class man, Sietse, a school caretaker, who objects to his boss, a school principal, criticizing the parents of a class:

> the principal entered, I got along with him very well, and he said to me: 'that 1-A class, how many parents were there?' 'Well', I said, 'two'. 'Yes, that's what you get with those anti-social folk', he said. And I got so angry! I said to him: 'now let me tell you something... He said... [Sietse here indicates that the principal tried to respond, but was interrupted by him]. 'No', I said, 'my own son is in that class!' 'O sorry', he said. I said: 'boy, you think first before you say anything'. Yes, I can say anything to him.

As Prins sees it this is the reaction of a working-class man whose class has, indirectly, been criticized, and who reacts in a gendered, masculine way. This provides a good example of how class and gender interact, how class struggle can be gendered.

Moreover, Holvino (2010: 249), like Yuval-Davis, wants to emphasize how intersectionality can be used to attend to processes at different levels of analysis – that simultaneity does not just apply to processes of identity but to institutional and social practice, too. Thus intersectionality can provide a broadly applicable way of looking at social issues at a number of different analytical levels.

However, before we accept the view that seems to have settled into orthodoxy, that intersectionality is not to be understood in an additive way, it is I think useful to remember Crenshaw's own early work on the issue. For example, she says at one point (Crenshaw 1991: 149):

I am suggesting that Black women can experience discrimination in ways that are both similar to and different from those experienced by white women and Black men. Black women sometimes experience discrimination in ways similar to white women's experiences; sometimes they share very similar experiences with Black men. Yet often they experience double-discrimination – the combined effects of practices which discriminate on the basis of race, and on the basis of sex. And sometimes, they experience discrimination as Black women – not the sum of race and sex discrimination, but as Black women.

This does, indeed, point to the need to consider the condition of black women in the condition of simultaneity but it also suggests that we need to be alert to a range of different situations; that sometimes it is a matter of considering one issue or the other, sometimes both in an additive way, sometimes both in a more complex way. We can also note that one of the legal cases that Crenshaw (1989) refers to in arguing for an intersectional view was that of de Graffenreid versus General Motors. Here a group of black women lost their case for discrimination which they argued was based on race and sex discrimination acting in combination. These women lost their jobs in a round of redundancy where the criteria for selection was length of service. Because black women were not recruited by the company until relatively recently they inevitably had less service than white women. Thus, while perhaps there was no selection of these women for redundancy because they were black women, the result was the same. This case was useful to Crenshaw's argument as it demonstrated how the courts refused to accept the argument that the combination of race *and* sex put these women at a disadvantage. However, an adequate understanding of the way in which these women were discriminated against could be obtained if we consider how as a *racial* group they were at a disadvantage. We might argue that the criteria for selection were indirectly discriminatory on 'racial' grounds alone, although it affected women. There are two issues raised by this. One is that of when we need to move beyond consideration of one 'line' of difference, and when we need to combine two or more lines to further the analysis. Crenshaw (1989: 149) uses the analogy of a road intersection and points out that accidents might be caused by the flow of traffic from either direction or from multiple directions. If we use this analogy we might argue that we need to consider particular combinations – or perhaps even recognize that sometimes there is no need to consider multiple dimensions at all. Sometimes racism, say, might be just racism. The other issue is the nature of the relationship between two lines of difference, where two are relevant. In the case of these General Motors workers, one could argue that an 'additionality' approach would in fact be appropriate – that the way in which gender segregation of labour *and* past racial discrimination combined to disadvantage this group. There is no need to examine the 'mutual constitution' of the group. Walby et al. (2012) also object to holding to the 'multiple constitution' test of intersectionality, preferring the term 'mutual shaping' – but even this seems to go further than this case warrants. There is a need to consider a range of cases: in some 'intersectionality' does not add to the analysis, in others an additive approach is sufficient and in yet others 'mutual constitution' (or at least mutual shaping) operate. In considering individual chapters in this book, I think it is useful to consider these possibilities. I think sometimes it is useful to consider these different dimensions independently, sometimes in an additive manner and sometimes as 'mutually constitutive'.

Which lines matter?

Crenshaw's work emphasized race and gender in a US context and Holvino (2010) writes as a 'woman of colour', the term she uses to emphasize the 'commonalities among Native American, Latina, Asian and Black/African American women, who share a status and an experience as ratio ethnic minorities in the USA' (Holvino 2010: 249). This raises the issue of how we conceptualize the lines of difference in any intersectional analysis, and when we can group multiple categories to form a single category. If we take the logic of the intersectional argument we can, of course, make a case for considering these groups of women of colour as different. The experience of a Latina might, in crucial respects, differ from that of an Asian. In grouping these together Holvino has adopted a particular strategy which of course makes sense in a US context. Without wishing to delegitimize Holvino's strategic move I would want to emphasize that other positions are possible and that context matters.

Holvino's work is useful in drawing attention to the need to consider the intersections of class, gender and race as well as other dimensions, such as nation and sexuality (2010: 259). To this list might be added disability and age. Clearly all of these can be relevant to a particular individual or to a particular group's experience. However, it poses a challenge in that one cannot address everything simultaneously. Analysts need to consider not only when and on what basis to group potentially different categories together, but also what lines of difference to focus upon. One solution is to see the social scientist's task as to give voice to particular groups; particularly marginalized groups who may otherwise not be heard. Here we might define a group as any body of people who see themselves as a group, on their own terms. In this case we need to let them tell us what lines of difference matter to them. Alternatively we might apply *a priori* categories in our analysis; theoretically determined lines of analysis. For example, a Marxist might identify class as an important line to focus attention on, independently of whether or not people see themselves in these terms. These need not be mutually exclusive positions, of course, and we might adopt one or another in the course of different investigations or combine them in the course of any one. The strategy to be adopted depends largely on one's purpose and to the extent to which it aligns with the explicit purposes of those it seeks to address. In this book I have largely adopted an *a priori* approach, but issues of sexual orientation, say, are clearly ones that emerge to a large extent from the groups themselves, rather than any prior theorizing. The book is wide ranging in that it considers a number of different lines of difference, and I hope I have demonstrated the relevance of each. Other lines could have been chosen, however, and any such selection is open to the accusation that particular lines of difference are not considered. Why not religion? Why not personality? I think the selection reflects what I see in the literature and it also reflects dominant debates in the public sphere. In particular it reflects the influence of social movements for change (particularly as they inform the chapters on gender, race and ethnicity, disability and sexual orientation).

The ordering of the lines

If we accept that there may be multiple lines of difference that we need to consider in intersectional analysis this raises of course the question of whether there is a hierarchy of differences. The mention of Marxists in the previous section raises the idea that class is the most important factor. Marxist feminists have of course sought to reconcile a position that gives due emphasis to class and gendered structures of inequality (e.g. Bryson 2004). However, one solution is to argue that it is not a question of one category being more important all the time but of untangling how each affects the other in particular contexts. Rather than assuming either that one dimension is most important or, alternatively, that all dimensions of inequality are of equal significance all the time (see also Walby et al. 2012) we need to consider what applies in a particular context. Again the solution to this problem of the ordering of the lines might lie either in *a priori* theoretical positions or in listening to the voices of particular groups. We might attend both to what 'sides' are put forward, what are the manifest and latent identities, and consider why latency might exist.

How we select what is seen as important or most significant in a particular context is a difficult issue. Rather than establish a hierarchy I think it is better to simply have a conversation, and multiple conversations, and precisely to seek to avoid one set of voices drowning out all others (see Belenky 1996). This, however, still leaves the issue of where to focus attention and how to deal with complexity.

The focus of attention

In a widely referenced intervention, McCall (2005) identifies three approaches to intersectionality, based on their stance towards categories. The first, the anti-categorical approach, seeks to destabilize categories while the second, the intracategorical, seeks to examine one particular intersection (e.g. black women) from the point of view of that category. The third, intercategorical approach, however, examines the interactions between categories. The example she gives is in looking at wage inequality by gender, class and race in four US cities, revealing a complex pattern of social inequality. Of these approaches the second seems most common in the preceding chapters.

However, McCall (2005) perhaps does not push her conception of inter-categorical examination far enough. The example she provides of this, from her own research, still rests upon a rather static formulation. It is as if, rather than focusing upon one cell in a two-dimensional array, she focuses on multiple cells, but each is still the intersection of the rows and columns. She simply encourages us to compare the values in each cell. What this does not do is examine the nature of the relationships between these different dimensions and these different cells. It presents the outcome of the intersection but does not address the mechanisms and processes that give rise to dynamic and fluid interactions. And yet if we follow her lead and the idea of the intercategorical analysis perhaps we can envisage a processual view, examining *how* race, class and gender come together in multiple ways – not just comparing different points of intersection, but examining the *processes* that create different kinds of intersection and affect the relationship between them.

The literature on intersectionality often considers particular points of intersection, adopting an intracategorical approach, and while this is to be welcomed perhaps it is not enough. The contents of this book are perhaps strongest in considering this intracategorical approach (even if this has been implicit), but I think more needs to be done to consider the ways in which solidarity as well as conflict emerges through interaction. It is apparent that solidarity can exist within the subject categories considered in these chapters – within the category of a particular organization, occupation, class, gender, sexual orientation, disability group, age group or ethnicity. What is perhaps less apparent is how solidarity might occur across these lines of difference. This might be seen as the radical democratic politics once advocated by Laclau and Mouffe (1985) as well as the social justice unionism advocated by Fletcher and Gapasin (2009). I think any such solidarity will always be contingent and fluid; that it may take many different forms at different times and in different places. The achievements made by the disability movement in achieving some coherent mobilization across what are considerable points of difference are considerable, for example, but the work of coalescing various movements into a coherent force that challenges the hegemony of neoliberalism is much more challenging. But politics and solidarity is driven by identification. To echo the title of a book of the 1970s, perhaps we need to move beyond the fragments (Rowbotham 1979). But whether we do so or not identity work is only finished at the individual level with death; and only finished at the collective level with the end of history.

References

Alcoff, L. (1988) 'Cultural feminism versus post-structuralism: The identity crisis in feminist theory', *Signs*, 13(3): 405–436.

Allen, A. (1999) 'Solidarity after identity politics: Hannah Arendt and the power of feminist theory', *Philosophy and Social Criticism*, 25(1): 97–119.

Anthias, F. and Yuval-Davis, N. with Cain, H. (1992) *Racialized Boundaries: Race, Nation, Gender, Colour, and Class and the Anti-Racist Struggle*. London: Routledge.

Archer, M. (2003) *Structure, Agency and the Internal Conversation*. Cambridge: Cambridge University Press.

Ashforth, B. E., Harrison, S. H. and Corley, K. G. (2008) 'Identification in organizations: An examination of four fundamental questions', *Journal of Management*, 34(3): 325–374.

Belenky, M. F. (1996) 'Public homeplaces: Nurturing the development of people, families and communities' in Goldberger, N. R, Tarule, J. Clinchy, B. and Belenky, M. F. (eds), *Knowledge, Difference and Power: Essays Inspired by Women's Ways of Knowing*. New York: Basic Books: 393–430.

Berger, P. L. and Luckmann, T. (1967) *The Social Construction of Reality: A Treatise in the Sociology of Knowledge*. London: Allen Lane.

Bradley, H. (2016) *Fractured Identities: Changing Patterns of Inequality* (Second Edition). Cambridge: Polity Press.

Brown, A. D. (2015) 'Identities and identity work in organizations', *International Journal of Management Review*, 17: 20–40.

Bryson, V. (2004) 'Marxism and feminism: Can the "unhappy marriage" be saved?', *Journal of Political Ideologies*, 9(1): 13–30.

Butler, J. (1990) *Gender Trouble: Feminism and the Subversion of Identity*. London: Routledge.

Corlett, S. and Mavin, S. (2014) 'Intersectionality, identity and identity work', *Gender in Management: An International Journal*, 29(5): 258–276.

Crenshaw, K. (1989) 'Demarginalising the intersection of race and sex: A black feminist critique of antidiscrimination doctrine, feminist theory and anti-racist policy', *University of Chicago Legal Forum*: 139–167.

Crenshaw, K. (1991) 'Mapping the margins: Intersectionality, identity politics, and violence against women of color', *Stanford Law Review*, 43(6): 1241–1300.

de Lauretis, T. (1984) *Alice Doesn't: Feminism, Semiotics, Cinema*. Bloomington, IN: Indiana University Press.

Erikson, E. (1980) *Identity and the Life Cycle*. New York: W. W. Norton.

Fletcher, B. and Gapasin, F. (2009) *Solidarity Divided: The Crisis in Organized Labor and a New Path toward Social Justice*. Berkeley and Los Angeles: University of California Press.

Gadamer, H.-G. (1989) *Truth and Method*. London: Sheed and Ward.

Giddens, A. (1991) *Modernity and Self-Identity: Self and Society in the Late Modern Age*. Cambridge: Polity Press.

Gouldner, A. W. (1957) 'Cosmopolitans and locals: Toward an analysis of latent social roles: I', *Administrative Science Quarterly*, 2(3): 281–306.

Hall, S. (1996) 'Who needs identity?' in Hall, S. and Du Gay, P. (eds), *Questions of Cultural Identity*. London: Sage.

Hancock, A. M. (2007) 'When multiplication doesn't equal quick addition: Examining intersectionality as a research paradigm', *Perspectives on Politics/American Political Science Association*, 5(1): 63–80.

Hearn, J. (2014) 'On men, organizations and intersectionality', *Equality, Diversity and Inclusion: An International Journal*, 33(5): 414.

Holvino, E. (2010) 'Intersections: The simultaneity of race, gender and class in organization studies', *Gender, Work and Organization*, 17(3): 248–277.

Jenkins, R. (2004) *Social Identity*. London: Routledge.

Kandola, R. S. and Fullerton, J. (eds) (1998) *Diversity in Action: Managing the Mosaic*, 2nd edition. London: Institute of Personnel and Development.

Kerner, I. (2012) 'Questions of intersectionality: Reflections on the current debate in German gender studies', *European Journal of Women's Studies*, 19(2): 203–218.

Kirton, G. (2013) *The Dynamics of Managing Diversity*. Hoboken: Taylor and Francis.

Laclau, E. and Mouffe, C. (1985) *Hegemony and Socialist Strategy: Towards a Radical Democratic Politic*. London: Verso.

McCall, L. (2005) 'The complexity of intersectionality', *Signs*, 30(3): 1771–1800.

Medina, J. (2003) 'Identity trouble: Disidentification and the problem of difference', *Philosophy and Social Criticism*, 29(6): 655–680.

Özbilgin, M. F. and Tatli, A. (2008) *Global Diversity Management: An Evidence-Based Approach.* Basingstoke: Palgrave Macmillan.

Prins, B. (2006) 'Narrative accounts of origins: A blind spot in the intersectional approach?' *European Journal of Women's Studies*, 13(3): 277–290.

Ricoeur, P. (1994) *Oneself as Another.* Chicago: University of Chicago Press.

Rorty, R. (1989) *Contingency, Irony, and Solidarity.* Cambridge: Cambridge University Press.

Rowbotham, S. (1979) *Beyond the Fragments.* London: Merlin Press.

Shields, S. A. (2008) 'Gender: An intersectionality perspective', *Sex Roles*, 59(5–6): 301–311.

Smith, B. (1983) *Home Girls: A Black Feminist Anthology.* New York: Kitchen Table: Women of Color Press.

Spelman, E. V. (1990) *Inessential Woman: Problems of Exclusion in Feminist Thought.* London: Women's Press.

Syed, J. and Özbilgin, M. (2015) *Managing Diversity and Inclusion: An International Perspective.* Los Angeles, CA: Sage.

van Knippenberg, D. and Haslam, S. A. (2003) 'Realizing the diversity dividend: Exploring the subtle interplay between identity, ideology and reality' in Haslam, S. A., van Knippenberg, D., Platow, M. J. and Ellemers, N. (eds), *Social Identity at Work: Developing Theory for Organizational Practice.* New York: Psychology Press.

Walby, S., Armstrong, J. and Strid, S. (2012) 'Intersectionality: Multiple inequalities in social theory', *Sociology*, 46(2): 224–240.

Yuval-Davis, N. (2006) 'Intersectionality and feminist politics', *European Journal of Women's Studies*, 13(3): 193–209.

INDEX